The Baby Business

The Baby Business

How Money, Science, and Politics

Drive the

Commerce of Conception

Debora L. Spar

HARVARD BUSINESS SCHOOL PRESS

BOSTON, MASSACHUSETTS

Copyright © 2006 Harvard Business School Publishing Corporation
All rights reserved
Printed in the United States of America

09 08 07 06 05   5 4 3 2 1

Library of Congress Cataloging-in-Publication Data
Spar, Debora L.
  The baby business : how money, science, and politics drive the
commerce of conception / Debora L. Spar.
      p. ; cm.
  Includes bibliographical references and index.
  ISBN 1-59139-620-4 (hardcover : alk. paper)
  1. Human reproductive technology--Economic aspects. 2.
Infertility—Treatment—Economic aspects. 3. Surrogate
motherhood—Economic aspects. 4. Adoption—Economic aspects.
  [DNLM: 1. Infertility—therapy. 2. Adoption. 3. Commerce. 4.
Genetic Services—economics. 5. Reproductive Medicine—economics. 6.
Reproductive Techniques—economics. 7. Socioeconomic Factors. 8.
Surrogate Mothers. WP 570 S736b 2005] I. Title.
  RG133.5.S666 2005
  362.198'178—dc22

                              2005030503

No part of this publication may be reproduced, stored in or introduced into
a retrieval system, or transmitted, in any form, or by any means (electronic,
mechanical, photocopying, recording, or otherwise), without the prior
permission of the publisher. Requests for permission should be directed to
permissions@hbsp.harvard.edu, or mailed to Permissions, Harvard Business
School Publishing, 60 Harvard Way, Boston, Massachusetts 02163.

The paper used in this publication meets the minimum requirements of the
American National Standard for Information Sciences—Permanence of Paper
for Printed Library Materials, ANSI Z39.48-1992.

To all those who weren't
And to Daniel, Andrew, and Kristina,
who are

Contents

Reconceiving Recess

IMAGINE A FUTURE SCHOOLYARD in a prosperous suburban town. Two little girls swing side by side, their hair streaming out behind them. A boy dangles from the monkey bars, taunting his brother below. And children scramble up the slide as parents flutter mildly from the bench.

Look closer now to see who these children really are. The two girls? Twins actually, but of a sort, for one is Caucasian and the other half-Vietnamese. The dangling boy has recently recovered from a life-threatening illness, saved by a bone marrow transplant from the brother conceived to match him. The children on the slide are from Russia, Guatemala, and Vietnam and bear no genetic relationship to the parents who watch them. If you could see even deeper, you might glimpse the genetic triumphs that lurk beneath the surface: the cystic fibrosis that never was. The diabetes cured by a harvested stem cell. The biological replica of a lost, beloved child. You might see the children that never were and those conceived, or designed, or discovered to replace them.

These children of the future are already among us. In 2001, nearly 41,000 children in the United States were born via in vitro fertilization

(IVF)—"test tube babies" in the older vernacular. Roughly 6,000 sprang from donated eggs; almost 600 were carried in surrogate, or borrowed, wombs. In 2003, Americans adopted 21,616 children from abroad and produced a handful of homegrown, biologically unrelated twins. All these children were conceived in a very different fashion from their parents. And all of them, through one means or another, were purchased.

It is difficult to conceive of a child as commerce. For even at the start of the twenty-first century—even in an age driven by technological advances and dominated by market capitalism—we like to believe that some things remain beyond both markets and science, that there are some things money can't buy. In economic terms, these things—like love, truth, kidneys, and infants—are defined as being inalienable: the people who "own" the assets have no ability to profit from them. In moral terms, they are things that we as a society have chosen not to sell, assets or attributes that somehow are more valuable than any price they might fetch. This prohibition seems particularly strong for children. Who, after all, could put a price on a child? Who could imagine selling one? Across the world, baby-selling is strictly prohibited, defined as a crime more egregious, more unthinkable, than slavery.

And yet every day, in nearly every country, infants and children are indeed being sold. Want a better baby? You can buy one—from a fertility clinic that will discard any undesirable embryos, or a high-tech service that enables you to choose your child's gender, or an expert surgeon who can correct the child's defects while he or she is still in the womb. Can't have a baby the old-fashioned way? There are dozens of fixes for that, too. You could, for example, select sperm from banks listing their donors' SAT scores and hobbies. You could purchase eggs from a woman of your choice, paying anywhere from $2,500 to $50,000 for the optimal genetic mix. You could hire a surrogate to carry your child, or find a ready-made child from an Internet site that displays hundreds of available orphans. In any of these cases, you could expect to choose your desired characteristics and pay accordingly: thousands of extra dollars, for example, for Ivy League eggs, a docile surrogate, or the most skillful prenatal surgeon.

Understandably, most of these transactions appear to be above or beyond the market. Orphaned children, for example, are never "sold"; they're simply "matched" with their "forever families." Eggs are "donated," and surrogate mothers offer their services to help the infertile. Certainly, the rhetoric that surrounds these transactions has nothing to do with markets or prices or profits. Quite possibly, the people who undertake them want only to help. But neither the rhetoric nor the motive can change the underlying activity. When parents buy eggs or sperm; when they contract with surrogates; when they choose a child to adopt or an embryo to implant, they are doing business. Firms are making money, customers are making choices, and children—for better or worse—are being sold. As of 2004, the total cost of adopting a healthy Guatemalan infant was around $25,000. The cost of contracting with a surrogate was roughly $59,000. Top-notch eggs were going for as much as $50,000.

As people—as parents—we don't like to think of children as economic objects. They are products, we insist, of love, not money; of an intimate creation that exists far beyond the reach of any market impulse. And yet, over the past thirty years, advances in reproductive medicine have indeed created a market for babies, a market in which parents choose traits, clinics woo clients, and specialized providers earn millions of dollars a year. In this market, moreover, commerce often runs without many rules. Because no one wants to define baby-making as a business, and because the endeavor touches deeply on the toughest of moral dilemmas, many governments around the world have either ignored the trade in children or simply prohibited it.

Like most personal prohibitions, however, bans on procreation, of whatever form, have inevitably failed. The demand for children is so deep, so intense, that many people will do literally anything to fulfill it. In 2002, for example, an American hairdresser named Sharon Saarinen traveled to Beirut for cytoplasmic transfer, a procedure in which her eggs were rejuvenated with genetic material from another, younger woman. In 1996, a fifty-year-old law professor was impregnated with eggs from two different donors.[1] She subsequently gave birth to twins, one of whom was half-Vietnamese. And in 2002, a British couple emptied their savings account and traveled to a clinic in the United States, where they tried to conceive a very particular child, one who could potentially contribute lifesaving blood cells to their dying toddler.[2]

In these cases—and thousands like them—the parents aren't motivated by commercial instincts, and they hardly see themselves as "shopping" for their offspring. Yet they are still intimately involved with both a market operation and a political calculation. Saarinen, for example, went to Beirut because cytoplasmic transfer had been banned in the United States. In addition to travel costs, she and her husband probably spent about $10,000 trying to conceive their high-tech child.[3] Clients like Jane Cohen, the mother of mixed-race twins, can easily spend between $50,000 and $100,000 for multiple rounds of IVF treatment and several batches of eggs.[4] They can also contemplate such arrangements only in the handful of countries—the United States, Israel, South Africa—that boast sophisticated IVF facilities and permit repeated egg donations. Meanwhile, preimplantation genetic diagnosis—the technique that permits parents to select embryos with specific genetic traits—is restricted or unavailable in many countries. It is also expensive, adding roughly $3,500 to the costs of assisted conception.

In many respects, there is nothing special about the economic status of these new-age kids. Poor parents across time and place have viewed their children as potential economic assets, weighing their eventual economic contribution—in the rice field or factory or manor—against the costs of carrying them through childhood. Parents have chosen their children's gender based on economic factors, using infanticide or abandonment to rid themselves of less-valued offspring. They have even, under the most desperate circumstances, used their children as direct assets, selling them into slavery or indentured servitude. In all these historical cases, however, parents were confined to the number and type of children that nature (plus some crude contraception) bestowed on them. If parents produced "excess" children, they frequently placed them out with other families; if families were childless, they borrowed or adopted those of others; and if families produced deformed or unwanted children they either abandoned them or bore the additional cost.

In the new age of babies, by contrast, reproductive science has created extraordinary ways of addressing both the quantity and the quality of children. Contraception and abortion, for example, have sharply reduced the number of unwanted babies. Fertility treatments have brought millions of babies to those who want them; and genetic engineering and prenatal treatment, together with sperm and egg donation, promise to shape the type of children born. In the past, therefore, the "market" for children lay with the commercial value of the children themselves, with their eventual ability to run the farm or care for their elderly parents. In the future, the market will lie—indeed already does lie—with the ability of some agents, be they doctors, fertility clinics, or adoption agencies, to provide and perfect *new* children for the parents who desperately want them.

As these markets evolve, they will drag in their wake a host of moral issues and a scramble for policy solutions. Already, many countries with the capacity to engage in high-tech baby-making have passed laws that constrain or even prohibit the use of these technologies. Italy, for example, recently passed legislation that prohibits sterile, gay, or single adults from using donor eggs or surrogate mothers. In Germany, egg transfer of any sort is illegal, as are surrogacy and treatments that involve manipulating the human embryo. The European Union pushed Romania in 2004 to curtail all international adoptions, and the United States maintains a controversial ban on federal funding for embryonic stem cell research.

In other areas of endeavor, such restrictions would likely kill the market at hand, or at least slow its growth. But in the baby trade, demand is too high and desire too deep to be stopped. If parents want children and nature doesn't comply, then they are likely to pursue these children through whatever means possible. They will cross international boundaries and undergo untested, unregulated treatments. They will mortgage their homes and drain their savings accounts. And they will violate national laws, confident that no one will ever detect their crime. For who can tell, after all, whether babies born in Bremen were conceived in Istanbul? Who would criminalize a product that turns out to be a child?

In the baby business, therefore, science, law, and commerce stand at odds with one another. There is a market in babies, a market driven by extraordinary scientific advances. Since the mid-1970s, advances in medicine, biology, and chemistry have made it possible to produce children through a variety of high-tech channels and to tinker with children's genetic makeup before they are born. Science has also made it possible for commercial entities to charge stiff sums for these procreative capacities, allowing some parents to pay up to $100,000 to produce what others make for free.

This market, however, remains largely unacknowledged. No one likes to admit to manufacturing babies or to earning profits in the process. No one wants to argue that the baby business *should* be seen as commerce, or that its practitioners should be held to some kind of regulatory standard. And thus the trade is pockmarked by legal inconsistencies and continent-spanning loopholes. In Denmark, sperm donors are anonymous; in Sweden, they must reveal their names. In Germany, all eggs removed from a woman must be reimplanted inside her. In Russia, these same eggs can be removed, sold, bartered, and exchanged. Louisiana refuses to recognize the validity of any surrogacy contract, whereas California has built a thriving commercial industry around surrogacy agreements.

So what's a would-be parent to do? It's easy. They travel, trolling the world in search of their child. And savvy practitioners appeal to these international clients, crafting businesses that capitalize on regulatory gaps. A group of Israelis, for example, opened a clinic in the Dominican Republic in 2004, offering low-priced and fully legal services in an "inviting sunny tropical" locale. Denmark's Cryos International Sperm Bank is the world's largest exporter of sperm. Guatemala places nearly three thousand infants and toddlers in foreign homes each year, generating total revenues estimated to be $50 million.[5]

Such businesses are not explicitly illegal. Indeed, most fertility clinics are eminently respectable enterprises, fully in compliance with their nation's laws and responsible for having produced thousands of babies that otherwise might not have been born. Guatemala has a massive regulatory system that oversees international adoption and tends to scores of children who might otherwise face life on the streets. Yet even if these enterprises do nothing but good—even if they save lives, and make families, and advance scientific discovery—they still pose questions that are frightfully complex. Because they raise issues that strike at the core of humanity—at what it means to reproduce and give birth and to love. They demand definitions—of life and parenthood—that have stubbornly resisted consensus and have pitted groups passionately against one another. And in the process, they force us to make choices: should we, as a society, prohibit women from selling their eggs, their wombs, their embryos, or their children? Should we allow parents to select the genetic traits of their children? And who, in a world of fluid boundaries and invisible trade, gets to decide?

The Baby Business does not try to resolve these moral issues. On the contrary, it argues that the moral issues surrounding birth and babies will never be resolved. As a society, we will never categorically decide when life begins. We will never agree on a common definition of a "good" family or a "defective" child. But while we differ and argue and plot, individuals will be making these decisions and acting on them. Couples will contract with surrogate mothers, for example, even if the legal status of their contracts remains vague. They will advertise for high-end eggs, travel abroad for untested treatments, and search for Korean orphans on Internet Web sites. The market, in other words, will function even if the morals are cloudy and the laws uncertain. People will still sell the basic components of baby-making. Other people will buy them. Indeed, as the growth of international trade shows, uncertainly even drives profits in the baby business, allowing commerce to flourish between gaps of authority.

The central argument of this book, therefore, is that despite popular protests to the contrary, and despite the heartfelt sentiments of parents and providers, there is a flourishing market for both children and their component parts. Eggs are being sold; sperm is being sold; wombs and genes and orphans are being sold; and many individuals are profiting handsomely in the process. *The Baby Business* does not insist that this market is either good or evil. It simply argues that it exists.

The second proposition follows naturally upon the first. If there is a market for babies, then we need to explore it as such. We need to understand who the baby-makers are and how they are structuring their trade. We need to examine who makes money in this industry and what defines the clientele. Harsh as it may seem, we need to view reproductive medicine as an industry, with all the commercial prospects and potential foibles that other industries display. We also need to look closely at the prices that prevail in this industry and the relationships between various market segments. Because at some level, the product in all these segments is exactly the same: parents want a healthy child. When they buy eggs, for example, they aren't really interested in the eggs per se, but rather in the person they suspect those eggs will become. When they contract with a surrogate, they don't really care about her personal lifestyle, but only about what her lifestyle implies for the health of the child she will carry. When they adopt, they are looking, almost always, for a child who is like themselves in some way, a child who will simply be theirs.

Theoretically, therefore, all these various would-be children are nearly perfect substitutes for one another. All the means of baby procurement, after all, produce a similar child, one whose genetic makeup can never be fully assured and whose long-term prospects remain a mystery. In economic terms, then, the price of these children should be roughly commensurate, with variation occurring in fairly predictable ways. It is reasonable to assume, for example, that eggs will always cost more than sperm, because egg extraction is considerably more complicated (and potentially dangerous) than sperm donation. It is also reasonable to assume that adoption will cost less than assisted reproduction, because adopted children are already "available" in some sense, and many parents have a preexisting preference for children who are genetically related to them.

Yet this kind of predictable variation does not explain the range of prices that prevail in the baby market. Eggs, for example, cost far more than sperm—$4,500 versus $300 on average, and $50,000 versus $2,950 for the top end of the market. Why are parents willing to pay such high premiums for eggs? Similarly, although some forms of adoption are indeed less expensive than fertility treatments, many are not. Adopting a six-year-old from the U.S. foster care system, for example, costs virtually nothing. Adopting that same six-year-old from Russia, however, runs about $25,000. Such variation cannot be explained by the customary laws of supply and demand. For the baby market does not operate like other markets do. There are differential prices that make little sense; scale economies that don't bring lower costs; and customers who will literally pay whatever they possibly can. In this market, moreover, the fundamental rules of commerce are conspicuously absent. We don't know where property rights lie, for example, or how contracts apply. We haven't decided whether people own their own genetic material or whether they have some fundamental right to "consume" the pleasures of parenting.

But still the market remains. It may be cloaked in different language, it may be fragmented and skating on the edge of illegitimacy, but it is a market nevertheless. *The Baby Business* takes this market as a given and then figures out how it works.

A third theme relates to the historical context of this trade. On the one hand, the science of procreation is new. It is a modern phenomenon, a post-industrial miracle that emerged from the high technologies of bio-chemistry, microsurgery, and genetic engineering. Certainly, this is the view that dominates most treatments of the topic. On the other hand, however, one can also see reproductive advances as only the most recent chapter in a very ancient tale. Indeed, efforts to control procreation are nearly as old as humankind itself. Using an astonishing array of means—from crocodile dung to amulets and Lysol—people, and particularly women, have eternally tried to control their reproduction, to have children at their schedule rather than nature's or God's.

Some of these efforts have been devoted primarily to contraception, others to conception. But in all cases, the business of birth control has been messy, subject not only to technical limitations but also, and more dramatically, to the dictates of law, morality, and power. Religious authorities have long cast judgment on any man-made intervention in the reproductive process, and states have frequently prohibited specific acts or behaviors. During the fifteenth and sixteenth centuries, for example, governments across Europe gradually clamped down on any form of contraception. In nineteenth-century America, even information about birth control was forbidden as "obscene." In our own day, governments in Australia, Germany, and many other countries have prohibited the use of surrogate mothers, and the U.S. government has sharply constrained many kinds of fetal research. In nearly all these instances, however, the market survives government's attempt at prohibition. The baby business may go underground for some time; it may cross international borders. But the market persists, time after time, from one technology to the next.

Such historical precedents suggest an ongoing interplay between business and government, markets and morality. In the reproductive industries, we should expect moral concerns to hold a far greater sway than they do elsewhere. We should expect religious voices to weigh in on all advances concerning conception or its control; and we should expect governments to respond, frequently and forcefully, to the concerns thrust before them. As a result, firms in the baby business should expect to face a more restrictive environment than do firms in other, less intimate areas. And to a large extent they do. Adoption agencies, as mentioned earlier, operate under a highly structured set of laws. Fertility clinics outside the United States are frequently prohibited from accepting single parents; scientists cannot legally clone a client's beloved child.

At the same time, however, history suggests that such restrictions are not immutable. When people want to control their reproduction, and when technology allows them to do so, markets generally trump morals over the long run. In this sense, the playground of the future is likely to grow larger over time. Will people protest when two lesbian mothers use cutting-edge techniques to conceive a child that is biologically "theirs"? Yes. Will moralists cringe when embryos are selected to produce marrow for a dying sibling, or when women in Cambodia bear infants for middle-aged lawyers in New York? Yes again. But will anyone ultimately stop the markets that continue to grow around these technologies? Almost certainly not.

Understanding this interplay leads to *The Baby Business*'s final argument. Bluntly put, the book suggests that governments need to play a more active role in regulating the baby trade. This doesn't mean that governments should control the industry, or ban it. On the contrary. Markets, as noted earlier, will dominate the baby business. Private enterprises will profit from baby-making technologies, and outright bans on these technologies are destined to fail. If there is demand for babies, there will be supply.

Such a market-based relationship, however, doesn't preclude the kind of governmental intervention that exists in a wide range of other industry sectors: in education, in health care, in drugs. Indeed, governments are active players in most advanced capitalist economies, setting the rules that allow economies to function and, theoretically at least, keeping an eye toward the common good. In this context, the baby trade, particularly in the United States, stands out as an extraordinary exception: one of the very few industries to operate with virtually no rules.

One could argue that laissez-faire makes sense here, that it is even the moral choice in a time of technological evolution and a sphere marked by intense personal desires. High-tech children are tumbling across the ever-expanding playground; overjoyed parents are watching with glee the fruits of technology's labor. The market for children is working, and those who operate in it have no wish for intervention. The problem, though, is that neither science nor morality will permit this market to remain open-ended for long. As reproductive technologies push the envelope of possibilities, they will create children—and mistakes—that demand restitution. They will blur the edges of what is now formally forbidden—cloning, for example, and fetal research—and what is allowed. In the end, of course, the market will still win. We will continue to buy, sell, and modify our children, generating substantial profits in the process. But this market will not reign forever unfettered. Instead, the pulling and hauling of politics will create—must create—a regulatory framework in which the business of babies can proceed.

Stories from the baby trade are difficult to ignore. When we hear of surrogate mothers pleading to get their infants back, or of parents desperate to produce a child whose bone marrow could save a dying sibling, we tend to personalize their plights, painting reproductive advances as either savior or curse, as Frankenstein incarnate or a miracle of love. *The Baby Business* moves away from such stark stereotypes, arguing that we need to understand reproductive medicine in a more familiar context, a commercial context in which competing firms simply use technology to meet their customers' needs.

We may not want to think of babies in this way. We may not want to think of ourselves, or our doctors, like this. In the end, however, it is far better to concede the commerce and examine it than to insist it does not exist. We are selling children. *The Baby Business* describes how.

CHAPTER 1

The Quest to Conceive

Attacking an Ancient Affliction

"Give me sons," cried Rachel to Jacob.
"Give me sons or I shall die."

—GENESIS 30:1

FOR MOST PEOPLE, the production of babies is one of the simplest tasks around. It happens quite easily, often by accident, and only requires, as political scientist Melissa Williams is fond of remarking, "things lying around the house." There are no messy market interventions to worry about, no technical requirements, not even much practice. Baby-making, after all, is the oldest production known to humankind, a process that is programmed into the biological fiber of our beings and defines our very survival.

For a significant minority of would-be "producers," however, the mechanics of baby-making break down. They want children—they crave children—but cannot produce them on their own. Over time, they form the ranks of the infertile, a group that includes roughly 15 percent of women and 10 to 15 percent of men.[1] According to the most recent U.S. data, 17 percent of all married women suffered from either infertility or impaired fecundity in 2002.[2]

Medically, the members of this group may have little in common. Some have been rendered infertile by ostensibly unrelated illnesses. A woman may have had cancer treatments, for example, that involved the removal of her ovaries; a man may have suffered exposure to chemical toxins. Others have genetic problems with their reproductive systems or randomly appearing maladies. Some men suffer from low sperm counts or impaired sperm mobility. Some women are allergic to their husbands' sperm or simply too old to produce viable eggs. And some infertile couples have no discernible medical problem at all. What joins this disparate community, therefore, is only their shared inability. They want to bear children, and they cannot.

At the start of the twenty-first century, one might be tempted to regard infertility as a relatively minor problem. Infertile people, after all, do not suffer from any life-threatening illness. They can pursue adoption, if they like, or enjoy the company of other people's children. They do not have to bear the financial costs of raising a child or the emotional strain of emergency room visits, temper tantrums, and adolescence. It doesn't sound all that bad, especially if one notes that birthrates have plummeted across the industrialized world and that even fertile couples are increasingly choosing to remain childless.[3]

To those who suffer from it, however, infertility is a wretched curse— a disease that isn't really a disease, with an outcome that seems to defy nature. Some resign themselves to their fate; others adopt. But many infertile couples become consumed with the desire to conceive, willing to do whatever it takes to create a child of their own. For most of these would-be parents, the economic value of their desire—the price of a child, in other words—is literally inestimable.

The Commerce of Conception

At a personal level, of course, such unmet demand is tragic: millions of people are fervently seeking to purchase what everyone around them, it seems, gets for free. At a commercial level, however, it is exceedingly attractive. For who wouldn't want to sell in a market of millions, each of whom is desperate to buy? In 2004, more than one million Americans underwent some form of fertility treatment, participating in what had become a nearly $3 billion industry (see table 1-1).

As a commercial enterprise, though, the fertility business remains rather odd. On the one hand, it is undeniably a business: fertility clinics earn profits, advertise their wares, and compete, albeit subtly, on the quality and reliability of their services. They boost cadres of technologists who push the boundaries of production and sit amid clusters of related providers: sperm banks, testing facilities, hormone suppliers, and the like. On the other hand, though, the entire apparatus of this for-profit structure is devoted to producing a distinctly noncommercial outcome: a child. And thus fertility providers tend to shy away from acknowledging the hard-core aspects of their trade. They don't reveal their financial rewards very openly. They don't revel in their sales figures or compensation schemes. Many providers, moreover, maintain an uneasy balance between the world of compassion and the world of commerce: they are making money, yes, but also creating lives. This ambivalence, a trademark of the baby business more generally, is particularly evident in the fertility field, where the demand for conception essentially knows no bounds.

TABLE 1-1

The U.S. market for fertility treatment, 2004

Product or service	Revenue (U.S. dollars, thousands)
In vitro fertilization	1,038,528
Fertility drugs	1,331,860
Diagnostic tests	374,900
Donor eggs	37,773
Surrogate carriers	27,400
Donor sperm	74,380
Total	2,884,841

Source: Author's calculations, based on data provided by the American Society for Reproductive Medicine, the Centers for Disease Control, Business Communications Company, and individual providers. Figures for IVF are for 2002. Revenues from preimplantation genetic diagnosis (PGD) are not included.

In most other industries, supply, demand, and price are locked into their familiar and predictable embrace. A high level of demand for any good or service drives up its price and induces other suppliers to enter the trade. An expanded supply then pushes prices downward, restoring some sort of equilibrium to the market. As long as suppliers can enter freely, the market thus works to dampen prices, preventing them, in most cases at least, from soaring too high. In the fertility trade, by contrast, supply is limited by the level of expertise involved, and demand doesn't function as it does in other markets. When people are buying bananas, for example, there is a price beyond which they simply will not go. Ten cents a banana is OK, fifteen cents still permissible. But if banana prices were to rise to, say, $5 a bunch, most customers simply wouldn't buy. Similarly, if Nike were to raise the price of even its most popular basketball shoe way above what adidas or Reebok were offering, customers would eventually turn to the competition. And as long as Nike is aware of this fact, it—and nearly every other corporation—will be careful not to raise prices too quickly or too high.

What drives this downward pressure, of course, is the combination of competition and substitution: the ability of customers to choose Reebok over Nike, or apples in place of bananas. Even those products that seem irreplaceable generally have substitutes at some price level. If housing prices are too high, for example, people will rent. If gasoline rises beyond some (admittedly high) level, people will eventually opt for smaller cars or learn to take the train.

Where fertility is concerned, however, demand knows no limit. If parents want "their" children—children made with their blood, their genes—then the possibility of substitution disappears. They don't want to adopt; they don't want to babysit; they don't want to make do. Instead, they want what to them is irreplaceable, and they will frequently pay whatever they can. They will mortgage their houses, sell their cars, deplete the family savings. In some cases, of course, the funds run out well before a child is conceived. In others, insurance steps into the breach, or potential clients step out, realizing that they don't have the money to buy. But when people can pay for fertility services, they generally do. Over and over and over again.

To be sure, there are other markets that resemble the fertility trade. The health-care industry, for example, is full of insatiable demand and inestimable costs. What is the value of a kidney to a patient who lacks one? Or of chemotherapy to a child suffering from leukemia? We simply cannot price these goods, and we cringe at the thought of subjecting them to the market. As a result, governments across the developed world have yanked health care from the roughest edges of commerce, either thrusting it fully into the public realm or erecting concrete regulatory boundaries. We prohibit, in nearly all countries, the sale of kidneys. We regulate the provision of chemotherapy and shield patients from the full cost of their treatment.

Yet in the world of reproduction, government responses have been mixed. In some countries—England, Australia, and Israel, for example—state authorities have treated infertility as a somewhat troubled offshoot of medicine. They cover the costs of infertility treatments, but only under strictly defined conditions and in accordance with carefully specified guidelines. The private provision of fertility services—the fertility market, in other words—is sharply constrained. Other countries prohibit much wider swaths of treatment, preventing public as well as private clinics from applying science to the reproductive process.

In the United States, however, regulatory and legislative authorities have largely ignored the market for reproductive services. There are very few restrictions on fertility treatments and little regulation of providers. Instead, the market for fertility in the United States is vibrant, competitive, and expanding in the absence of any kind of formal controls. Because the United States is such a large and technically advanced market, moreover, it serves as a magnet for infertile couples around the world. Would-be parents from Japan, for example, can travel to Virginia and pay for the donor eggs or gender selection techniques that are unavailable at home. Gay or lesbian couples from England can hire American surrogates, buy American eggs, and produce their children in a customer-friendly California clinic. Price in these cases is rarely an issue, and supply slips unnoticed across international lines.

The quest to conceive, therefore, is more than a personal prayer or a biological drive. It is a global industry that is quietly growing, a business that thrives on technology and refuses to acknowledge its market roots. It is an industry that sells salvation of the most primal sort and yet exists in a white-robed cloister of vials and drugs and probes. And it is an industry, most notably, that thrives on people's excruciating desire to buy—to find someone, somehow, who will give them children before, like Rachel, they die.

Genesis: The Historical Treatment of Infertility

It seems appropriate that one of the first ancient references to infertility occurs in Genesis, and among the founding families of Western theology. Jacob's wife, like many of her Biblical peers, was unable to bear a child. After praying to God and begging her husband, she resorted in the end to a method common in her day—sending Jacob "unto" her maid and then adopting the resulting child as her own. Sarah did likewise, sending Abraham to her maid, Hagar, saying, "I shall obtain children by her."[4]

Such explicit and persistent stories bear witness to infertility's long history. For eons, societies have worshipped procreation; they have revered and been awed by the power to reproduce. One of the oldest vestiges of worship, in fact, is the fertility goddess, a symbol that crossed cultures and continents in the ancient world. Depicted usually as a pregnant (or at least particularly robust) female, the fertility goddess played a central role in worship ceremonies.[5] Paleolithic tribes arranged cowrie shells in the shape of a female "portal"; the Romans lit torches and built fires to honor Diana, the goddess of fertility; the Scandinavians revered Freyja, daughter of the sea god who controlled life and death.[6] In all cases, their prayers before these deities were largely the same: for children, for reproduction, for life. When women bore children in these societies, therefore, they were perceived as following the ways of both God and nature. And when their wombs were barren, life had gone astray.

Accordingly, the ancient world looked harshly on women like Rachel. Because fertility remained so closely tied to womanhood, childless women were regarded with a mixture of pity and scorn. The Bible paints childless women as tragic and incomplete; ancient Egyptians described them as "mothers of the missing ones."[7] Frequently, infertile, or "barren," wives were compared with their agricultural equivalents: a "field without crops," according to many depictions, or a "tree without leaves."[8]

Unlike trees or fields, however, childless women were also typically held responsible for their fate. Because ancient societies did not know how to explain either conception or childlessness, they interpreted infertility as either an act of God or a sign of sin. According to this logic, women like Rachel were childless because they deserved it in some way, because God had determined that they were unworthy of conception. And men who were married to unworthy women were free, in many cultures, to kill or abandon them. In ancient India, a husband could tie up his childless wife and burn her. In China, the childless wife was not permitted to die at home.[9] Elsewhere—in pockets of Greece and Turkey and Bali—depending on the mood of the time and creed of the ruler, sterile women were forced to commit suicide, "disgraced, hated, and maltreated" by societies that equated childlessness with godlessness.[10]

Bewitched and Bewildered

By the fifteenth century, several new theories had emerged to explain this unnatural state. One was that childlessness could be the work of witches as well as God; that it could be imposed upon innocent couples by living, evil forces. Particularly in western Europe, where witch hunts raged from roughly 1435 to 1750, God-fearing Christians believed that witches—often childless women themselves—could perform "knot-tying" ceremonies at weddings, tying a magical leather cord that would subsequently render a couple incapable of producing children. Witches were also believed to interfere with reproduction more generally, and to have the power of rendering men impotent.[11]

In 1487, the central text of the witch trials, a Dominican publication titled *Hammer of the Witches*, made this link in startlingly clear terms. Witches, it argued, "surpassed all others in wickedness." They performed contraception and abortion, crimes against the church, and frequently were guilty of seven major sins. Sin number 2 was making men impotent. Number 3 was performing sterilization and castration.[12] Presumably, such sentiments reduced the wife's burden a bit, because the possibility of impotence at least dragged husbands into the fertility equation. But this equation still painted male infertility as distinctly unnatural—the product, ironically, of women's ill deeds.

As the furor over witches eventually subsided, a growing rationalism groped to discover other scapegoats for barrenness. One popular theory settled on sex, or at least on too much of it or not the right sort. According to this view, the existence of childless prostitutes suggested that sex itself could lead to infertility, because "slippery" wombs might easily prevent conception.[13] According to one early treatise on fertility, for example, "common Whores have none, or very rarely any children; for the Grass seldom grows in a Path that is commonly trodden in."[14] "Whores" also engaged in contraception and abortion, practices that were condemned by prevailing authorities and believed (with some justification) to result in permanent sterility.[15] Prevailing religious attitudes then completed the package: infertility befell impious women, who engaged in prostitute-like behavior and indulged in too much sex. Such women were no longer hanged or driven to suicide, but society's scorn remained largely unchanged.

For thousands of years and millions of women, therefore, infertility remained a silent and irrevocable curse. Shamed by their condition, childless wives confessed their problem to midwives or shamans or quacks, willing to engage in whatever remedies were thrust upon them. They drank potions of mule urine and rabbit blood and doused themselves with herbs believed to induce pregnancy. They kissed trees, slid on stones, and bathed themselves in brackish water thought to resemble the blood of childbirth.[16] When all else failed, they prayed, adopted, or, like Rachel, employed another woman to bear "their" child. Mostly, though, they resigned themselves to their barren state, seeking slender solace in the belief that it was God's will. The demand for children remained persistent and harsh, exacerbated by the lack of other options for women and the status that heirs conferred upon men. But supply was simply not forthcoming. For centuries, science could not determine precisely how babies were conceived. And it certainly could not compel that conception when nature dictated otherwise.

This unfortunate state of affairs began to shift ever so slightly in the late seventeenth century, as science slowly joined nature as a source of physical knowledge. In 1684, an anonymous author published *Aristotle's Master Piece*, a popular compendium that drew on both emerging science and ancient Greek theories to describe procreation as a physical blending of male and female "semence," the seeds that were purportedly released by both partners in conception.[17] The *Master Piece* was eventually reissued in dozens of editions, followed in due course by a stream of "marriage manuals" that explicitly linked conception to the "mingling of seed," and pregnancy, for the first time, to pleasure.

The Expert Midwife (1694), for example, cautions, "*Sterility* happens likewise, from the Womans Disgust . . . or her dullness and insensibility therein."[18] So, too, was the conclusion of *An Inquiry into the Causes of Sterility in Both Sexes*. "When the female is not capable of gratification from debility, or against inclination," its author intoned, "she is scarcely or ever fruitful."[19] Although evidence for this theory was slight, a logic was nevertheless laid out: conception depended on the mixing of fluids, and fluids didn't emerge without orgasm. What's most interesting about this reasoning (aside from the fact that it's wrong) is that its proponents, for the first time, were painting infertility not as an act of God, sin, or malice but rather as a physical condition amenable to scientific remedy.

Insofar as conception did occur, however, these seventeenth-century manuals assumed that the product of this mingling was a tiny, nearly perfect human. Building on the theories of Aristotle and Hippocrates, they believed that babies sprang from something akin to eggs and that they lived in some inchoate form, waiting for the seed that would catalyze growth. In 1681, for example, one eminent researcher wrote that "the egg is weak and powerless and so requires the energy of the semen of the male to initiate growth."[20] Others, known as animalculists, argued that each drop of semen contained a microscopic human, waiting only for the nourishment that eggs provided.[21] Both schools, though, reasoned that conception was more akin to growth than creation. The child already existed. It simply needed its parents to mix their fluids in the appropriate way, producing the food or spark or spirits (depending on one's theory) that would allow the child to grow. In this view, infertility became a physical, almost a mechanical, problem. Childless women were not necessarily hexed any more, or evil. They just had to have the right kind of sex.

Remedies and Apparatus

Such views persisted well into the late nineteenth century. They also gave rise to a small but rather lucrative treatment industry, the precursor to today's self-help books and fertility clinics. Most of this field was comprised of marginal medical "experts," people—mostly men—without any specialized training or knowledge. Most of them advertised their wares widely and loudly. Few of these treatments offered even the dimmest prospect of success.

One of the most ingenious of this lot was James Graham, an innovative Scotsman who built a sizable fortune on "electrotherapy" and other "never failing prescriptions" for fertility. After practicing for some time in Philadelphia, Graham ventured back to England and won fame in 1779 for apparently curing the Duchess of Devonshire's infertility. The grateful duchess rewarded him well, and Graham moved to London, where he invested in a high-profile "Temple of Health." In the temple, men listened to lectures on potency as they sat on chairs that emitted mild electrical shocks. Women attended separate lectures or indulged in Graham's other electrical cures—the "magnetic throne," for example, or an "electrical bath." They purchased Dr. Graham's "aetherial balsam," a concoction, he related, "of rich gum, with . . . ether, electricity, air, or magnetism."[22] Or they bought his *Lecture on Love; or Private Advice to Married Ladies and Gentlemen*. If all else failed—and if the patient was extremely wealthy—recourse could be had to Graham's "celestial bed," a vibrating sensation that couples could rent for 500 guineas a night. According to Graham, "[the] superior ecstasy which the parties enjoy in the Celestial Bed [was] really astonishing . . . the barren certainly must become fruitful when they are so powerfully agitated in the delights of love."[23] One could only hope. At current rates of inflation, 500 guineas is worth approximately £22,700, or about $37,500.

Other remedies were less expensive, although not necessarily any more effective. In the eighteenth and nineteenth centuries, women who suffered from "obstructions" or "female weakness" were regularly advised to get exercise, take cold baths, or confine themselves to bed. They could doctor themselves with more modern equivalents of ancient cures—herbal tonics, for example, or special teas—or buy from an ever-expanding list of commercial products. Indeed, "female" illnesses became during this period one of the most attractive targets for patent medicines, concoctions that had little basis in science but thrived instead on the growing use of proprietary labeling and mass-market advertisement.[24]

Meanwhile, medical science was slowly moving into the field of fertility. In 1672, Renier de Graaf, a physician experimenting on rabbits, found small follicles (now called Graafian follicles) containing the animals' ovaries, and in 1677 Anton van Leeuwenhoek identified sperm under his microscope.[25] In 1707, a serious treatise on infertility, *De Sterilitate*, demonstrated a growing understanding of physical impediments to fertility, including ovarian sclerosis and tubal blockages.[26] And in 1797, *An Inquiry into the Causes of Sterility* painted childlessness as a physical ailment and "the cause of as much evil in the world, as any of those diseases to which we are liable."[27]

Making the Connection

It wasn't until the nineteenth century, however, that changing mores and advancing medicine allowed for a more explicit link between sex and procreation and more precise advice regarding the mechanics of reproduction. Part of this shift was simply the result of advancing science: as researchers probed more closely into the human body, they began to grapple with the biology of birth, with the organs and actions and chemicals that turned "animalcules" into babies. What enabled this science, though, was not just advancing knowledge. It was also the advance of medicine into both the bedroom and the female body. Until the late nineteenth century, after all, "feminine" illnesses were considered so private and so personal that male doctors were loath to investigate them too closely. Reproductive ailments were particularly tricky, because prevailing wisdom still treated them as acts of God. Around the turn of the century, though, a growing band of doctors began to differentiate themselves from the healers, apothecaries, and midwives who had tended to illness in the past.

Part scientist, part clinician, these new doctors defined themselves as professionals, university-trained specialists who understood the body's inner workings. Although their training in many cases was quite perfunctory (some medical schools in the 1800s required only several months of training), they explicitly differentiated themselves from less-educated practitioners, and particularly from the midwives, who had long relied on personal and informal training.[28] In Europe, doctors grouped themselves into professional guilds. In the United States, they gathered into professional societies and formed the American Medical Association in 1848. Slowly, some of this group began to specialize in women's illnesses, peering into parts of the female anatomy that for ages had been both physically and socially taboo.

Initially, this emerging cadre of experts focused on the most obvious aspects of reproduction: the position and timing of intercourse. They advised their patients to restrict themselves to the missionary position, arguing that conception that occurred with the wife on top would result in abnormal or otherwise deformed offspring—"Dwarfs, Cripples, Hunch-back'd, Squint ey'd, and stupid Blockheads," according to one source.[29] They also stressed the timing of sex, urging couples to concentrate on the wife's most fertile moments.*

Accordingly, the mid-nineteenth century saw a small wave of texts dedicated to the science of reproduction and the treatment of infertility. In the spring of 1844, for example, a doctor named Frederick Hollick began giving lectures in New York on "woman's diseases." Using life-sized papier-mâché models, Hollick gave his audiences a complete tour of human anatomy, including, he boasted, "the development of the new being in the womb at every stage." After lecturing to packed audiences along the East Coast—"upwards of four hundred ladies . . . in one day!" he reported—Hollick retired to a literary career, publishing a series of illustrated advice books for women. His counsel—relatively sound, if not precise—was echoed by other popular manuals of the time, including Thomas Low Nichols's *Esoteric Anthropology* (1853) and William Alcott's *Physiology of Marriage* (1855).[30] On a more technical level, Augustus Gardner's 1856 text, *The Causes and Curative Treatment of Sterility*, pub-

---

*Unfortunately, even though their theory was correct here, the details were not: until quite recently, doctors believed that women were most fertile in the days just after their periods, exactly when they are *least* likely to conceive.

licly located crucial elements of female anatomy and repudiated the prevalent notion that women needed to have orgasms to conceive.[31]

This era also witnessed the birth of reproductive surgery, crude attempts to "fix" the female organs that had only recently been identified. In 1855, Dr. J. Marion Sims presided over the opening of the Woman's Hospital, the first U.S. medical facility devoted entirely to feminine complaints. Sims, who had risen to prominence after devising a surgical cure for a particularly miserable complication of childbirth, firmly believed that all reproductive problems were mechanical ones, amenable to the right form of surgical intervention. He also believed in the powers of experimentation, having arrived at his first cure after years of trying one method and then another on the slave women that neighbors brought to him. "I went on improving the methods of operating," he later recalled, "eliminating first one thing and then another till I had got it down to a very simple practice."[32]

Throughout the 1850s and 1860s, Sims and his associates continued to experiment, working now with the poor and immigrant women who filled the public wards. They operated on hundreds, maybe even thousands, of women, removing ovaries or clipping cervixes to fix what they described as the purely physical impediments to reproduction.[33] Sadly, most of these "cures" proved as ineffectual as their medieval predecessors. Records from Sims's famous Woman's Hospital show virtually no evidence of subsequent pregnancies, and modern medical knowledge suggests that Sims was almost certainly operating far from the source of his patients' problems.[34] But in treating infertility as a surgical situation, Sims and his colleagues had finally and permanently repainted childlessness as a medical condition—as the realm of doctors and specialists rather than witches and gods.

Failing to Produce: The Causes and Conditions of Infertility

Today, modern science confirms the biological basis of infertility. Couples are not childless because of who they are or what they've done, but because they suffer from some underlying physical flaw. Occasionally, that flaw can result from particular actions that one of the partners has engaged in or fallen victim to. Occasionally, emotional or psychological concerns can impede the reproductive process. But in the vast majority of cases, infertility is a fairly straightforward, utterly physical condition.

Essentially, infertility results when a given couple is unable to produce a viable embryo—a sixteen-cell mingling of egg and sperm that will subsequently embed itself in the mother's womb and evolve into a living child. A formal definition comes from the American Society for Reproductive Medicine, which states that "a marriage is to be considered barren or infertile when pregnancy has not occurred after a year of coitus without contraception."[35] Sometimes the problem comes from the sperm, sometimes from the egg, and sometimes from the channels that either bring the two together or allow their product to flourish.[36]

For sperm, the problem usually resides in either quantity or speed. Some men produce too few sperm, or sperm that tend to perish before they reach the egg. Some men have had operations that have destroyed their bodies' ability to produce sperm, or have suffered exposure to toxic chemicals (in war, or certain industries, or as a result of prolonged chemotherapy) that have led to the same result. When sperm production is normal, men may still have physical problems that block the sperm's passage from the testes. In very rare cases, a man may produce sperm that actually engender an allergic reaction in his partner. Overwhelmingly, though, male infertility springs from a simple physical flaw: the inability of the man's sperm to penetrate or fertilize the egg of his desired partner.

Female infertility is more complicated, tracing as it does the more complicated biology of female reproduction. Whereas almost all male infertility is caused by problems with the mechanics of sperm production, female infertility can reside in one of three sites: the eggs, the fallopian tubes, or the uterus. Because all are necessary components of reproduction, all are also equally capable of contributing to infertility.

Statistically, female infertility stems most frequently from problems with the fallopian tubes: the microscopic channels that serve, under normal conditions, to bring a woman's eggs into her uterus. Because the tubes are small and delicate, they fall prey to a wide range of ailments, any one of which can seal the tiny opening and prevent pregnancy.[37] For example, endometriosis, a relatively common affliction of the uterus, can cause bits of the uterine lining to slough off and block the fallopian tubes. Ectopic pregnancies, in which the embryo implants in a tube rather than the uterus, can also cause blockage or even destruction of the fallopian tubes. So can pelvic inflammatory diseases (PIDs), illnesses that occasionally result from sexually transmitted diseases.

Although less common, uterine disorders are in many ways more devastating than tubal ones, because the uterus is inherently more difficult to circumvent. In cases of uterine infertility, a woman may suffer from a misshapen or scarred womb, or one that is physically unable either to secure the developing fetus or carry it to term. She may have had to undergo an early hysterectomy, usually as a result of either cancer or advanced endometriosis. Occasionally, a woman may even be born without a womb.

Most remaining cases of infertility are attributed to ovarian disorders. More treatable than uterine problems, they are also more enigmatic, tied to personal decisions as well as physiology. Traditionally, ovarian problems have emerged from the same kind of biological misfortune that haunts other instances of female infertility. Barren women were born without ovaries (rarely) or suffered from hormonal imbalances that rendered egg production either scarce or nonexistent. Their bodies refused to ovulate or to produce viable eggs. These conditions still apply, and they account for an estimated 33 percent of total female infertility.[38] Increasingly, though, ovulatory disorders are linked directly to age and with the inescapable correlation between fertility and youth.

In the aggregate, female fertility peaks at around age twenty-seven and then declines dramatically after thirty-five. Although many individual women are capable of bearing children much later in life, the statistical chances of doing so decline precipitously over time. An average twenty-eight-year-old woman, for example, has a 72 percent chance of conceiving after a year of effort. An average thirty-eight-year-old, by contrast, has only a 24 percent chance. Put differently, female fertility drops 20 percent after the age of thirty, 50 percent after thirty-five, and 95 percent after age forty.[39] These stark numbers speak to both a growing cause of childlessness and a growing demand for market-based solutions. That is because women who suffer from age-related infertility aren't barren in the traditional sense; they have the physical means to carry a child and even, sometimes, to produce one.[40] They just don't have sufficient eggs to make conception as easy as it once might have been.[41]

For women who suffer from age-related infertility, the emotional toll appears to be particularly high. These are women, after all, who could have had babies if they had started earlier, women who may have put off childbearing to pursue a career or other personal goals. Acknowledging infertility in these cases is especially tough. As Diane Aronson, a former executive director at RESOLVE, a U.S. national infertility association, recounts, "I can't tell you how many people we've had on our help line crying, saying they had no idea how much fertility drops as you age."[42]

Regardless of the cause, however, and regardless of age, infertility wreaks inestimable havoc on those who suffer from it. Although it does not have physical effects in the manner of, say, cancer or tuberculosis, and although childlessness is not itself life threatening, it tends to produce an emotional reaction akin to major illness. In studies conducted at Boston's Beth Israel Deaconess Medical Center, for example, Dr. Alice Domar, an expert on the connection between women's physical and psychological health, has shown that infertile women register abnormally high levels of depression, similar to those induced by cancer, HIV, and heart disease.[43] One infertility sufferer recounts, "When you take away being able to have a child biologically, it is like having to face death—almost like having half of you die . . . because having kids is the main way that people deal with the fact that they *are* mortal."[44] Other women (and men) express similar sentiments—of worthlessness, despair, lack of hope or desire.

On a personal level, such unsatiated demands are the stuff of tragedy. Infertility wrecks many of the marriages it affects; it drains bank accounts and often challenges the sexual identity of its victims. Yet commercially, such deep-seated demand is also undeniably attractive. In 1982, 4.5 million women in the United States reported that they suffered from infertility. This number rose to 4.9 million in 1988 and 6.2 million in 1995.[45] Historically, these women have always existed: since Rachel's time, we know, a significant percentage of both women and men have struggled with the burdens of barrenness. But because there were no cures for their condition, there was also no market. As science has slowly decoded the mechanics of reproduction, however, the prospects for treatment have grown exponentially, carving out markets that never really existed before.

Women who suffer from missing or damaged fallopian tubes, for example, can now avail themselves of in vitro fertilization (IVF), a popular and hugely successful technique described later. Men with low sperm counts can employ intracytoplasmic sperm injection (in which a single sperm is injected directly into the egg) or can venture with their partners to a thriving array of sperm banks. Women with uterine malfunctions can hire gestational surrogates, a practice described in chapter 3. In all these cases, the underlying dynamic is exactly the same: there is a demand for conception and a growing supply of technological fixes. There is, in other words, a market.

Searching for a Cure

To be sure, there has always been a market of sorts for fertility treatments. Someone, after all, sold the amulets and potions prescribed in medieval times. Someone carved the fertility statues and peddled the balms and elixirs that the Victorians prized. None of this activity, though, amounted to very much; it was composed of a very small number of people selling superstition or "cures" that were essentially worthless.

By the turn of the twentieth century, however, matters had begun to change. For the first time, doctors and scientists started to grapple with the physical causes of childlessness and with various treatments that actually worked. As these treatments evolved, they formed the critical supply side of the fertility industry, allowing demand at last to meet its match. Three developments in particular gave birth to the baby business. First was an increased understanding of the biology of reproduction. Second was the discovery of hormones and the development of endocrinology. Third, and most spectacular, was the invention of in vitro fertilization, a technique that shocked the world in 1978 and thrust the business of baby-making into a political and social maelstrom.

The first of these breakthroughs, by contrast, was much quieter. And it began, oddly enough, with gonorrhea, a sexually transmitted disease that caused discomfort but not major illness among its male sufferers. Gonorrhea had been around for centuries, a covert disease that doctors traditionally treated with various emollients and elixirs. In the latter decades of the nineteenth century, though, infection rates began to soar, a result of shifting sexual mores and a thriving commercial sex trade in America's urban cores. At around the same time, doctors also noted a marked increase in certain cases of infertility. Young women, newly married and previously healthy, developed abdominal pain and infections soon after marriage. Unable to conceive, they also had husbands who had previously been "cured" of gonorrhea.

Initially, doctors refused to see any connection between these two facts: infertility, they insisted, was a woman's disease, and gonorrhea had nothing to do with it. But gradually, both anecdote and eventual examination provided the link. Many men who had been "cured" of gonorrhea, the microscope revealed, no longer produced sperm. Infertility in these cases was thus both male and biological; it was caused, quite simply, by disease.[46]

This finding, together with developments from the growing field of gynecology, focused scientific attention on the biology of reproduction and the physical impediments to conception. Quietly, even furtively, a small band of doctors began to experiment with artificial insemination and with various ways of repairing a woman's fallopian tubes.[47] Although their advances were modest, infertile couples rapidly descended on this emerging corps of specialists, searching (and paying) for whatever treatment was available. In 1906, for example, one early gynecologist, Dr. Robert Tuttle Morris, was overwhelmed with patients after he successfully transplanted a small sliver of one woman's ovary into a previously infertile patient. "I wished that surgeons everywhere could have seen some of the pitiful letters received from women who had lost their ovaries," he later recounted. "I was offered extremely large sums of money contingent upon obtaining like results in other cases."[48]

Help Through Hormones

The second and more significant boon to commerce, though, emerged in the 1930s, when developments in endocrinology created, for the first time, a mass-market approach to childlessness. Over the previous few decades, scientists had begun to experiment with what were then called the "ductless glands"—organs that seemed to produce bodily secretions that were linked, in turn, to behavior. The researchers didn't know quite what these substances were or how they functioned.

But they could demonstrate some causal, often sexual, relationship: castrating a rooster, for example, changed the bird's sexual attributes, whereas reimplanting the testicles—even inside the animal's abdominal cavity—restored his normal behavior.[49]

In 1905, a group of British scientists labeled these mysterious substances "hormones" and helped to launch a research program around them. Initially, much of this research concentrated on the possibility of concocting hormonal extracts—of using, say, testosterone derived from a fertile male to treat an infertile one. Then it migrated slowly to a more process-oriented phase, in which scientists tried to understand the role hormones played in regulating the body's functions. In both phases, though, the research rapidly revealed a commercial side—a business based on selling either hormonal extracts or hormonal treatments.

Not surprisingly, this first phase of commerce combined serious research with a fair amount of quackery. Surgeons experimented with gland transplants; scientists offered preparations based on glandular extracts; and charlatans sold over-the-counter elixirs such as "spermin."[50] These treatments flourished in the first two decades of the twentieth century, as researchers slowly began to isolate and identify the body's major internal secretions. Then, in 1923, two scientists at Washington University in St. Louis succeeded in extracting estrogen.[51] More specifically, they demonstrated that, like the pancreas or thyroid, a woman's ovaries produced a distinct and critical substance; a substance that was key to the entire process of reproduction. With estrogen, women were physically capable of conceiving and carrying a child. Without it, the entire process was doomed from the start. Estrogen, in other words, controlled a woman's fertility.

It is difficult to overestimate the importance of this research. By identifying estrogen, the St. Louis scientists had unlocked at last the chemical basis of reproduction—the keys, in fact, to the creation of life. And once they understood how these keys functioned, subsequent researchers could begin to fix the process when it broke.

Technically, human reproduction depends on a complex and intimate blend of hormones. It begins (ironically, perhaps) in the brain, where the tiny hypothalamus gland secretes a substance known as gonadotropin-releasing hormone. This hormone prompts the pituitary gland (also located in the brain) to produce two other hormones: follicle-stimulating hormone (FSH) and luteinizing hormone. These substances, in turn, regulate the production of the more familiar reproductive hormones: estrogen and progesterone. Essentially, estrogen is the substance that launches conception: once the ovarian follicles receive the appropriate hormonal signal, they produce estrogen and release an egg into the fallopian tubes. Progesterone, by contrast, typically ends the cycle, preparing the womb for pregnancy and preventing any more eggs from ripening.

For conception to occur, all these hormones must be secreted, in the right amounts and concentrations, at precisely the right time. If any of the hormones is missing or weak or overactive, the entire process stalls and pregnancy becomes virtually impossible. On the male side, a similar though less intricate calculus applies, with sperm production dependent upon an appropriate level of testosterone.

As these processes became better understood, so too did actual "cures" for infertility suddenly seem within reach. Because if the reproductive cycle depended on the interaction of particular hormones and if these hormones could be extracted or synthesized in the laboratory, then treatment became akin, theoretically at least, to normal pharmaceutical procedure: identify the problem, prescribe the proper medication, dose the patient, and await results. Such treatments avoided the uncertain risks of surgery and the discomfort that surrounded artificial insemination. Like antibiotics, which were also emerging as marvels of the laboratory, hormones promised scientific fixes for age-old ills. And because the science was good at last and the ills so common, the market for these fixes was potentially vast.

The problem, however, was that hormones proved exceedingly difficult to extract, much less produce. Initially, scientists attempted to retrieve the key secretions from their animal equivalents—crushing bulls' testicles, for example, to extract testosterone, or using cows' ovaries to produce estrogen. But the magnitudes involved in this method were staggering. To generate one-hundredth of an ounce of testosterone, for example, scientists had to process nearly a ton of bulls' testicles. To get estrogen, they needed the ovaries of eighty thousand cows.[52] The price of these extracts reflected the cost of their production: $200 for a gram of progesterone in the 1930s, far too much for the average woman to afford.

Accordingly, the great commercial race in the 1930s and 1940s lay in the quest for synthesis, for some way of re-creating the body's secretions in the laboratory and multiplying the amounts that nature had bequeathed. Much of this work was done in a cluster of universities involved with the early hormonal research. Even more of it, however, migrated into the expanding pharmaceutical industry, into firms that saw the commercial benefits that were certain to befall the mass production of hormonal therapies. Both Schering-Kahlbaum and Parke-Davis, for example (now descended to Schering and Pfizer, respectively), rose to prominence with the commercial production of estrogen in the 1930s. G.D. Searle, now a unit of Monsanto, was instrumental in the mass production of both progesterone and cortisone.[53]

Initially, these firms and their competitors concentrated on finding more efficient sources for their prized secretions. They discovered, for example, that the urine of pregnant women yielded a particularly high concentration of estrogen; and that the roots of the *Dioscorea*, a wild Mexican yam, could be used to produce progesterone. Over time, these companies also learned how to create the underlying chemical compounds, manipulating the molecular structure of the cholesterols that become hormones. Eventually, these discoveries began to reduce the price of hormonal treatments and widen the market. By the late 1930s, most major U.S. cities contained at least one private infertility practice, along with hospital-based clinics for poorer patients. And hormones were among the most effective tools in their kit.

Test-Tube Pioneers

Meanwhile, even as hormone therapy was rapidly defining the twentieth-century market for fertility treatment, scientific developments were leading toward the third major breakthrough in the baby business. In 1944, John Rock, one of the nation's leading fertility specialists, announced that he and his research assistant had managed to fertilize four human eggs in vitro (literally, "in glass"). Using eggs donated from women undergoing hysterectomies, Rock and his assistant had matched the eggs in a petri dish with semen left over from earlier artificial inseminations. After more than a hundred attempts, four of the matches worked, combining to create tiny fertilized ova. The results were greeted, not sur-prisingly, with a mixture of awe and horror.

Within the fertility community, Rock was already regarded as a mav-erick. A staunch Roman Catholic and professor at Harvard Medical School, he was passionately committed to researching the underlying causes of infertility and curing what he regarded as one of the saddest human plights. He was a master of tubal surgery—an extremely delicate operation—and had pioneered an innovative hormonal treatment known as the "Rock rebound." By the 1930s, though, Rock had begun to despair of tubal repair: the operation only worked in less than 7 per-cent of cases and offered no hope, obviously, to women whose fallopian tubes were missing or irreparably damaged.[54] Looking back at some early and highly experimental attempts at "ovarian transplants," therefore, Rock began to play with the idea of circumventing the fallopian tubes entirely; of extracting an egg from an otherwise healthy woman, fertil-izing it outside her body, and then reimplanting the tiny embryo into the mother-to-be.[55] In 1944, he achieved the first two stages of this extraor-dinary three-stage process. After that point, the experiment was stalled.

As word of Rock's experiments slipped into the mainstream press, hundreds of infertile women sent their pleas to Boston, begging the doc-tor to cure them or even to use their eggs and wombs as the site for fur-ther experiments. Sadly, there was little that Rock (or anyone else) could do at this stage. But the scientific promise he offered emboldened both the victims of infertility and those who hoped to serve them. In the 1950s, childless couples rushed to their doctors with unprecedented speed. Mainstream magazines routinely discussed the trauma of infertility and the treatments made possible through medical advances. A 1950 arti-cle in *Look*, for example, speculated that "babies born by proxy mothers are a distinct possibility."[56] A 1947 article in *Parents* asserted that "nowa-days specialists are effecting gratifying 'cures' of the apparently infertile."[57]

In the midst of this excitement, not surprisingly, fertility clinics mul-tiplied, increasing from 52 in 1949 to 119 by 1955.[58] The profession be-came more organized and in 1944 launched its own society, the American Society for the Study of Human Sterility. By 1958 this once-tiny group had grown to include 840 members, hosted an annual scien-tific conference, and published a highly regarded journal peppered with advertisements from the growing ranks of associated products: pregnancy tests, basal thermometers, and fertility drugs.[59]

Supplying Demand

It is useful to recall at this point that the surge of interest in infertility represented a shift of supply rather than demand. The clamor for cures that emerged in the middle decades of the twentieth century was part of the eternal demand for offspring—the same demand that had driven Rachel to desperation and pulled her Victorian heirs to the improbable pleasures of Graham's vibrating bed. Although the data are sketchy, reliable estimates suggest that the rate of infertility in mid-century America was no higher than rates in nineteenth-century America or medieval Europe or ancient Greece.[60] Instead, what had exploded by the early postwar period was the supply side of the equation: the number and type of providers who actually offered solutions for infertility rather than vague promises of relief.

Many of these solutions were undoubtedly exaggerated. In 1947, for example, physician Joseph Wassersug assured readers of the journal *Hygieia* that "expert workers" in the field of infertility were able to cure 50 percent or more of their patients.[61] Another specialist told readers of *Look* magazine that success rates were roughly one-third and rising rapidly.[62] Albert Q. Maisel, in *Parents*, asserted that "pregnancy follows treatment in from thirty-five to more than fifty percent of all cases."[63]

But even granting a substantial discount for exaggeration, it is clear that the supply of solutions was simply greater in the 1950s than ever before. Doctors could reliably offer their childless patients a growing menu of options—from hormone therapies to artificial insemination and tubal surgery. Not all of these worked. In fact, roughly two-thirds of the infertile couples who sought treatment during this era were likely to remain childless, victims of conditions that science still could not fix.[64] Yet in the aggregate, the supply of fertility treatments had finally begun to approximate the demand. And because postwar couples were particularly eager to start their families and because they had a newfound confidence in the power of both markets and science, would-be parents gratefully bought whatever the growing baby business could provide. In 1952, one observer estimated that there were two thousand doctors offering fertility treatments in the New York metropolitan area alone, toting up "many millions every year . . . from the hopes and heartaches of the childless."[65]

Advances in hormonal therapy brought new options and more business in the 1960s, when researchers perfected the drugs that would become Clomid and Pergonal. Through mechanisms that scientists didn't fully understand, both of these drugs worked to stimulate ovulation in women who did not otherwise ovulate; they were endocrinological catalysts, in other words, that could induce pregnancy in previously infertile women. Although both drugs (and particularly Pergonal) substantially increased the chances of multiple births, they were also extremely effective, generating pregnancy rates of around 14 to 15 percent per cycle in women who otherwise had virtually no hope of conception.[66] Because these odds were so much higher than those offered by any previous remedies, women frequently underwent six to eight cycles of treatment before either conceiving or giving up.

As word of these drugs spread, infertile couples mobbed fertility clinics, eagerly paying thousands of dollars to receive the new treatments. In 1970, after one participant in a Pergonal trial gave birth to quintuplets, other clinics involved in the trial were rapidly booked solid. In Los Angeles, one doctor reported, "We don't have a vial in the house."[67] By the turn of the century, Pergonal had been replaced by later-generation drugs such as Follistim and Gonal F. These drugs were among the most common fertility treatments and, at between $1,050 and $5,600 per cycle, also the most profitable.[68]

Tempest in a Test Tube

By all accounts, Louise Brown was a perfectly ordinary child: a blond, blue-eyed little girl born on July 25, 1978, in Oldham, England. The circumstances surrounding her birth, however, were anything but ordinary. For Louise was the world's first child born from in vitro fertilization, the first of what would soon become an army of "test-tube babies." Her birth set off both a firestorm of criticism and a burst of commercial activity.

The details of the birth and the criticism are legendary now, providing perhaps the central story of technology's advance into reproduction.

Louise's parents—Lesley and John Brown—were a working-class couple from Bristol. John worked as a truck driver; Lesley stayed at home. They had been childless for a decade, victims of blocked fallopian tubes that prevented Mrs. Brown from conceiving. In technical terms, Mrs. Brown suffered from a simple and common reproductive flaw. It was the same flaw, in fact, that John Rock had tried fervently to address in the 1940s: a malfunction of the fallopian tubes that befell a couple who were otherwise perfectly capable of conception. As Rock had realized, the only way to cure such a couple's infertility was to circumvent the tubes themselves, allowing the egg and sperm to mingle in some other medium. Rock proved that such mingling was possible but moved on to other pursuits before demonstrating how the resulting embryo—a tiny, delicate, sixteen-cell creation—could be transferred to the mother's womb. This task fell to a later generation of specialists, who quietly worked on the second phase of Rock's experiment for the next several decades.

Two of these doctors—Patrick Steptoe and Robert Edwards—were responsible for Louise's birth. Working together since 1967, Steptoe and Edwards were determined to complete Rock's mission: to fertilize an egg outside a woman's body and transfer it to her uterus. To do so, they realized, would involve at least three components, each medically radical in its own right: they would need to remove the woman's eggs at the right time (as Rock had done), fertilize them in a medium that could sustain the egg outside the body, and then administer the precise hormones that would convince the woman's body that conception had occurred. Without this chemical conviction, the womb would reject the fertilized egg in what would become essentially a high-tech miscarriage.

Quietly, the pair had been working for more than a decade, experimenting with different combinations of fertility drugs, different methods of egg retrieval, and different schedules for both retrieval and transfer. Nothing worked. Between 1967 and 1975 Steptoe and Edwards performed at least eighty in vitro procedures without achieving a single pregnancy.[69] When one woman finally became pregnant in 1975, the pregnancy was ectopic and had to be terminated. The two doctors continued to tinker with their methods, at last arriving at the combination of tactics that produced Louise.

Doubts and Dilemmas

For the Browns, of course, the technology proffered by Steptoe and Edwards was nothing short of miraculous. "It was like a dream," recalled the new dad. "I couldn't believe it."[70] For many outside observers, however, it was somewhere between a nightmare and unmitigated sin; it was emblematic of both technology's gruesome advance and the abnormal intervention of humankind into nature's realm. Some ethicists, for example, worried that the separation between sex and reproduction was too fundamental to replace by technical means; that creating children outside the body would eventually undermine the very meaning of life. At the University of Chicago, biologist Leon Kass argued that "this blind assertion of will against our bodily nature—in contradiction of the meaning of the human generation it seeks to control—can only lead to self-degradation and dehumanization."[71] Similarly, Paul Ramsey, a leading Protestant ethicist, pronounced, "Men ought not to play God before they learn to be men, and after they have learned to be men they will not play God."[72]

Feminists, meanwhile, split into two contentious groups. Some, led most famously by Shulamith Firestone in her *Dialectic of Sex*, embraced IVF as the first step toward liberating women from their reproductive biology. Others painted IVF as the self-serving creation of men and commerce. Like potions and hormones and tubal surgery, they argued, it was just another "hubristic and harmful technology," born of a conspiracy between the "collective male ego and the corporate and medical and pharmacological purses."[73] By promoting the idea that a woman could find happiness only in motherhood, it "perpetuate[d] the cycle of depression, despair, hope . . . [and] promote[d] a fetus-centered ideology."[74]

More damaging criticism came from the Roman Catholic church, which was explicit in its denunciation of any form of assisted reproduction: "From a moral point of view procreation is deprived of its proper perfection when it is not desired as the fruit of the conjugal act, that is to say of the specific act of the spouses' union."[75]

Chastened by such critics, governments in the United States, the United Kingdom, and Australia launched high-profile inquiries into the implications of IVF, promising to arrive at an appropriate set of guidelines. In all three countries, the inquiries dragged on for years, becoming intimately intertwined with debates over abortion, fetal research, and state funding. In the end, the three countries reached widely disparate yet similarly inspired conclusions. The British ultimately decided that in vitro techniques, including the freezing and donation of embryos, could "be regarded as an established form of treatment for infertility."[76] Children born as a result of these techniques were to be considered fully legitimate in the eyes of the law, and a new state agency, the Human Fertilisation and Embryology Authority, was established to regulate both fertility research and fertility services.

In Australia, state parliaments arrived at their own set of conclusions and recommendations. In South Australia, for example, clinics were permitted to treat only patients who were considered medically infertile, and a new regulatory agency was given sweeping powers to govern reproductive technology. In Victoria, treatment was limited to infertile heterosexual couples, and a separate agency was established to license fertility centers and approve fertility specialists. In effect, therefore, the Australians, like the British, decided to permit in vitro fertilization but regulate its practice.

In the United States, by contrast, the political system was still reeling from the 1973 *Roe v. Wade* decision. Faced with fervent—occasionally even violent—opposition to abortion or fetal research, the federal government had suspended funding for fetal research in 1974, pending the recommendations of a soon-to-be-created National Ethics Advisory Board. During the waning days of the Nixon administration, oversight for these policies fell to Health, Education and Welfare (HEW) Secretary Caspar Weinberger, whose conservative views on reproductive matters were well known. In 1976, responsibility moved to Joseph Califano, President Carter's secretary of health and human services, another public opponent of abortion. Califano established a revamped commission and launched his own round of hearings, which most in the field of reproductive medicine regarded as an extended excuse for an eventual ban. Surprisingly, though, Califano's commission reported positively on IVF, recommending in March 1979 that the government end its moratorium on funding.[77] Even with this report, however, Califano and the National Institutes of Health were reluctant to act. "It was a political hot potato," recalls one leading fertility specialist. "No one would touch it." And so, amazingly, the "short-term" moratorium stayed in place. No federal funds in the United States flowed to IVF research.

Yet by this point, the seduction of the test tube was far too strong to be resisted. Only two years after Louise Brown's birth, doctors in Melbourne, Australia, announced the birth of Candice Elizabeth Reed. Eighteen months later, America's first test-tube child, Elizabeth Jordan Carr, entered the world. By the spring of 1983, roughly one hundred fifty babies had been conceived in vitro.

Birth of the Baby Market

At this stage, the success rates for IVF were still slim—roughly 10 to 15 percent in 1987.[78] Costs were relatively high—around $5,000 per cycle—and social critics shunned IVF as a mechanistic intervention in the work of God. In commercial terms, it wasn't a particularly vigorous market.

The birth of Louise and her siblings, though, demonstrated that IVF could work and that technology could indeed address some of the toughest cases of infertility. Accordingly, observers in the field quickly realized that supply was now poised to meet a deep and latent demand. If doctors could provide IVF services, they reasoned, infertile couples would clamor to consume them, regardless of the price or social acceptability. The demand was simply that strong. And thus the late 1980s saw a slow but steady entry into the fertility trade, a stream of private clinics and medical schools willing to eschew federal funding in favor of a reproductive practice.

Some of these providers came directly from the federal government, victims of the ambiguous ban on federal funding. Dr. Joseph Schulman, for example, left a prestigious job at the National Institutes of Health to launch the Genetics and IVF Institute, a private clinic in Virginia. Others were medical renegades who had withdrawn to the margins of American practice. And still others were mainstream clinics or medical schools that simply identified a need for their services.

The very first American IVF center, for example, was launched in Norfolk, Virginia, where Howard and Georgeanna Jones, two of the country's most respected fertility specialists, had gone to spend their retirement years. Yale Medical School began to offer IVF in the Yale In Vitro Fertilization Program in 1982; Columbia followed suit with its own clinic in 1983. Then came more explicitly commercial ventures such as IVF Australia, a chain of clinics launched by an American businesswoman who had herself conceived at one of Australia's first IVF centers.

As the centers multiplied, IVF slipped from an oddity into a niche. The doctors perfected their techniques, produced more children, and trained more doctors to enter the growing trade. Although prices stayed firm, demand was more than strong enough to meet the expanded supply, especially as success rates increased. Quietly, doctors began to see the field of reproduction not only as a cutting edge of medicine but also as a distinctly profitable endeavor—expanding, unregulated, and catering to a population that seemed ever eager to pay. Between 1995 and 1998, the number of in vitro procedures performed in the United States rose by 37 percent, from roughly 59,000 to roughly 81,000. During this same period, the number of fertility clinics rose from 281 to 360.[79] Fertility, by this point, was far more than a mysterious blessing, a hormonal reaction, or even a developing science. It had become a thriving business as well.

The only constraints on the baby business, in fact, were those that would trouble it for the next ten years and that continue to define the boundaries of this trade. The first of these constraints is science. Because despite the vast achievements in the field of fertility treatment, despite what one practitioner has described as a "revolution" in medical success rates, fertility clinics still can't treat countless cases of involuntary childlessness. Some of these cases are due to the patients' age or a particular medical condition. More, however, are consigned to the category of unknown causes, devastating the parents and frustrating their doctors. What complicates these cases from a commercial point of view, however, is that unknown causes and unsatisfied parents can, cruelly perhaps, bring the greatest financial rewards—the rewards of charging for round after round of expensive treatments, none of which leads to the desired result.

This central irony drives the second constraint on the baby trade. Babies, it turns out, are relatively expensive to produce. As chapter 2 describes in greater detail, the average price for a cycle of IVF in the United States was $12,400 in 2003. The lowest cost for donor eggs (in the Midwest or outside major urban areas) was between $3,000 and

$4,000. These are hefty prices to pay, even in a rich nation like the United States. As a result, many people who presumably would *like* to enter the baby business are forced by their finances to the sidelines, because the price—of IVF, donor eggs, a gestational surrogate, or a foreign adoption—is simply too high for them to pay.[80] In this market, therefore, price acts harshly as a constraint on demand. The desire is there, as we know. So, increasingly, is the supply. Yet the price of this supply is still too high for many potential buyers, leaving supply and demand to meet at a point well below their full potential.

Theoretically, of course, governments could solve the price constraint. They could, like the Danes and the Israelis, fold fertility treatment into their national health systems, covering their cost through private funds. Or, like fourteen U.S. states, they could mandate insurance coverage for fertility treatment, dramatically lowering the cost to affected patients. Yet any policy of this type runs straight into the third constraint that faces the baby market. This is the constraint of politics, the constraint that has made U.S. lawmakers and U.S. administrations exquisitely wary of treading too close to the baby trade. They don't want to prohibit it and thereby risk the wrath of those for whom assisted reproduction is the only path to conception. Yet they also don't want to condone its farthest reaches, because assisted reproduction is undeniably what its critics claim it to be: a technological intrusion into nature's most intimate process. It is an intrusion, moreover, that raises excruciating questions about women's bodies, women's rights, and the ability of parents to manipulate and perhaps even market their offspring.

The moral content of these questions has made the baby business too sensitive to legislate in the United States. But it hasn't stopped the market itself. Instead, as subsequent chapters will show, the baby business is thriving and expanding, rapidly developing the medical solutions for even higher-tech births. This market, though, remains hampered by the three constraints just described: by the limits of its science; by the dilemma of unmet demand; and by a political system that has left the baby business to wander through an unsustainable thicket of legal and commercial uncertainty. We will return to these constraints in the chapters that follow.

CHAPTER 2

A Cluster of Cells

Mechanics of the Modern Fertility Market

By the action of Modern Industry, all family ties among the proletarians are torn asunder, and their children transformed into simple articles of commerce and instruments of labor.

—KARL MARX, *THE COMMUNIST MANIFESTO*

IN FERTILITY, as in any market, we must start at the very beginning, where supply and demand collide to produce some kind of market exchange. We need to understand what drives demand in the fertility trade; what determines supply; and how the price of desire is set. We need to explore who is making money in this industry, and how.

The first piece of analysis is painful but simple. In the fertility market, as described earlier, demand is nearly constant. Roughly 10 to 15 percent of all adults experience some form of infertility. It may stem from the female or the male, or it may be unexplained. Commercially, it doesn't much matter: the crucial fact is that 10 to 15 percent of any given population suffers from a condition that subsequently gives rise to a specific demand. They want children, and they can't have them.

Not all of these people seek treatment, of course. In fact, in the United States, only 36 percent of infertile women seek treatment for their infertility.[1] However, for this 36 percent—or a total in 2002 of about 2.8 million women—the quest to conceive becomes an endless, bottomless demand, driving them in many cases to pay whatever they can: to take out a second mortgage, wipe out their savings, or give up a lucrative job.[2] At the extreme, some couples will pay as much as $100,000 for round after round of high-tech treatment. More commonly, they will pay whatever their own, more limited funds will allow, choosing between fewer or less-expensive treatments.

Thus demand in this market is not exactly what economists would call price insensitive: fertility customers care about price, and they purchase more services when the price goes down. But frequently, people buy on hope rather than on performance, and they base their spending largely on their available resources. Or to put it somewhat more crudely, when would-be parents enter the baby market, they don't necessarily think about the *value* of a particular service or treatment. They can't, because the value of what they are buying has no price. Instead, they think much more simply about what they can afford to pay.

And thus demand in the fertility trade clusters into three linked but separate segments. First are those for whom money is truly no object—wealthy couples or individuals who are willing to pay almost literally whatever the market will bear. Second are equally determined clients with more limited means. And third are those armed with generous insurance plans, able to "afford," like the wealthy, whatever their insurance covers. What binds these segments is their shared determination to do whatever it takes to produce a child. What differentiates them is their precise bottom line—the point at which they run out of the funds or the energy to continue.

Meanwhile, supply in this industry also bears its own distinctive contours. It has, first of all, been growing over the past two decades at a dizzying rate. In 1986, there were roughly 100 fertility clinics in the United States, performing a total of 10,000 cycles of assisted reproductive technology (ART). By 2002, there were 428 clinics performing as many as 115,000 cycles. In 1986, U.S. revenues from fertility treatment totaled approximately $41 million.[3] By 2002, these same revenues were approaching nearly $3 billion. And this number doesn't include the ancillary players in the trade: consultants, lawyers, equipment suppliers, and various types of counselors.

At its core, however, fertility is still a market where entry remains limited and size matters. Yes, there has been a scramble to enter the market, and yes, increasing numbers of physicians now offer fertility services to their eager patients. But the central players in the industry are reproductive endocrinologists, specialists who can enter the profession only after years of formal training, and the absolute number of clinics is therefore limited by their supply. Moreover, much of the fertility industry is increasingly marked by significant economies of scale, meaning that firms or clinics must serve a large number of clients simply to cover their fixed costs.

As a result, production in the fertility trade is rather concentrated, and a handful of big players—in hormones, in clinics, in sperm—accounts for a growing percentage of the total business. These are the players that generate the largest volumes, the greatest economies of scale, and the highest profits. They are also the players that have been able to keep their prices remarkably stable over time: in 1986, the price for an in vitro fertilization cycle was roughly $5,000 to $6,000 at a top-of-the-line private clinic.[4] In 2003, the average price was $12,400, or only slightly more than the inflation-adjusted price of the older $6,000 service.[5]

What makes this calculation particularly interesting is that the IVF industry expanded dramatically over this same period, growing from a tiny and experimental niche of research to an established branch of treatment. One might therefore have expected prices to decline. (Think, for example, of the early years of the computer industry, when prices fell dramatically as manufacturers rushed to supply demand.)[6] Yet instead, IVF prices nudged slightly upward, bearing evidence of both the suppliers' power to raise prices in this market and the buyers' willingness to pay.[7] In this regard, the fertility industry looks somewhat like a luxury trade, with a handful of powerful suppliers (think of Tiffany's, Armani, or DeBeers) catering to a well-heeled clientele.

Yet fertility, of course, is not a luxury good. Indeed, for those who lack it, fertility is a necessity of life—a basic human right, according to many advocates.[8] And because markets are political structures—because they are conceived and shaped in a democracy by competing political demands—the fertility market also bears signs of another kind of demand: a politically expressed demand for lower prices, greater access, and expanded choice. Although this demand has been relatively quiet (infertile people are far less politically active than cancer sufferers or AIDS patients), it has still made a mark in the industry, affecting how the market develops and what suppliers can do.

The most obvious manifestation is insurance coverage, a kind of two-edged sword for the fertility trade. On the one hand, when insurers cover infertility as a medical illness, they nearly guarantee a greater demand for fertility treatments: people who previously couldn't afford treatment suddenly enter the market, and people who bought minimal services now buy more. Thus, political demands in this industry can translate easily into expanded commercial demand. On the other hand, though, insurance coverage comes at a cost, forcing providers to charge only what the insurers will pay. Accordingly, insurance—and even the *threat* of insurance—acts to cap prices in the industry and put an even greater premium on volume. Tiffany's and Armani, by contrast, have no such worries.

Political pressures also raise the ever-present specter of regulation. Because infertility treatments have a substantial medical component and often involve procedures that incite moral debate, the industry is a natural candidate for government oversight. In most parts of the world, such oversight is already in place. In the United States, by contrast, federal regulation is minimal, confined to a single piece of legislation (the Fertility Clinic Success Rate and Certification Act of 1992) without any means of enforcement. Still, as with insurance, the threat of regulation hangs heavily over the industry, prodding suppliers to conform to a fairly rigorous regime of self-regulation and often to act as if they were anticipating a regulatory response.

At the same time, regulatory differences between the United States and other countries have also created gaps and opportunities in an increasingly global market. Because U.S. brokers can pay unlimited fees for egg donation, the high end of the global egg trade has gravitated rapidly toward the United States. Because Danish sperm is subject to rigorous standards and guaranteed by the government to remain anonymous, a Danish sperm bank has been able to corner much of the global market for exported sperm. In this fashion, players in the fertility trade skate along the edges of government decree, responding to and often profiting from the political variations they face.

Contours of the Market

Overall, then, the fertility trade is a wide and disparate market, defined by clusters of providers specializing in distinctive competencies. There are component suppliers in the trade: assembly operators and manufacturing centers, surgical experts and diagnosticians. There are clinics that cater to particular clienteles, along with a growing legion of consultants, marketers, and reproductive lawyers. All these segments operate under the same broad rubric that defines the baby trade. All of them are selling into a market where "whatever it takes" is often the going price. They are selling to clients joined by their desire to buy but divided sharply by their ability to pay. They are selling a product that is simultaneously hope and medicine. And they are selling in an environment constantly subject to ethical concerns and political oversight.

Each of the segments involved, however, experiences these factors in a different way. Each of them faces a slightly different aspect of the demand for children, a slightly different threat of regulation, and a different calculation of entry costs and the value of scale. To understand the modern fertility market, therefore, we need to probe beyond an abstract notion of supply. We need to break the market into its component parts, looking at how each operates and how together they meet and shape the ever-present demand.

The Market for Sperm

Arrayed along the fertility trade's bottommost rung are those that supply its most basic components: sperm, eggs, and hormones. These are among the industry's oldest firms and its most profitable. They are also its most unapologetically commercial, seeing no contradiction between the products they sell and the profits they reap.

Commercial sperm banks, for example, have been a feature of the fertility landscape since 1970, when the first for-profit bank opened its doors in Minnesota. As in other segments of the baby business, many of these firms began life as nonprofit, in-house clinics—service centers, really, for the growing treatment of male infertility. Both technically and commercially, their function was simple. Men would produce sperm in a laboratory setting, and the labs would capture and preserve it for future use.

The market for this service was small and quiet at first, composed almost entirely of men who couldn't inseminate their wives through natural means. For them, sperm banking was entirely a nonmarket operation; it was only a step in the process of artificial insemination (AI). Before long, however, observers of the field noticed that there was an additional demand for insemination, one that transcended both the marital link and the normal bounds of markets. Many women, it appeared, were eager to obtain sperm that did not necessarily come from their husbands. Some of these women had husbands with genetic diseases; others had husbands who couldn't produce sperm under any conditions; still others had no husband but a desire to produce children nevertheless. In each of these cases, sperm banking solved a problem and created a market.

The commercial market started slowly, as reproductive clinics edged into the business of intermediation. Initially, the clinics used sperm only from their patients' husbands. Then they began taking donations from friends or family. And then they realized that a more impersonal system could actually enhance both the quantity and the quality of the sperm supply. By moving toward the market—soliciting donors and paying them a nominal fee—the clinics could reduce their dependence on their patients' circles of friends and impose a more anonymous form of quality control. Using donated sperm, women (and their husbands) wouldn't actually have to choose a *man* to father their child. They only had to choose his sperm.

If we consider this progression in purely economic terms, it parallels the growth of any market. At stage one, production occurs only within the boundaries of the family. At stage two, barter appears, bolstered by the personal ties of relationship. And then at stage three, the producers begin to specialize, selling the components of production across an impersonal, rule-bound market.[9] Presumably, neither the suppliers nor the customers of donated sperm wanted to see their relationship as part of a commercial transaction, but that's what it was. By 1980, there were seventeen frozen-sperm banks across the United States, offering more than one hundred thousand samples for sale.[10] They furnished the raw material for twenty thousand babies that year, charging roughly $66 per specimen.[11]

The donors of this raw material typically were students or young professionals, men who were reviewed by the sperm banks and chosen by virtue of their physical and genetic characteristics. Some of the banks prided themselves on providing particular types or quality of sperm; the Repository for Germinal Choice, for example, offered only the sperm of exceptional donors, including Nobel Prize winners and Olympic athletes.[12] Others carved more discrete niches, such as selling primarily to lesbian couples or providing more information (photos, videos, personal notes) about particular specimens. In 1988, the U.S. government conducted its first and only survey of the artificial insemination market, finding that nearly eleven thousand physicians provided artificial insemination services, 22 percent of whom employed commercially purchased semen.[13] By 1999, there were more than one hundred sperm banks in the United States alone, few of which retained any direct link to the clinics that had spawned them.

Medically, artificial insemination is one of the simplest means of addressing male infertility. Commercially, it is also one of the most straightforward operations, a standardized procedure in which the customer—a straight couple, a lesbian couple, or a single woman—chooses a particular donor from an array of possibilities. Most sperm banks charge a standard fee for each specimen (usually \$200–\$300) and reveal a set list of their donors' characteristics. California Cryobank, for example, provides twenty-four pages of information, including religion, hair texture, occupation, and years of education. For an additional \$20, recipients can purchase an audiotape of the donor answering questions in his own voice. Fairfax Cryobank in Virginia offers extended donor profiles for \$7 to \$15, with health histories that span three generations. It also provides a personal shopping service in which clients send photos of the person they'd like their child to resemble.[14]

Although the process of collecting sperm is low tech, the storage side of the equation is considerably more complex. After it has been collected, sperm is washed and then frozen to minus 80 degrees Celsius. Then it is flash-frozen to minus 196 degrees and suspended in a tank of liquid nitrogen. Under federal regulation, all sperm must be kept in storage for at least six months while the donor is repeatedly tested for HIV, hepatitis, and other sexually transmitted diseases. The costs associated with these procedures are significant, as are the resulting economies of scale. The business of sperm banking, therefore, has tended to be dominated by a small number of relatively large firms, each armed with a sizable donor base, highly specific technical expertise, and an inherent interest in expansion. In 2000, the *Wall Street Journal* estimated the global market for sperm exports to be worth anywhere between $50 million and $100 million a year.[15]

One of the leaders in this market is Cryos International Sperm Bank, a firm from Aarhus, Denmark, that sells its sperm around the world. Launched in 1991 by a soft-spoken economist named Ole Schou, Cryos began as a local firm, soliciting donations from Danish university students and subjecting them—and their sperm—to a rigorous process of testing and evaluation. In April 1991, the company delivered its first samples to the Mermaid Hospital, a private Danish hospital. Two weeks later, the hospital reported five pregnancies, and word of the "Danish stuff" began to spread. Other fertility clinics, in Denmark and abroad, called Cryos and were stunned to discover that Schou could deliver high-quality sperm virtually overnight. "They had no idea," Schou recalls, "of what service and competition were all about." Cryos expanded its business, selling to Norway, Greece, Italy, and even the Middle East. "They say that you can't sell sand in the Sahara," Schou says quietly. "Sperm is even harder. But we sell it."[16] By 2002, Cryos was exporting sperm to more than fifty countries and realizing a contribution margin—the percent of revenues left to cover fixed costs and profit—of roughly 80 percent.[17]

In Denmark and most of its export markets, Cryos competes on the quality of its product and the anonymity of its donors. It identifies them only by number, sells sperm only to doctors, and reveals nothing except the minimal physical characteristics of its donors: height and weight, hair and eye color. Under Danish law, moreover, the donors' full identity can never be revealed. According to Schou, it is this promise of anonymity, together with high-quality assessment and customer service, that has made "the Danish stuff" so popular around the world. Most recipients, he argues, don't want to know their donors. And they never want their offspring to know that Daddy arrived via FedEx.

In the U.S. market, though, this calculus apparently breaks down. Many couples, as well as a growing number of single women, are eager to know their donors and are even willing to pass this information on to their children. Accordingly, sperm banks in the United States market their product in a very different way. Rather than limit the information they disclose, firms such as California Cryobank and the Genetics & IVF Institute instead provide potential recipients with a veritable smorgasbord of detail: hobbies, family history, favorite foods, handwriting samples—"everything," says Dr. Keith Blauer of the Genetics & IVF Institute, "except their address, telephone number, and name."[18]

Some banks go even further, differentiating themselves by offering "known" donors: men who have agreed to let their offspring contact them after they turn eighteen. For example, Xytex, a large bank based in Georgia, provides its clients with photos and the names of their donors. Rainbow Flag Health Services makes its transparency explicit, promising potential clients, "Your child will grow up without secrets. They will not grow up fantasizing that their 'father' is the lost King of Bavaria or Charles Manson."[19]

All these banks, however, operate along similar financial lines. Donors are wooed through promotional material scattered around college campuses or other attractive locales. They contribute a fixed number of times over a relatively short period and receive around $75 per specimen. Each specimen yields between three and six vials of sperm, and each vial sells for $250 to $400—a gross markup for the banks that averages roughly 2,000 percent.[20] Much of this revenue goes to covering the banks' fixed costs: donor screening, specimen storage, and the paperwork involved in tracking large numbers of anonymous, identical-looking "products." Today, the breakeven point for a sperm bank is approximately ten thousand units a year, and the smaller banks—those linked only to a particular clinic, for example, or a small cluster of doctors—are facing increased financial pressure. As these pressures mount, and as the banks jostle to provide a growing array of donor types, the sperm bank industry is likely to proceed even further down the paths of specialization and consolidation. And in the end, predicts Dr. Cappy Rothman of California Cryobank, "only the biggest will survive."[21]

The Market for Hormones

A second and equally well established line of commercial supply comes from hormones, the complex chemical substances that regulate reproduction. As described in chapter 1, hormones were an early break-through in the quest to conceive and an early contributor to the fertility trade. They remain critical, used on their own in some cases of infertility, and together with IVF or IUI (intrauterine insemination) in others. The current world leader in the market is Ares-Serono, a Swiss company that marketed the first hormonal treatment for infertility in the 1960s and ramped up its revenues to $420 million by 1988.[22] By 2004, Ares-Serono had achieved worldwide revenues of $2.5 billion and a net income of nearly $500 million, making it the third-largest biotech company in the world. Fertility treatments accounted for 32 percent of the company's sales.

Unlike sperm banks, which frequently market their product to the final consumer (the woman or couple who are choosing the sperm), hormone suppliers sell almost exclusively to the doctors and clinics that operate along the market's second tier. Would-be parents seldom choose "their" fertility drug, or even a particular drug regime. Instead, they tend to take, and purchase, whatever the doctor prescribes.

Commercially, then, fertility drugs behave very much like other pre-scription pharmaceuticals. Companies like Ares-Serono concentrate their marketing resources on the doctors and clinics that channel their product to the end consumer. They spend a great deal of money on research and development ($468 million for Ares-Serono in 2003) and protect this in-vestment through a combination of patents, brands, and powerful entry barriers.[23] They don't need to worry about price, because most of their customers are willing to pay—again and again—even if the drugs don't lead to the desired outcome. In the United States, a single unit of follicle-stimulating hormone (FSH) costs between $50 and $80. Patients generally use three to seven units per day for seven to ten days, depending on their age and how well they respond to the hormones. The total cost of hor-mones for each cycle, therefore, ranges from $1,050 to $5,600, and many women undergo three or four cycles before turning to higher-tech means.

In 1995, a shift in Ares-Serono's product portfolio shed light on its commercial prowess. Late in 1994, the company had decided to move its manufacturing focus from Pergonal to Metrodin, a related hormonal compound that reportedly produced fewer side effects. In the course of this shift, however, available stocks of both Pergonal and Metrodin de-clined, causing fertility centers and drugstores to run short. Patients undergoing hormone therapy at the time were squeezed. Many panicked, scouring mail-order pharmacies for any overlooked stocks and often paying higher than normal prices.[24] Fertility centers turned away new patients, and some enterprising doctors managed to import the drugs from abroad.[25]

It was a classic market reaction to monopoly power. Publicly, some doctors railed against the company's action, arguing that "the new drug is no more effective than the old" or that "it has created needless anxiety for many patients."[26] Others threatened to boycott Metrodin or to shift to new entrants like Humegon, a fertility drug that won FDA approval in 1995. Yet, in the end, Ares-Serono released its new drug, and fertility clinics scrambled to prescribe it. Indeed, they continued to prescribe it even as the price of the new product climbed steadily. According to one fertility specialist, "They did what they always do . . . they bought the doctors with grants, and dinners, and research prizes."[27] Any short-term discontent over prices subsided, and competition remained limited.

In the mid-1990s, a trickle of developments seemed to suggest a more finite future for hormones. Researchers at Australia's Monash University, a leading site for reproductive breakthroughs, managed to remove immature eggs from a woman's ovaries without using drugs or surgery. They then matured the eggs in a test tube and fertilized and transferred them. In other words, they completed a successful round of IVF without any hormone treatment at all.[28] If such experiments could be replicated on a large scale, they could reduce the market for fertility drugs, or at least create a plausible substitute for them.

In the meantime, though, hormones remain a quiet but critical component of the fertility trade. Between 1982 and 1992, Ares-Serono saw its sales rise by an average of 22 percent a year.[29] The company sold $260 million worth of fertility drugs in 1991 and then watched sales more than double again between 1992 and 2003. In 2003 alone, the company's sales rose by 31 percent, to $519 million. Its profits were $390 million, an astounding 75 percent of sales.[30]

The Market for Eggs

A third area of supply is newer, more complicated, and far more controversial. This is the market for eggs, a market that emerged only in the early 1990s but rapidly became the most differentiated and competitive link in the supply chain.

The market for eggs was a distinct and almost certainly unplanned offshoot of IVF technologies. Initially, as described earlier, IVF was a miracle technology for couples like the Browns—couples who were capable of producing both sperm and eggs and lacked only the fallopian tubes to bring the two together. For couples having other reproductive problems, IVF was essentially useless. Over time, however, both couples and their doctors began to contemplate another use of IVF, a use that was technically quite similar but socially astounding: they began to think about taking the eggs of one woman and transferring them to the womb of another. They began to think, in other words, of sourcing donor eggs for infertile women just as artificial insemination relied on donor sperm.

Medically, the move was simple. Once doctors knew how to fertilize eggs and transfer the resulting embryo back into a womb, the only additional complexity came from the need to coordinate two women's reproductive cycles. This they did with hormones, using Pergonal or its equivalent to cause superovulation in the donor, and progesterone to prepare the recipient's womb for pregnancy. The greater complication came from finding these donors—women who were willing both to give away their eggs and to undergo a fairly rigorous medical procedure to do so.

At first, most of these women came from the intended recipient's friends and family. A healthy sister, for example, would donate her eggs to a sibling who had lost her ovaries to cancer. Or a college roommate would offer eggs to a friend whose ovaries had ceased to produce. In all these cases the donation was just that—a donation. And the donated eggs, combined with IVF, could allow an otherwise infertile woman to carry and bear a child. Genetically, of course, the child that resulted from borrowed eggs wasn't related to his or her mother. Yet for women who had no other way of conceiving, the combination of IVF and donor eggs was a godsend. They could undergo pregnancy, bear their husband's offspring, and give birth to a child who otherwise could not have been conceived. It was another medical marvel. As one recipient reported, "I have just given birth to a miracle child."[31]

This miracle, however, depended on more than medicine. It also needed eggs—healthy eggs, to be precise, ideally produced by a young woman whose ovaries were at the peak of their production. The doctors who performed these procedures also liked to have multiple eggs, increasing the likelihood that at least one would be fertilized and implant; and the recipients generally wanted eggs that looked like them—eggs, in other words, that bore particular genetic characteristics: the intended mother's hair or eyes, for example, or her desired level of educational achievement. Sometimes, suitable donors could be found—the sisters or roommates who volunteered their eggs and were medically able to provide them. In most cases, however, donors simply weren't available, interested, or able. The demand for donor eggs thus grew steadily during the 1990s, tracking the growth of IVF centers and the increased social acceptance of test-tube kids. But the supply was sharply limited.

The sources of this shortfall were obvious. Unlike sperm donation, which involves at most a fifteen-minute commitment and a small dose of embarrassment, egg donation is an arduous procedure. The donor must agree, first, to a three-week regimen of hormone therapy, involving daily injections that prompt her ovaries to produce an overabundance of eggs. During this time, she makes frequent visits to the doctor's office, giving blood samples and having ultrasound exams that help the doctor to determine when her eggs are "ripe." Then, when the eggs are ready to be harvested, the donor undergoes a brief procedure in which the doctor plucks the eggs from the ovaries using a small ultrasound probe connected to a needle. Although the procedure usually entails only the discomforts of mood swings and abdominal swelling, some donors suffer from hyperstimulation, a painful condition in which the ovaries produce too many eggs and the body swells with fluid. Others develop bleeding or, very rarely, an allergic reaction to the hormones.[32] The long-term implications of egg donation are unknown.[33]

As long as egg donation remained truly altruistic, therefore, it was destined to be plagued by severe shortages. Why would a healthy young woman put herself at any risk to help an infertile stranger? Why would someone undergo surgery just to give away a piece of herself? There was simply no mechanism to push supply anywhere close to the level of demand.

Elsewhere, of course, similar mismatches between supply and demand are mediated quite effectively through the market. If people clamor to purchase frilly pink tulips and the tulip harvest is meager, then the price of tulips will rise until it equilibrates demand. This equilibration proved tricky in the egg market, though, because people couldn't quite determine whether eggs were something that could, or should, be sold. Virtually every country, for example, prohibits the sale of kidneys and other human organs, which explains why they are constantly in short supply.[34] Some countries also prohibit the sale of blood. Yet others, including the United States, permit the commercial "donation" of both blood and sperm, on the grounds that they are renewable body parts rather than organs.

So which regime made sense for eggs? Initially, it appeared that eggs might be classified more as organs; the United Kingdom, for example, pursued this policy route, along with several other European nations. But no restrictions were forthcoming in the United States, and so both price and commerce eventually crept into the equation, softly and subtly at first, and then with explicit vigor. Around 1990, a handful of fertility clinics began quietly advertising for potential egg donors. They posted notices for "healthy women willing to help infertile couples" and offered to pay a fee of about $2,500 to cover "time and inconvenience." Almost as soon as the ads were posted, "donations" appeared: from graduate students, young mothers, struggling actresses. Most of the women expressed a fervent desire to help other women in need; some had watched relatives struggle with infertility or felt particularly grateful for a stroke of compassion in their own lives. Nearly all, though, were clearly also responding to the financial incentives inherent in a lump-sum payment for several weeks of "work."

At this point, a small group of outsiders began to realize that eggs, like sperm, had the makings of a market. One example was Shelley Smith, a former actress working as a family counselor in Beverly Hills. After conceiving her own children through egg donation, she decided in 1990 to go out on her own, serving as a broker between potential egg donors and would-be recipients. In 1991, Smith started placing ads in publications geared to young actresses, offering an "extremely rewarding financial and emotional opportunity" to young women with the right kind of eggs. Rather than operate as a fertility specialist—something she wasn't—Smith became an intimate intermediary. She handpicked her "angels," screening for attractiveness, intelligence, good health, and "heart." She gave them psychological tests and a battery of interviews, plus tokens of appreciation—chocolates, a massage, sometimes a diamond necklace—after their egg retrieval. Then she offered her donors, regular and premium, to an upscale clientele, couples who were picky about their eggs and willing to pay $4,500 to Smith's Center for Egg Donation in addition to the donors' fee and normal IVF charges. When Smith opened her doors in 1991, she was the only independent egg broker in Los Angeles. But competition quickly emerged, from large-scale players like Bill Handel's Center for Surrogate Parenting and the Virginia-based Genetics & IVF Institute, as well as a slew of small-time brokers.

By 2004, the baseline figure of $2,500 per donation had slowly given way to substantially higher prices and a more differentiated pricing structure. Most large fertility centers offered their own in-house egg programs, complete with a full menu of potential donors and prices that typically ranged between $3,000 and $8,000. These figures followed strong geographical trends, with fees in smaller cities hovering still around $3,000 to $4,000; those in Washington, D.C., averaging about $5,000; and those in New York, the highest-priced market, hitting between $7,500 and $8,000.[35] The centers recruited donors using discreet ads in local newspapers and provided potential clients with both physical and social descriptions of each option. At the Genetics & IVF Institute, for example, clients could learn their donor's ethnic background, education record, occupation, and special interests. All donations, though, were strictly anonymous, with clients and their eventual offspring never learning the origins of their genetic material.

Other suppliers, by contrast, offered a more hands-on approach. At the Center for Egg Donation, for example, clients from around the world searched an online database of donors, complete with name, SAT scores, and glossy photos of both the donor and her own family. They could meet the donor if they chose to and even arrange for occasional contact after their child was born. Although the center's Beverly Hills location led to an apparent cluster of blonde and blue-eyed eggs, it also offered harder-to-find types, including Jewish, red-headed, and South Asian prospects.

Finally, like the Repository for Germinal Choice, the turn-of-the-century egg market also boasted an elite tier: boutique dealers in the highest-end eggs. In 1999, for example, a small ad posted in Ivy League campus newspapers raised eyebrows with its explicit offer of $50,000 for a very specific kind of egg: the donor had to be at least 5'10", with an SAT score of 1,400 and no family medical problems. The ad was placed by Thomas and Darlene Pinkerton, a California couple who left the real estate business to launch a high-end egg service called A Perfect Match. More recently, another Pinkerton ad promised $100,000 to a Caucasian woman "with proven college level athletic ability" willing to "give the gift of life and love."[36] Some larger agencies, such as the Boston-based Tiny Treasures, hover somewhere between the Pinkertons and the rest, specializing in Ivy League donors with SAT scores higher than 1,250.[37]

Clearly, such services cater to buyers' desire to choose—down to musical preferences—the kind of genetic bundle they are purchasing. Some also cater to particular kinds of buyers—Asian couples, for example, or homosexuals. Meanwhile, because commercial donation remains illegal in most other industrialized countries, U.S. firms have risen easily to the top of the global egg trade. At the Center for Egg Donation, 30 percent of business in 2003 came from abroad, and the number was steadily rising.

Production Centers

Dr. Merle Berger is unabashed about his job. The founder of Boston IVF, the largest fertility center in the United States, Berger is a pioneer in reproductive medicine. In more than thirty years of practice, the doctor has helped thousands of people create the children they desperately want. He is a professor at Harvard Medical School and the author of more than fifty scientific articles. Yet Berger describes his profession in a distinctly nonmedical way. "I manufacture embryos," he announces.[38]

Today, Berger and his colleagues sit at the heart of the global fertility business. Doctors by training, they run the largest and most visible sector of the baby trade: the fertility clinics that oversee treatment for approximately 1.2 million people a year in the United States alone. Inherently, all these facilities are chameleons of a sort. They are medical facilities and counseling facilities, the sites of high-tech research and intimate personal tragedy. They employ prize-winning scientists, hard-core marketers, and a bevy of lab technicians. At their core, however, all fertility centers do essentially one thing: they manufacture embryos that turn into babies.

To achieve this result, fertility centers employ a large and growing bundle of techniques: physical examinations, batteries of tests, and sometimes counseling sessions. If the problem can be identified (as in roughly 90 percent of cases), then specialists at the center lay out a suggested course of treatment. Because of the uncertainties involved, however, the treatments are in many ways more like options; patients try a particular method, check monthly for results, try a few more rounds, try another method or another, and move on. In the tougher cases, the doctors function almost as engineers. They tinker with the production process, trying different combinations and techniques. Patients, meanwhile, also tinker—at least initially—with the clinics they select and the procedures they pursue. Once they have settled on a particular practice, however, patients rarely leave. Instead, they tend to become involved in an increasingly personal relationship, relying on *their* doctor, *their* clinic to provide the product they desperately want.

Consider, for example, the case of David and Vivian, a professional couple in their early thirties who were unable, for unexplained reasons, to conceive.[39] Vivian had hormone treatments and intrauterine insemination (IUI) at Massachusetts General Hospital, and became pregnant with twins. But the twins died during the third trimester, leaving Vivian desperate to try again. In sixteen months she had five more rounds of hormones and three more IUIs. Then she switched to IVF, got pregnant on the second try, and miscarried. Frustrated, she and her husband finally left MGH for Saint Barnabas, a New Jersey clinic that Vivian believed to have "the highest success rate." At Saint Barnabas, Vivian and David paid $379 for each test, compared with a $10 copayment in Massachusetts. But they didn't care. The couple spent more than $100,000 on further treatments before adopting their son, Dmitri, in Russia.

Or take Patricia and Isaac, another young and highly educated couple who couldn't conceive a child.[40] Patricia's two sisters and mother had given birth in their late thirties, so she and Isaac had presumed that becoming pregnant would not be a problem. In the early years of their marriage, therefore, they focused on education and jobs, trying only after several years to have a child. When Patricia did not become pregnant, the couple underwent scores of tests and then rounds of fertility treatments. After three cycles of Clomid, Patricia turned to IVF and became pregnant after her second round of treatment. Sadly, though, the embryos—twins—implanted in her fallopian tubes, and the pregnancy had to be terminated. Soon after, Patricia was diagnosed with early-stage breast cancer and underwent a bilateral mastectomy. Throughout this ordeal, she stuck persistently by her doctors at a leading fertility clinic, even though she worried that she was becoming "deprioritized." As of March 2005, she was planning to pursue one or two more cycles. She was nearing forty at the time and had been trying to conceive for three years.

And finally, consider Katherine and Noah—also young, well educated, and trying desperately to create a child.[41] Because Katherine had several aunts who had struggled to conceive, she and Noah had wasted no time. "From our wedding night," Katherine recalls, "I was trying to get pregnant." When nature didn't work as they had hoped, Katherine went to a local fertility clinic, where she had three rounds of IUI. Then the couple moved to a new city, where she jumped to IVF treatment. She had three rounds in rapid succession but achieved only a brief pregnancy, which soon ended in miscarriage. So Katherine underwent surgery for endometriosis, tried IUI again, and enrolled in a class for stress management. When the juggling became too much to handle she quit her job but continued treatment at the same fertility center with the same specialist. The doctor, Katherine said, remained positive. "He seems to think," she recalled, "that we have no reason to stop what we're doing."

Notice what all these cases have in common. The clients' demand for the "product" is exceedingly strong. They are willing to try anything—repeated rounds of hormones, multiple surgeries, pregnancy right after cancer—and they are essentially unwilling to give up. Or as Katherine laments, "This whole process has a twenty-four-seven hold on my life. I cannot just forget." Each of the couples is determined to produce a child from their own gametes—"After all this," notes Patricia, "it's really hard to give up having a genetic child"—and price is simply not a critical constraint.

Notice, too, the loyalty that each of the clients retained for the provider. Even when they were spending considerable sums of money, for example, Vivian and David didn't take their case to a different center. Even after five years of complex and frustrating treatment, Patricia was only beginning to consider other options, such as egg donation or adoption, or other potential providers. In this regard, the fertility trade functions very much like the medical trade in general. That is, the people who purchase fertility services don't see themselves as participating in a commercial relationship. They switch providers only reluctantly; they don't argue about price; and they generally don't blame the doctors when treatment fails.[42] Such tendencies are further reinforced when insurance is paying the bill for fertility treatments, as happens now across Europe and in several U.S. states.[43]

The view from the clinics, by contrast, is more commercial. Although nearly all fertility centers tout their medical expertise and their patient-focused environments, they also reveal a distinctly financial bent. To begin with the obvious, in the United States, at least, fertility is emphatically a for-profit endeavor. Nearly all the major sperm banks are for-profit, as are all the hormone providers and most of the egg banks. The fertility clinics themselves occupy a more mixed landscape, because many remain linked with major research universities and their affiliated teaching hospitals. All the doctors at Boston IVF, for example, are on staff at Boston's Beth Israel Hospital and hold teaching appointments at Harvard Medical School. All the doctors at Manhattan's Center for Women's Reproductive Care are affiliated with Columbia University. Similar connections link Yale Medical School and the Yale Center for Reproductive Medicine and Infertility.

Yet in many of these cases, the fertility centers are not themselves bundled into the hospitals' nonprofit status. Boston IVF is a stand-alone, professionally managed private corporation, as is the Center for Women's Reproductive Care. The doctors, therefore, wear at least two hats: clinicians or researchers at major teaching hospitals, and employees of for-profit fertility centers. Some then multiply these hats even further. Boston's Berger, for example, along with some of his colleagues, has additional financial interests in an egg donation firm (Dream Donations), an embryo testing laboratory (Embryonics), and a consulting business (IVF Performance). Dr. Cappy Rothman, who teaches at the UCLA School of Medicine, is also a cofounder of the IVF Center at Century City Hospital and medical director of California Cryobank, one of the world's largest sperm banks. Generally, the rationale for these overlapping structures is in part scientific synergy, and in part pure profit. "I was dismayed," recalls Berger, "that physicians could only make money from what they do with their hands."[44]

Commercial Clinics

Outside the world of academic medicine, fertility clinics are even more overtly commercial. They compete actively in the market for infertile patients, often relying on carefully nurtured relations with a circle of referring physicians. "We wine and dine them," reports one lab director, "and tell them how good we are." "We do newsletters, dinners, parties at medical meetings," recounts another.[45] Many of the clinics hire high-powered marketing consultants and advertise their services on billboards, in magazines, online, and on the radio. "We've tried everything," one doctor says, laughing.[46]

Some even compete directly on price. The Advanced Fertility Center of Chicago, for example, offers a money-back guarantee for patients who do not produce a baby after treatment.[47] The ARC Family Building Program, a nationwide network of doctors, offers several standardized options, including the Three-cycle Plus program and the Affordable Payment Plan. According to the company's Web site, the Plus program includes additional services such as "assisted hatching" and the opportunity to purchase a money-back guarantee. The Affordable Payment Plan "can make your fertility care less expensive than a second car."[48]

Other efforts are subtler. Most of the clinics' Web sites, for example, feature gauzy photos of infants and joyous couples rather than syringes and invasive medical procedures. Many tout optimistic success rates and book their physicians to speak at infertility gatherings organized by local advocacy groups. Like other businesses, they are increasingly turning to incentive schemes and performance measures to gauge their own productivity. At several Northeastern practices, for example, doctors' pay is aligned with three quantitative goals: patient satisfaction, financial performance, and birthrates. As a result, says a beaming outside consultant, "The whole clinic is obsessed with outcomes."[49]

Finally, across the United States, private fertility practices are increasingly consolidating into networks such as IntegraMed, a publicly listed company that provides member clinics with management advice, pharmaceutical products, and in-house financing. One doctor who joined his practice to IntegraMed in 1997 expected his annual caseload to rise by 80 percent, allowing him to keep his practice open "52 weeks a year, fully staffed all the time, offering even the most exotic reproductive technologies."[50]

Of Medicine and Markets

This business in births is neither inherently bad nor completely new. On the contrary. As noted earlier, there has long been a deep-seated demand for fertility treatments and a small, if historically rather useless, supply of solutions. What complicates this particular area of the baby market, however, is the fine line it walks between commerce and medicine, between treatment for an illness and purchase of a much-desired good. In other realms with similar characteristics—the market for donor kidneys, for example, or cancer treatments—the state traditionally has intervened to establish guidelines. Kidneys, we know, can never be sold. Cancer treatments are mediated through the health-care system and subject to a well-established (if occasionally inequitable) set of rules. In the fertility trade, by contrast, private rules reign. The fertility centers themselves set the rules that guide their conduct, working under the auspices of the ASRM (American Society for Reproductive Medicine). In the United States, at least, the federal government is essentially silent, offering only the merest of parameters: fertility centers must report their success rates to the Centers for Disease Control; they must abide by basic laws forbidding malpractice and fraud; and, in fourteen states, insurance companies must cover (or offer to cover) some form of infertility treatment for their policyholders.[51]

Outside these boundaries, the centers are free to operate and compete. There are no constraints on their advertising (other than basic prohibitions on fraud or misrepresentation) or on tactics for attracting their clientele. To be sure, this same degree of openness characterizes nearly all aspects of U.S. business; indeed, it is this very openness that is frequently cited as driving the vitality of U.S. commerce. But in the fertility trade, the underlying business model plays out strangely.

Consider, for example, the conundrum that occurs every time a client fails to become pregnant. The client—let's call her Sally—is determined to conceive a child. The doctor—we'll call him Dr. Welby—wants to help Sally and earn revenue at the same time. He also has some knowledge about Sally's statistical chances of achieving pregnancy, knowledge that presumably is accurate in the aggregate although not necessarily relevant to her situation. In many cases, these three dimensions work perfectly well together. Dr. Welby uses his medical expertise to diagnose Sally's problem and prescribe an appropriate course of treatment; Sally undergoes the treatment and pays Dr. Welby; and some months later, the proud mother carries her infant home.

When the treatment doesn't work, however, this happy equilibrium can fall seriously out of balance. Imagine that Sally is forty-two years old and her eggs are only marginally viable. Dr. Welby prescribes an initial course of treatment with Gonal-F (a leading brand of FSH) at about $3,000 a cycle. Sally undergoes three cycles without becoming pregnant. Commercially, this state of affairs is rather beneficial to both Dr. Welby and Ares-Serono, the producer of Gonal-F. They earn revenues from each cycle, and Sally is unlikely to complain about what, to be blunt, is a repeated purchase of a service that doesn't work. In fact, even if Dr. Welby were to advise Sally to stop the treatment, using his professional judgment to conclude that Gonal-F isn't going to help in her case, she might very well insist on trying again. And again, and again, and again. Indeed, fertility specialists regularly describe women who continue with treatment well after the chances of success have declined. To quote one industry insider, "Talk about a big business . . . it's carrots hanging out there, because it's so hard to say when enough is enough."[52]

Note the dilemma that is thus inherent in the product. If Dr. Welby were selling, say, potato chips, his commercial incentives would be straightforward: he would want to continue selling his product to Sally, convincing her each time of the desirability of her purchase. If she didn't like the plain chips, he'd try to sell the barbecue flavor, or the salt and vinegar—anything to keep her coming back. By contrast, if Dr. Welby were only practicing medicine, both Sally and the state would eventually put limits on what he could sell. If the cancer treatment didn't work, she would abandon it (or die). If the ulcer medication was too expensive, she (or her insurance company) would look for less-expensive alternatives.

Where fertility treatments are concerned, however, there are few incentives to stop treatment. Sally is determined to keep trying, the state has no guidelines, and the business side of Dr. Welby would be foolish to say no. The only constraint comes from price: at roughly $3,000 a month, Sally will eventually run out of money. If Sally is wealthy, however, or has devoted all her savings to pursue a child, "eventually" may not come for quite some time. And during that period, Dr. Welby can continue to sell multiple rounds of a product that probably won't work.

Now consider what happens next. Sally despairs of hormone treatment and asks Dr. Welby for more aggressive treatment. She wants to try IVF, or its even higher-technology sibling, ICSI (intracytoplasmic sperm injection). Dr. Welby again faces a dilemma. Commercially, he has every interest in encouraging Sally to proceed: depending on where he is located, Dr. Welby charges between $6,000 and $14,000 for each round of in vitro fertilization, and most women undergo an average of three cycles before either conceiving or giving up.[53] Financially, therefore, IVF is a great boon to Dr. Welby. Indeed it is IVF that provides infertility centers with the bulk of their profits. Most centers, according to industry experts, try to perform between three hundred and four hundred cycles of IVF per year just to break even (see table 2-1).[54] The revenues from these cycles cover the centers' fixed costs: nurses, laboratories, counselors, office rent. After that point, revenue from additional cycles translates almost directly into profits. And at $6,000—or $14,000—a cycle, the profits for the largest clinics can be considerable.

Whenever Dr. Welby dons his marketing hat, therefore, he faces a statistical and moral conundrum. On the one hand, he dearly wants to convince Sally that the likelihood of success in her case is high. He wants her to believe that his practice is particularly good at producing babies and that IVF is a particularly attractive path for her to pursue. All these arguments are easy to make, because most women in Sally's position desperately want to believe that fertility treatments will cure their condition. In fact, they tend to overestimate their chances of conception by an extremely wide margin.[55] So Dr. Welby will not have a hard time convincing Sally about the benefits of treatment. Moreover, his own preferred method of treatment—IVF—is indeed increasingly successful: on

TABLE 2-1

Top twenty U.S. clinics by number of cycles, 2002

Clinic	Number of cycles
Boston IVF (Waltham, MA)	2,648
Reproductive Medicine Associates of New Jersey (Morristown, NJ)	2,301
Shady Grove Fertility Reproductive Science Center (Rockville, MD)	1,941
Weill Medicine College of Cornell University Center for Reproductive Medicine and Infertility (New York, NY)	1,755
Reproductive Science Center (Lexington, MA)	1,564
Brigham and Women's Hospital Center for Assisted Reproduction (Boston, MA)	1,389
IVF Lincoln Park (Chicago, IL)	1,376
Huntington Reproductive Center (Pasadena, CA)	1,099
Program for In Vitro Fertilization, Reproductive Surgery and Infertility (New York, NY)	1,039
Highland Park IVF Center (Highland Park, IL)	1,006
Presbyterian Hospital ARTS Program (Dallas, TX)	963
Cooper Center for In Vitro Fertilization, P.C. (Marlton, NJ)	892
Reproductive Biology Associates (Atlanta, GA)	855
Reproductive Science Associates (Mineola, NY)	817
Center for Advanced Reproductive Services at University of Connecticut Health Center (Farmington, CT)	814
IVF Michigan (Rochester Hills, MI)	803
Midwest Reproductive Medicine (Indianapolis, IN)	763
Women and Infants Hospital, Division of Reproductive Medicine and Infertility (Providence, RI)	745
Institute for Reproductive Medicine and Science, St. Barnabas Medical Center (Livingston, NJ)	734
Fertility Center of New England, Inc., New England Clinic of Reproductive Medicine (Reading, MA)	719

Source: Compiled by author from data in Centers for Disease Control and Prevention. Division of Reproductive Health. *2002 Assisted Reproductive Technology Success Rates: National Summary and Fertility Clinic Reports.* Atlanta, GA, 2004. Note that clinic-level data does not include cycles for women older than forty-two, and that "cycles" includes only those using fresh nondonor eggs.

average, in vitro fertilization results in a live birth more than 25 percent of the time.[56] And so again, what makes financial sense for Dr. Welby will also strike a happy chord with Sally.

Clinic-specific success rates, on the other hand, pose a more complicated issue. For "success" is a tough thing to measure in the fertility trade, and the numbers that might look best to Sally are not necessarily those that will either enhance her own chances or generate a healthy revenue stream for Dr. Welby. For example, in 2001, 27 percent of all IVF cycles performed in the United States resulted in a live birth.[57] This suggests that a woman like Sally has roughly a 1-in-4 chance of becoming pregnant using IVF. Yet if Sally is, say, twenty-six years old, aggregate statistics (see table 2-2) suggest that her chances of having a baby through IVF are actually more than 38 percent. If she is forty-two, they plummet to 9 percent.[58] Which are the relevant figures? Does Sally want the average, or the average for her age group? If Dr. Welby specializes in older women and thus has a lower pregnancy rate than his competitor, is this good news or bad news for Sally? Does it suggest that Dr. Welby's clinic is better or worse than the clinic down the street?

TABLE 2-2

Average pregnancy success rates, by age, per cycle of ART

Age	Pregnancy rate	Live birth rate
22	38.6	36.2
26	43.2	38.1
30	41.3	36.4
34	37.9	32.0
38	29.7	23.2
42	16.0	9.0
46	2.2	1.1
Average	33.0	27.0

Source: Centers for Disease Control and Prevention. Division of Reproductive Health. 2001 *Assisted Reproductive Technology Success Rates: National Summary and Fertility Clinic Reports.* Atlanta, GA, 2003, Figure 10.

Even pregnancy and birth rates, moreover, don't tell the full story of success, because recent research indicates that children conceived via IVF may carry a higher risk of birth defects. One Australian study, for example, found that IVF babies were twice as likely as naturally conceived infants to have multiple major birth defects.[59] Others report higher rates of rare urological defects and increased risk of early childhood cancers.[60] IVF also leads to a much higher rate of multiple births— 37 percent, according to one recent study—which itself leads to more complicated pregnancies and a greater chance of premature or underweight births.[61]

How much of this information should Dr. Welby relate to Sally? Under the law, virtually none is required: his only obligation is to report the pregnancy and birth rates of his clinic to the Centers for Disease Control (CDC), which then aggregates the data and publishes it in an annual report. If a particular clinic chooses not to reveal its data, the CDC has virtually no powers of compulsion; in 2000, for example, twenty-five U.S. clinics made no report to the CDC, including Genetics & IVF Institute, one of the nation's largest centers.[62] Under ASRM guidelines, meanwhile, Welby need only get informed consent from his patients, use medically acceptable techniques, and follow informal guidelines with regard to the number of embryos transferred at any time.[63] Even at a personal level, the landscape is murky, because Sally, after all, doesn't care about aggregate statistics. She just wants the chance to have a baby.[64]

As Dr. Denny Sakkas of Yale IVF explains, "Infertility is a hit or miss business . . . If you end up with a baby, nothing else matters. Unfortunately, a negative result is more likely than a positive one . . . It's a strange area to be in. Sixty to seventy percent of patients' treatment will fail. And you know that."[65]

Dr. Welby and his real-life counterparts therefore face what Dr. Richard Berkowitz, a reproductive specialist at New York's Mount Sinai hospital, describes as a "real Catch-22." "The doctors want to get the patients pregnant," he recounts. "The patients want to be pregnant. So the patients shop for the doctors who have the best pregnancy rates."[66] This dynamic pushes fertility clinics, almost inexorably, to put the most positive spin they can on their technologies and data, touting procedures that frequently have a low probability of success and an unknown potential to do harm. As Dr. Mark Sauer, a leading expert at Columbia-Presbyterian Medical Center, puts it, "Our mission is to make a woman pregnant, with almost a whatever-it-takes attitude."[67] Stories from the popular press drive this attitude even further, glorifying "miracle" babies and the doctors who produced them.[68] Stories from the other side—of couples undergoing round after round of expensive but ultimately futile treatment—are considerably less common.[69]

All fertility practices, therefore, need to wrestle with the commercial dilemmas that come from this gap in perception. If the clients of fertility services truly shop around for the clinic or doctor with the "best" statistics, then the clinics will be under implicit pressure to shape their practices toward particular statistical outcomes. Such manipulation is relatively easy. If clinics want to boost their pregnancy rates, they can refuse to treat women over a certain age, or women whose levels of FSH are higher than a certain level. They can encourage patients to withdraw from the program if they don't get pregnant within a certain period of time, or they can skip less-expensive options in favor of IVF.

One could describe these tactics simply as good medicine: if a woman has reached a certain age and her hormone levels have dropped below a certain level, then perhaps doctors should encourage her either to withdraw from fertility treatments or to pursue only the most aggressive routes. But clearly, such tactics also reflect a commercial motive, for if patients choose fertility clinics by statistical rates of success, then clinics will be constantly tempted to discard those cases that damage their success rates. As one laboratory director asserts, "Fertility clinics are there to make money. You're not going to pursue something that's going to hurt you. And if your success rate drops, you're going to lose patients."[70] Columbia's Sauer is even more direct. "Everybody," he asserts, "knows how to inflate the numbers . . . If a program wants to maintain a very high success rate, they can and do literally select the best patients to treat."[71]

When insurance enters the picture, the dilemmas become even more profound. Recall that in some states, coverage of fertility treatments is mandated by law: insurance companies in those states must include at least some IVF services in their basic insurance package.[72] As they do in other areas of health care, therefore, insurance companies have arrived over time at benchmarks for reimbursement. In Massachusetts, for example, a state with particularly generous coverage, insurance providers generally cover a prescribed course of treatment involving three rounds of Clomid, three rounds of the more powerful FSH, and then—and only then—IVF treatment. As a result, clinics based in Massachusetts operate under a fairly strict set of commercial constraints. They can't recommend IVF (except in certain carefully defined cases) before the patient undergoes the prescribed rounds of Clomid. They can't charge a forty-three-year-old woman much more than a twenty-eight-year-old.[73] If they are looking toward the bottom line, therefore, they will be drawn almost inevitably toward volume.

In other words, if clinics face a cap on how much they can charge for each fertility procedure, it is in their economic interest to treat as many patients as efficiently as they can.[74] Essentially, they are in a volume business. The availability of insurance expands the pool of potential patients but limits the amount of revenue that each one can generate.[75] In states like New York and California, by contrast, less generous insurance coverage changes the financial incentives of fertility treatment.[76] Here, clinics tend to be less interested in how many patients they treat, concentrating instead on the upper end of the market—on the patients who are wealthy enough to dispense with insurance mandates and pay whatever it takes (see table 2-3).

In the fertility trade, therefore, as in sperm and hormones, specialization and consolidation have already proceeded apace. The most successful clinics are either very high volume or very high tech, whereas the others—smaller, less sophisticated, less commercial—increasingly are being squeezed by declining profit margins and an increased pressure to merge.

All the clinics, moreover, are affected by the constraints laid out in chapter 1. They are, first of all, racing to keep up with a science that, for the past twenty years, has been progressing by leaps and bounds. This means that they are constantly forced to invest in this new science: in the most newly minted doctors, the best-trained technicians, the most sophisticated laboratory equipment, all of which raises their costs. At the same time, though, they must reckon with the reality that their customer base is sharply limited by these same costs and, ironically, by the success

TABLE 2-3

The costs of IVF

Procedure	Jones Institute of Reproductive Medicine, Norfolk, Virginia	Brigham and Women's Hospital Center for Reproductive Medicine, Boston	Columbia University Center for Women's Reproductive Care, New York	Center for Reproductive Medicine and Infertility (Cornell), New York
Initial evaluation	$920–$1,410	$286	$300–$400	$400–$500
Cycle stimulation	$5,720	$2,569	$2,000–$5,000	$8,900
Pregnancy tests	$350	Included in cycle	$105	$285
Egg retrieval	$2,499	$4,645	$2,780	Included in cycle
Medications	$3,000	$2,000–$4,000	$2,000–$5,000	$2,500–$5,000
ICSI	$2,420	$2,000	$2,000–$2,950	$2,500
Cryopreservation	$1,650	$800	$1,300	$1,000, plus $250 per quarter
Total number of cycles for women aged 41–42 (2002)	17	183	92	280

Source: Jones Institute, Billing Office at Columbia University Center for Women's Reproductive Care, Brigham and Women's Hospital, Center for Reproductive Medicine at New York Weill Cornell, Centers for Disease Control.

that science has brought. In other words, because fees for IVF remain so high, demand is lower than it otherwise would be. And because IVF procedures are increasingly successful—leading to a greater percentage of pregnancies in a shorter time—the pool of patients is actually shrinking. As one doctor wryly remarked, "Most infertility practices today have a hard time replacing the patients we 'lose' to pregnancy."[77]

Once again, the market's third constraint—politics—theoretically could widen this market, using insurance policies, as states like Massachusetts already do, to lower prices and expand the patient population. To date, most states have been wary of going this far, and most clinics have been happy to resist. But if pressures along these lines increase, then more of the fertility trade will be pushed toward the volume end of the market, toward that commercial state where, as Boston IVF's Berger acknowledges, they simply "manufacture embryos."

The Specialty Trade

Away from the glow of the spotlight, meanwhile, a number of smaller businesses are also growing around the business of conception. Some of these are exceedingly high tech, developed on the back of painstaking breakthroughs in reproductive science and genetics. Some are more mundane, serving primarily to accommodate the needs of small sectors of the infertile population. Together, they compose the final tier of the fertility trade.

One piece of this market centers on techniques for handling and preserving eggs. In 1997, doctors at Reproductive Biology Associates, an Atlanta-based fertility center, announced that a thirty-nine-year-old woman had given birth to twins conceived from the frozen eggs of a twenty-nine-year-old donor. Several months later, the center announced that another patient had given birth to a child produced from her own previously frozen eggs.[78] These announcements were not completely without precedent. Indeed, since 1986, sporadic reports of successful egg freezing had emerged from reproductive specialists scattered around the globe: a single pair of twins in Singapore, a smattering of isolated births in Australia and Europe. But none of the doctors involved had been able to duplicate their successes, and most acknowledged that the technology for freezing eggs remained highly unreliable.

The problem, it appeared, lay with the very high water content of eggs: during the freezing process, the water tended to crystallize, destroying the delicate spindle that contained the egg's crucial cytoplasm. In the early 1990s, however, researchers in Italy began to experiment with techniques for dehydration, adding sucrose during the freezing process to absorb water from the egg and limit the formation of ice crystals. As these techniques improved, they pushed success rates for egg freezing higher, eventually making it possible for clinics like Reproductive Biology Associates to offer egg freezing to a select group of patients: young women about to undergo chemotherapy, for example, or couples who needed to wait between the time of egg retrieval and implantation.[79]

Quickly, though, interest in egg freezing spread far beyond the patients for whom it was medically necessary. Well attuned to the ticking of their own biological clocks, young women began to consider egg freezing as a possible way to delay childbearing for an extended period— a way, at last, to beat the fertility decline hovering in their mid-thirties. And fertility clinics realized that egg preservation, theoretically at least, represented a whole new market for reproductive services.

As the technology matured, these prospects grew more exciting. By 2002, a leading British fertility specialist publicly announced that egg freezing technology would work "just as well for the Bridget Jones generation who want to freeze their eggs to keep their reproductive options open."[80] In Atlanta, the doctor who had helped to conceive the first well-publicized products of frozen eggs predicted that "within two years we'll have egg banks all over."[81] "We have been overwhelmed," reported one of his partners, "by calls from women who want to delay having children."[82]

Meanwhile, a new host of entrepreneurs was also taking note. In Milwaukee, a fertility specialist launched Egg Bank USA in 2002, charging $7,000 to remove ten to fifteen eggs from a young woman and store them for eventual use. In Los Angeles, the CHA Fertility Center announced a similar service, targeting "women in their 30s who are busy in their professional lives" and offering what the *Wall Street Journal* described as "egg banking for the masses."[83]

Watching from the outskirts, a Harvard Business School student named Christina Jones realized that the potential market among her friends and acquaintances was huge. Having already launched and sold several software businesses, the thirty-four-year-old Jones poured $300,000 of her own money into research and began in 2002 to assemble "the best-of-breed components for premium egg freezing services."[84] Armed with an exclusive license for cutting-edge cryoprotectant technology, Jones's firm, Extend Fertility, jumped into the egg market in the spring of 2004, offering full-service egg retrieval and storage for $15,000 plus annual storage fees. At the time of launch, Jones predicted that egg freezing would rapidly become "bigger than IVF."[85]

A more contentious segment of the market revolves around sex selection. Technically, choosing the sex of one's baby is no longer particularly complicated. Embryologists can determine an embryo's gender while it is still in vitro. Ultrasound technicians can tell as early as twelve weeks after conception. And a new crop of screening techniques promises to differentiate male from female sperm.[86] All these techniques have created the quiet possibility of commercial sex selection.

In Virginia, the Genetics & IVF Institute began to offer "sperm sorting" on an experimental basis in 1998, using a patented technology called MicroSort to select those sperm most likely to produce either a girl or a boy. Originally, this high-tech method of staining and then separating sperm was developed by researchers at the U.S. Department of Agriculture, who were working on ways of fine-tuning the breeding process of cattle and other livestock. But doctors at the Genetics & IVF Institute seized upon the obvious commercial applications in humans and negotiated an exclusive license for all human uses of MicroSort. Because the technology in this case was subject to review by the U.S. Food and Drug Administration, the Institute could not leap as quickly into the sex selection market as it had elsewhere. So it launched well-publicized trials instead, asking potential clients through radio and magazine ads, "Do you want to choose the gender of your next baby?" By early 2004, more than four hundred presorted babies had been born this way, each at a cost of roughly $2,500.[87]

Meanwhile, developments along the cutting edge of infertility treatment promise to create both new modes of conception and expanded nodes of commerce. In 1992, for example, researchers in Belgium pioneered the technique known as intracytoplasmic sperm injection (the abbreviation, ICSI, is pronounced "icksy"). Using tiny needles and micromanipulators (tools that lessen the hand's movement), the scientists were able to isolate a single sperm and inject it directly into the egg. The egg was fertilized, and a child was born. Subsequent experiments demonstrated that ICSI was extremely successful in dealing with male-related infertility, and, as word of the technique spread, other fertility centers began to attempt it. Most achieved the same kind of success that the Belgians had predicted, with overall pregnancy rates of about 32 percent.[88]

And thus a rash of centers began to use ICSI as a marketing tool, racing to offer it before their competitors had fully mastered the technique. Financially, the new treatment was a boon: centers typically charged an additional $1,000 to $1,500 to perform the procedures. Technically, ICSI allowed many more couples to achieve pregnancy, especially if they suffered from male infertility. Yet medically, the prospects were uncertain. Because ICSI essentially allowed infertile men to father children, it seemed to destine those (male) children to the same genetic fate. According to several studies, male children born via ICSI lacked the same gene that their fathers did, meaning that they, too, were likely to be infertile.[89] By this point, however, demand for the technique was strong and soaring. Tens of thousands of children were born using ICSI during the 1990s, and thousands of additional parents were increasingly eager to try.[90]

Even more controversial—and potentially lucrative—is preimplantation genetic diagnosis (PGD), a technique that allows doctors to screen eight-cell embryos for genetic traits. In practice, PGD is already being used to select among embryos with a high probability of fatal genetic disorders: parents who carry the gene for cystic fibrosis, for example, or Tay-Sachs disease, can use PGD to identify which of several in vitro embryos are free of these dread defects. In theory, though, PGD can do much, much more. It can screen for defects in embryos produced by older women. It can identify embryos with Down syndrome. And potentially, it can enable parents to select their children's genetic makeup long before they're born. The vast possibilities of PGD are described in chapter 4. For now, it suffices to mention that PGD screening currently adds an average of about $3,500 to the total IVF bill.[91]

Conceiving the Market

It is entirely possible—even plausible—to conceive of the reproductive market as a small, profitable enclave of sophisticated science. It is a market, first of all, that remains irrelevant to 85 to 90 percent of the population, those lucky enough to conceive their children the old-fashioned way. Nearly by definition, then, it shouldn't share the traits that characterize the markets for potato chips or sneakers.

Even in medical circles, fertility remains a niche market, one that is unlikely to expand beyond a small fragment of potential customers. Most of these potential customers, moreover, never avail themselves of any form of treatment: as noted earlier, only 36 percent of infertile women in the United States seek medical assistance, and only 1 percent resort to ART.[92] The others keep trying, give up, or move on to other pursuits.

Those that do enter the market, by contrast, are decidedly wealthier and better educated than average.[93] They are clearly members of a global elite, interacting in what feels very much like a luxury market: $12,400 for an average cycle of IVF, $3,500 for PGD, up to $50,000 for Ivy League eggs. The firms that serve this clientele, meanwhile, are highly concentrated and distinctly profitable. The global market for sperm is dominated by a small number of high-volume, high-profit firms. So is the market for hormones, where companies like Ares-Serono and Organon (a subsidiary of Akzo Nobel) face limited competition and almost no downward pressure on price. Egg brokers and fertility centers are newer entrants to the fertility trade, but already they seem to be evolving along a similar course, with smaller centers consolidating into networks like IntegraMed, and larger centers like Boston IVF reaping the substantial profits of scale.

The fertility industry presumably could stay this way for quite some time, settling into a small and highly lucrative corner. It could continue to serve a relatively small portion of the population, pushing along technology's edge to refine the science of conception. It could retain a kind of Tiffany's mentality, selling hugely valued products to couples willing to pay.

Yet experience both outside the United States and in other industries suggests that the fertility trade could also follow a very different route, one that embraces a larger market in exchange for substantially lower prices and a modicum of regulation. Consider the fact that about 75 percent of fertility's potential customers are not yet buying the product: only 15 percent of infertile women in the United States have used fertility drugs; only 5.5 percent have employed artificial insemination, and only 1 percent have tried IVF.[94] Consider, too, that recent developments promise to extend the benefits of fertility treatment beyond the infertile population. Soon, perfectly healthy young women could regularly choose to freeze their eggs, hedging against the "risks" of a late marriage or a prolonged career. Soldiers could routinely freeze their sperm before going off to war, and homosexual couples could use assisted reproduction to conceive and bear their genetic offspring. Such applications could add millions of customers to the fertility trade—but only if prices come down and access is widened.

Already, we see early signs of this connection in states like Massachusetts, where generous insurance coverage has dramatically increased demand for fertility services. We see it as well in countries like England, Denmark, and Israel, where state funding has likewise reduced the price and expanded the demand for treatment.[95] And we see it across high-tech industries like personal computers and DVD players, where goods that were initially considered expensive luxury items migrated over time to the mass market, earning their manufacturers considerably greater reward. This is the mathematical reasoning that drives most of American capitalism, the reasoning epitomized by Henry Ford's 1908 decision to manufacture the all-black, mass-produced Model T car. In most areas of medicine, such reasoning is clearly inapplicable: no matter how low the price falls for open heart surgery, demand for the service is unlikely to rise by very much. In fertility, by contrast, demand could well soar, driven both by the 75 percent of infertile couples who currently choose not to pursue treatment and the more amorphous pool of fertile individuals who might selectively employ the techniques of assisted reproduction.

If the market is left purely to its own devices, however, this kind of widening is unlikely to occur. Although some clinics will move aggressively into the volume market and some, like the members of the ARC Family Building Program, will begin to play with price, there is still considerable room at the top end of the market and little incentive for treatment providers either to reduce prices or to attract government intervention.

There also is little reason for any of these providers to engage with the social, medical, and ethical issues that emerge from their science. For example, should there be age limits on infertility treatment? Should new procedures be subject to testing protocols? Should multiple births be controlled or limited? Without any outside pressure, the market will tend to answer no to these questions and yes, repeatedly, to the desires of potential clients. Yes, a sixty-three-year-old woman can choose to undergo IVF treatment. Yes, a family with one daughter can choose to conceive a son. Yes, a couple can proceed with the birth of IVF-induced quintuplets. And perhaps they should. But one could also argue that these are not the kinds of questions that markets answer best. Because what happens when the sixty-three-year-old gives birth to a severely deformed child and then sues the fertility clinic for damages? What if hospitals and insurance firms balk at covering the intensive care costs for quintuplets? Without accepted guidelines, private firms and independent physicians are likely to pass along the costs of decisions they are not fully authorized to make.

In the United States, much more so than in Europe or Canada, the private market has already pushed the social and scientific boundaries of assisted reproduction. Only in the United States can a young woman "donate" her eggs for $50,000. Only in America can two gay Britons pay tens of thousands of dollars for the privilege of conceiving "their" child in a third-party womb. Yet even in the United States the market for conception has certain limits, some of which, ironically, may work against the pursuit of profits. The market for fertility hormones, for example, would almost certainly be widened by federal guidelines mandating insurance coverage. Even if prices were capped below current levels, an increase in demand would significantly mitigate any downward pressure on profits.

Similarly, greater regulation of fertility clinics could actually expand the market for fertility services, in addition, potentially, to making it safer and more equitable. Recall that in the United States, only 1 percent of women with fertility problems employ IVF and other high-tech treatments. In Denmark, by contrast, where the state guarantees three free cycles of IVF to all infertile women under the age of forty, demand for the treatment is widespread: in 2001, 3.9 percent of all Danish babies benefited from some sort of assisted reproduction.[96] Similarly, although privately funded researchers in the United States have contributed mightily to the emerging science of assisted reproduction, so have researchers from the United Kingdom, France, Israel, and Australia—all countries where fertility clinics and access to fertility services are regulated much more tightly than in the United States. On these grounds, there is little to suggest that regulation of the fertility industry is destined in any way to diminish scientific innovation.

Finally, although most U.S. fertility practices are delighted to remain in the gray area of private regulation, history suggests that over time clarity is far more profitable than ambiguity. For as long as conception remains a furtive trade—a business cloaked in the garb of science—it will remain vulnerable to both the excesses of its fringes and the attacks of its critics, to the doctors who push science beyond what society will accept and the fundamentalists who react to the advance of reproductive technology by pushing for complete and outright bans. We will return to these issues in chapter 7.

CHAPTER 3

Renting Wombs for Money and Love

The Emerging Market for Surrogacy

Sing, O barren woman, you who never bore a child;
burst into song, shout for joy, you who were never in labor;
because more are the children of the desolate woman
than of her who has a husband.

—ISAIAH 54:1–2

IN 1985, the tragic story of Baby M grabbed all the tabloid headlines. It was a Solomonic tale, a story of love and greed that centered on a tiny child born to one mother and yet claimed under law by another.

The details were straightforward. A professional couple, Bill and Betsy Stern, decided not to risk the dangers of childbearing when they learned that Betsy was suffering from multiple sclerosis. Determined to have a child "of their own," however, they contracted with a surrogate mother, a twenty-six-year-old woman named Mary Beth Whitehead, and agreed to pay her $10,000 in exchange for the conception and birth of "their" child, the genetic offspring (via artificial insemination) of Bill Stern and Whitehead.

The pregnancy was uncomplicated, and Whitehead abided by the terms of her contract for nine months. Four days after the baby was born, though, Whitehead came to visit the Sterns and disappeared with the child, later arguing, "I signed on an egg. I didn't sign on a baby girl."[1] The Sterns called the police; Whitehead threatened to leave the country; and for weeks the drama played out in the courts and international media. Eventually, Bill Stern won sole custody of his daughter, and Baby M went home.*

Baby M was followed in due course by scores of other children who entered the world on shaky legal legs in the last decades of the twentieth century, born of one set of parents and yet claimed—biologically, emotionally, or contractually—by another. Some of these children were conceived in altruism, with one biological mother producing what another could not. Many, though—indeed most—were conceived in the market as well as the womb, the products of desire combined with the ability to pay.

In a physical sense, surrogacy is the antithesis of mainstream fertility treatment. For in most of these procedures—hormone treatment, artificial insemination, IVF, and egg donation—the desired result is a complex mixture of conception, pregnancy, and baby. Most women undergoing IVF, for example, don't just want a baby, or even "their" baby. They want to give birth to that baby, to experience the rituals of pregnancy and labor that have traditionally defined both motherhood and birth.[2]

This longing defines the contours of even the most advanced fertility treatments, where pregnancy is generally seen as a critical element of success. Even if a woman has undergone IVF using donated eggs, she can still carry and give birth to "her" child. The donor typically remains invisible in this relationship, and money is rarely mentioned. In surrogacy, by contrast, the physical relationship is reversed, and the economic one apparent. Instead of giving birth to her child, the intended mother borrows—

---

*Technically, the New Jersey court invalidated the surrogacy contract and awarded Mr. Stern primary custody only after concluding that it was "in the best interests of the child." Mary Beth Whitehead retained parental and visitation rights.

employs, rents, purchases—the womb of another. The pregnant woman is not the mother in a surrogacy arrangement; the paying woman is.

This physical role reversal raises a whole new slate of commercial and political questions, many of which were epitomized in the grueling fight over Baby M. First, even more than IVF or other forms of assisted reproduction, surrogacy pushes against traditional definitions of parenthood. For whatever reasons—social, historical, biological—we tend to think of the connection between birth mother and newborn as more intimate than that between a sperm or egg donor and the eventual offspring. We think of the woman who carries and gives birth to a baby as that child's mother, regardless of the child's genetic parentage. But in a surrogacy arrangement, the birth mother is not the intended mother, and may not even be the genetic mother, of the child.

Second, when the birth mother relinquishes this child, she frequently receives compensation—not for the *child* exactly, but for her labors in the course of production.[3] This exchange makes surrogacy overtly commercial and raises charges of commodification that are difficult to dismiss. Are surrogate mothers selling their children? Are they selling, or at least renting, their bodies? And if they are, should anyone be trying to stop them?

In some countries, governments have already answered yes to these questions. Surrogacy contracts are banned, for example, in Germany, France, and several Australian states. Their enforcement is sharply constrained in Canada, Israel, the United Kingdom, and many of the U.S. states that have taken legislative action in this area.[4] The U.S. federal government, by contrast, has been markedly reluctant to impose any kind of law on the emerging market for surrogacy, preferring to leave the dilemmas of surrogacy to local legislatures and courts. As a result, surrogacy in the United States has grown in a piecemeal and highly disparate fashion, with states adhering to and insisting upon a wide range of rules. Yet because demand in this market can be intense, couples are entering into surrogacy arrangements even when they suspect that the underlying contract is either void or unenforceable. They are also crossing state boundaries in search of sympathetic courts, and relying on the lawyers and brokers who have understandably clustered around these jurisdictions.

Practically, surrogacy is one of the simplest means of solving infertility. The intending parents can acquire whatever eggs or sperm they most desire and transfer the resulting embryo to a womb most likely to succeed. They can circumvent the risks of pregnancy in an older or medically impaired mother and still create a child related to either or both of the intended parents. Commercially, surrogacy offers a seductive way for lower-income women to profit from their bodies without—theoretically at least—selling either their bodies or their children. Politically, however, surrogacy is troubling, for it involves an economic relationship that sits deep within a moral calculus. What, the debate over surrogacy asks, can legitimately be sold in a market transaction? Who decides? And how can any state or authority weigh the desires of having a child against the dangers of selling one?

Background: The Ancient Art of Surrogacy

As a substitute means for producing children, surrogacy is an ancient practice. Women across the globe have long used others to bear the children they could not conceive, relying on a combination of tradition, coercion, and affection to create the desired result. Ironically, the techniques they used mimic the variations in modern surrogacy.

Sometimes, infertile women simply adopted at birth the "surplus" children of a neighbor or friend. Where resources were scarce and contraception limited, it simply made economic sense for children, like grain or military service, to be distributed more evenly across a small community. In Vietnam and Greece until quite recently, for example, women who bore large numbers of children frequently gave their later-born to those unable to conceive.[5] In colonial America, mothers often "put out" their younger children, placing them with smaller or childless families where they would learn a trade or provide an extra set of working hands.[6] Such transactions occurred well outside the market, and neither woman—the birth mother nor the adoptive mother—received financial compensation for her services.

Elsewhere, surrogacy assumed a more intimate connection, one more akin to today's version of the process. Infertile women chose surrogates, often their maids, to bear children for them. History records these transactions most vividly in the book of Genesis, as we've seen, where Rachel commands her husband to consort with her maid. "Behold my maid, Bilhah," she cries, "Go in unto her, and that she may bear upon my knees, and I also obtain children by her." Sarah likewise relies on her maid Hagar to conceive Ishmael.

In Biblical surrogacy, therefore, as in many contemporary surrogacy arrangements, the child was genetically related to the father who would raise him. The birth mother, by contrast, was neither a pure volunteer nor a paid provider. She was a servant in most cases, or sometimes a second wife or concubine of the father. As Pamela Laufer-Ukeles points out, the surrogate mother in these situations was essentially more of a surrogate wife.[7] Frequently, she was acknowledged as the mother of her biological children, who were simply raised in the household of another woman.

Another form of surrogacy arose in the Middle Ages, when wealthy women regularly turned their newborns over to wet nurses: nursing mothers who, for a fee, would assume the care and feeding of an additional child. Typically, the child would live with the wet nurse during the first year of life, with the natural mother making only occasional visits.[8] In many respects, this relationship is the closest antecedent to modern-day commercial surrogacy. The surrogate generally has no long-term involvement with the child; she is employed for a specific task and paid a nontrivial fee. The surrogates tend to be poorer than the mothers they serve and to have their own biological children. Wet nurses, though, were a well-accepted feature of the medieval landscape, paid providers of a service that many women either preferred or were forced to outsource.[9]

Over time, of course, preferences changed. Shifting mores reified the notion of motherhood across the industrializing world, creating what historian Carl Degler has referred to as a "cult of domesticity."[10] Wet nurses went the way of concubines as Western couples settled into stable patterns of monogamous, multichild households and as women, particularly mothers, were discouraged from entering the workforce. Such patterns were cemented by religious beliefs—Catholic, Protestant, and Jewish—that sanctified childbearing only in the context of marriage. Children born out of wedlock were frowned upon, as was any form of physical contraception.[11]

This situation prevailed until the final decades of the twentieth century, when technology combined with shifting social norms to re-create the option of arm's-length conception.

Baby-Makers: The Birth of Commercial Surrogacy

At its core, traditional surrogacy is a low-tech operation. All it entails, as the Biblical wives understood, is a woman willing (or coerced) to have sex with another woman's husband and then willing (or coerced) to let this other woman raise the resulting child. In purely practical terms, the only problem stems from the lack of willingness in the absence of coercion. Given that pregnancy and childbirth impose significant costs and sometimes even physical danger, why would any woman undertake the risks of conception without the benefits of a child?

In Biblical times, the incentive was coercion: Bilhah was Rachel's maid, after all, and presumably had no choice. In other cases, altruism may provide sufficient reward, with friends or sisters producing offspring for those who cannot. But generally, we should expect markets to fail in the area of surrogacy. For without either incentive or coercion, the supply of surrogate mothers is unlikely to equal their demand.

Theoretically at least, the missing piece of this puzzle is money. If women could be *paid* to serve as surrogates, then financial compensation could presumably replace coercion as a workable incentive. Market failure could be surmounted by using the basic lever of commerce—money—to increase the supply of potential surrogates. And surrogacy could become a fee-for-domestic-service arrangement, much like infant care or housecleaning. Historically, though, the intimate nature of surrogacy's task has rendered such arrangements impractical. Few women have wanted to be paid for what was essentially sex plus pregnancy and a baby. Few men (or their wives) have wanted to contract for such services. Thus not even money has traditionally been able to create a market for surrogacy.

In the latter decades of the twentieth century, though, surrogacy underwent a significant revival. Part of the impetus for this resurrection came from technology; part from commercial enterprise; and part from shifting moral norms. Together they created a vibrant, albeit controversial, market for motherhood.

The first piece of this market was artificial insemination (AI), a procedure, as described in chapter 2, that was perfected and brought to market in the 1980s. Commercially, AI was a very big deal for all forms of assisted reproduction. The sperm banks were the first blatantly for-profit entities in the world of infertility (aside from the elixirs and vibrating beds); they were the first to cross the boundaries of marriage in pursuit of a child and to offer components that came from a stranger.

For surrogacy, however, the implications of AI were particularly profound. In the past, the only way for surrogate mothers to produce children was to engage in sexual relations with the prospective father—a messy business under any circumstance and one that held little appeal for the wives of the husbands involved. With AI, however, conception was removed from sex, making it possible for a man to impregnate a surrogate without even necessarily meeting her. This physical distancing made surrogacy a considerably more attractive option. Combined with the ever-increasing numbers of sperm banks, AI also made surrogacy more feasible, allowing infertile couples to procure both sperm and eggs from outside, unrelated sources. In economic terms, then, the emergence of commercial AI enhanced both the demand for and the supply of surrogate mothers.[12] And once demand and supply were in place, the market followed readily.

Early Movers

One of the first to recognize the commercial potential for surrogacy was Noel Keane, a Michigan attorney with a small general practice. In 1976, Keane noticed that many of his clients had become aware of the reproductive potential of AI. Having despaired of conceiving children by other means, these couples began to ask Keane to find them surrogates, women who would be willing to undergo AI and then give the child to the biological father. Keane agreed to assume this broker role and placed advertisements in Michigan papers, offering prospective mothers a fee for the service of surrogacy. With this act, he effectively launched a market, searching for a supply (of mothers) to meet the demand that was already apparent.

Just as his business was launching, though, Keane encountered problems. Some newspapers refused to take his ads, worried about the propriety of advertising for mothers. Others ran highly critical stories, describing Keane as a charlatan or baby-trader. These commercial tussles, though, paled before the legal obstacle that Keane soon faced. Under Michigan law, he discovered, the sale of babies is illegal. Practically, this ban meant that any payment for surrogacy was essentially payment for a baby, because the nonbirth mother in a traditional surrogacy arrangement had no genetic relationship to "her" child. Instead, even when the child was the genetic offspring of her husband, the mother-to-be was still an adoptive mother—precisely the kind of mother who was expressly prohibited from buying a baby.

Realizing that the law would inevitably criminalize the surrogacy services he had been arranging, Keane quickly tried to move toward a more altruistic model. Convinced that surrogacy itself was not illegal in Michigan, he eliminated the payment, offering potential surrogates the chance to give the gift of life without any financial compensation. But altruism, it appears, was far less attractive than cash. The supply of surrogates "dried up as quickly as they had sprung," Keane later noted, leaving him with a business model now shorn of its business.[13]

Over time, Keane managed to restructure his offerings. He fought a legal battle in Michigan and then decamped for jurisdictional purposes to Florida, where a more lenient state law neither prohibited payment to surrogates nor required that the child in question be born in Florida.[14] He was also joined by a small but defiant band of competitors, each striving to carve a commercial niche in the still murky field of surrogacy.

For example, Bill Handel, a high-profile Beverly Hills lawyer, built a successful surrogacy practice based on the notion of psychological compatibility. Working with a female psychologist, Handel wrote contracts that he presumed were legally unenforceable, relying instead on the surrogate not to change her mind.[15]

In Kentucky, Dr. Richard Levin used his state's relatively lenient adoption laws to launch a heavily publicized commercial surrogacy practice as early as 1979. With a license plate reading "Baby 4 U," Levin made no secret of his commercial intent, publicly announcing that he would pay appropriate surrogates several thousand dollars for their services. He then made the rounds of local and national talk shows, often with his surrogates in tow, presenting them as "modern-day Florence Nightingales, ministering to the needs of infertile couples."[16] Customarily, brokers like Levin charged around $15,000 for their intermediation, bringing the total cost of surrogacy to somewhere between $20,000 and $45,000.[17] Levin also charged differential prices for his surrogates, arguing with customary brashness that "you have to expect to pay more for an engineer."[18]

Commodities and Critique

In the early 1980s, this group of brokers produced a handful of high-profile babies: one hundred by 1983, according to Keane, and five hundred by 1986.[19] Baby M was among this initial group, as were several other hotly contested infants. Observers at the time generally cautioned that the baby business had gone way too far and that intermediaries like Keane and Levin were essentially commodifying both women and children.[20]

"When women's labor is treated as a commodity," wrote critic Elizabeth Anderson, "the women who perform it are degraded . . . In this practice the natural mother deliberately conceives a child with the intention of giving it up for material advantage."[21] Similarly, Gena Corea, who refers to surrogates as "breeder-women," proclaimed in a 1987 press conference, "The rise of the surrogate industry does not take place in isolation. It is part of the industrialization of reproduction. It is part of the opening up of the 'reproductive supermarket.' "[22]

On the other side, supporters of surrogacy framed their arguments in terms of either parental desperation (those who turned to surrogacy had no other means of producing a much-wanted child) or the freedom to contract (if individuals were allowed to procreate and to contract, then surely they should be able to procreate under contract). These arguments played out in both academic and public forums, pitting market advocates against the defenders of women's rights. Interestingly, most feminists aligned with traditional conservatives in this debate, arguing that women's rights did not include the right to sell procreative services.[23] More libertarian feminists, by contrast, sided with the more radical free marketers, insisting that freedom for women included the freedom to contract for labor, be it working in a factory or bearing a child.[24]

The raging debates, however, belied the relatively small size of the market. Yes, there were some brokers making considerable profits; yes, there were women selling surrogate services for $10,000 a round, and couples willing to pay considerably more. But the business was still relatively small:

about thirty commercial surrogacy agencies as of 1988, making about one hundred matches a year.[25] Such sluggish growth reflected the uncertainties that remained. Were surrogates selling their labor or their bodies? Were couples buying a service or a child? Without clear legislation on these issues, contentious surrogacy cases were destined to wind up in the courts, where judges were similarly likely to hand down very disparate decisions. This lack of predictability squeezed the market. Some women—out of altruism, guilt, or pure desire—were willing either to serve as unpaid surrogates or to sign surrogacy contracts whose terms remained effectively unenforceable. But they were few and far between—the fodder for talk shows, perhaps, but not the makings of a market.

As the debates over surrogacy continued to rage, however, scientific developments were already rendering them largely moot. By the mid-1980s, new technologies for conception had supplanted the traditional model of surrogacy, creating a substitute with far greater commercial potential. This substitute, of course, was gestational surrogacy. And by splitting the baby-making process into three fully separate components, it revolutionized the business.

The Promise of IVF

The spark for this revolution came from in vitro fertilization (IVF), the breakthrough technology described in chapter 1. Thrust onto the world stage with the 1978 birth of Louise Brown, IVF unleashed an intense social controversy and a rapidly expanding commercial market. It was IVF, far more than AI or hormones or even traditional surrogacy, that pitted the proponents of assisted reproduction against an increasingly determined band of adversaries; it was IVF that drove the prospects for a prosperous reproductive trade.

For surrogacy, the implications of IVF were subtler but equally immense. What made traditional surrogacy complicated, after all, was that the surrogate mother was also the genetic mother of the child she bore. Like Rachel's maid, the surrogate was indeed giving "her" child to another woman, one with no genetic link to the child in question. It was this central asymmetry that made surrogacy a legal and ethical morass, because the surrogate undeniably had a greater claim on the child than the intended mother.

Accordingly, when surrogacy arrangements were contested, the surrogate mother nearly always won back the rights to the child, qualified only by the competing rights of the contracting father, who had an equal biological claim. The intended mother, by contrast, had only a contractual right to the child, a right that most courts found exceedingly difficult to uphold. In the infamous Baby M case, for example, the New Jersey Supreme Court ultimately ruled that "a contractual agreement to abandon one's [i.e., the surrogate's] parental rights . . . will not be enforced in our courts . . . There are, in a civilized society, some things that money cannot buy."[26] Note that the court here held a commercial right (the contract) against a biological right, and the biological right won.

In this context, the great beauty of IVF was that it raised the possibility of splitting the genetic mother (the woman who provided the eggs) from the surrogate mother, of letting the surrogate carry a child who genetically was not hers. Legally, this split meant that the connection between the surrogate and the baby would be far less powerful than under traditional surrogacy arrangements. Commercially, it implied that the supply of components for gestational surrogacy could be both divided and enlarged. When parents contracted for a traditional surrogacy arrangement, after all, they essentially needed to purchase a single package of egg-bundled-with-womb. By contrast, if the same parents were to engage in a gestational contract, they could instead acquire two separate components: the egg from one source (including, in many cases, the intended mother) and the womb from another. IVF provided the technical means of bundling these components into a child.

The Womb but Not the Egg

In the mid-1980s, the missing piece of this puzzle was eggs, arguably the most fragile component of the process and the least developed commercially. But as chapter 2 describes, once IVF raised the prospect of selling eggs apart from pregnancy, supply began to grow. Quietly, brokers and fertility clinics began to search for two different and sharply differentiated sources of supply: women willing to sell eggs without pregnancy, and women willing to carry and give birth to a genetically unrelated child.

As matters turned out, the supply of both of these components grew as a result of their unbundling. In other words, women were considerably more interested in providing eggs if they didn't also have to undergo pregnancy, *and* they were more interested in serving as surrogates if the child they carried was not genetically theirs. By removing the traditional link between egg, womb, and mother, gestational surrogacy thus reduced the legal and emotional risks that had surrounded traditional surrogacy and allowed a new market to thrive.

Once again, it was brokers like Noel Keane and Bill Handel who seized the lead, moving from an informal business of personal contacts to a more specialized portfolio of hired surrogates and donated eggs. Freed from the constraints of the egg-and-womb package, they became more discriminating in the surrogates they chose, looking now for eggs with particular genetic traits and wombs attached to a certain personality. They found these surrogates, once again, by discreetly placed ads, offering a typical fee of $10,000 to cover what was now billed simply as a pregnancy. Rather than "conceiving a child" for another couple, the new brand of surrogates were only "carrying." Accordingly, they were held to (and compensated for) a very different kind of arrangement.

In one of Keane's typical gestational contracts, for example, the surrogate agreed to assume all the risks of pregnancy, refrain from intercourse during the insemination period, refrain from drugs, alcohol, and tobacco during the pregnancy, undergo amniocentesis or abortion at the contracting parents' discretion, and accept a lower payment for a stillborn child.[27] The complete contract ran to fifty pages, a far cry from the half-page that had served Keane's traditional surrogates in the early days. By 1986, Keane had opened a Manhattan branch—the Infertility Center of New York—and claimed to be interviewing five prospective couples every Saturday morning.[28] These couples were paying roughly $25,000 to $45,000: a $10,000 fee for the surrogate, $15,000 for the broker, and all expenses.[29]

Before long, Keane and Handel were joined by many of the more specialized boutiques described in chapter 2: differentiated egg brokers like Tiny Treasures; egg and surrogacy brokers like Shelley Smith; and agencies, such as Growing Generations, that specialized in gay couples. As these services proliferated, the underlying economics of surrogacy began to change.

First, and most importantly, the separation of eggs and wombs allowed the supply of both components to increase. In 1995, for example, the assisted reproduction program at New York's Columbia-Presbyterian Medical Center had five egg donors on file. By 1998, the program's director reported that he was receiving fifty to one hundred calls a week from potential donors, and now had five hundred donors on file.[30] To be sure, not all women who used gestational surrogates used donor eggs as well; many mothers-to-be, in fact, used their own eggs. But the possibilities of gestational surrogacy, combined with IVF more generally, allowed the commercial egg market to prosper and grow.

Second, ironically, this same separation also allowed the price of eggs to increase, from the $2,500 offered for the earliest donations to the stratospheric heights of the infamous $50,000 Ivy League offer. Normally, we would expect that an increase in supply would lead before long to a *decrease* in price: more young women selling eggs should mean that the price of eggs would go down. But here, the ability to differentiate among eggs—to choose a blonde-haired or cello-playing donor—meant that the price of many eggs actually rose.

Meanwhile, differentiation in the egg market had subtly stabilized the market for wombs. In a traditional surrogacy arrangement, after all, the birth mother is providing two essential components: the genetic material that will form the child, and the physical environment in which the baby will be conceived and carried. The contracting parents, therefore, presumably want a surrogate with both the "right" genetic makeup (race, physical characteristics, intelligence, and so forth) and the ability to sustain a healthy pregnancy. Contractually, they also want to ensure that the surrogate will not change her mind after giving birth. Finding this precise combination of attributes is understandably a very costly proposition.

When traditional surrogacy gives way to gestational surrogacy, by contrast, the parents' demands upon the surrogate decline. They no longer care about her genetic proclivities, because they're acquiring those elsewhere. They don't care what she looks like, and they are less worried that she will claim the child at birth or that courts would be inclined to find in her favor. All they really need is a healthy woman, willing to undergo pregnancy and to adhere to certain standards of behavior—no drinking, no smoking, no drugs—during its course.

This set of demands apparently appealed to a much wider range of women, and once gestational surrogacy became feasible the pool of

potential surrogates grew apace. More women were willing to provide
pregnancy-without-eggs than pregnancy-with-eggs, and more couples
were happy to embrace gestational surrogacy as an alternative to other
forms of fertility treatment. In 1981, when surrogacy was still almost entirely of the traditional sort, an estimated 100 children had been born as
a result of these arrangements. By 1986, that number had risen to approximately 500.[31] By 2002, the U.S. Centers for Disease Control reported 1,210 attempts at gestational surrogacy in the year 2000 alone,
double the number that had been attempted only three years earlier.[32]

The price of surrogacy, however, remained relatively steady throughout this period, settling at roughly $20,000 per pregnancy. Many of
these new surrogates were women of color, able now to bear the primarily white children of assisted reproduction. By 2000, 30 percent of
gestational surrogacy arrangements at the largest U.S. program involved
surrogates and couples from different racial backgrounds.[33]

Taken purely on commercial terms, then, the combination of IVF
and surrogacy had created a more hospitable market for contractual
pregnancy. The customers in this market had more choice than they had
had in the past and much greater control over the product they desired.
The suppliers, meanwhile, were more diverse than they had been in the
past, and more able—in some cases at least—to charge a higher price for
a differentiated product. The coercion that had prevailed in Rachel and
Bilhah's day was gone, replaced by a discreet set of brokers offering psychological testing, hefty fees, and occasionally even chocolates.

Issues of Exploitation

Or so it seemed. Yet many of surrogacy's harshest critics were hardly
mollified by the changing nature of the trade. In fact, many observers
saw the expanding market as further evidence of commodification, of
the exploitation of (poor, nonwhite) women by their richer or more in-
dulgent sisters.[34] Central to this argument was a rejection of genetics as
the definition of motherhood. For even in gestational surrogacy, the
critics argued, the birth mother developed a powerful bond with "her"
child, a physical and emotional bond that gave this woman every bit as
much claim to the child as either the genetic mother or the contractual
one. Accordingly, taking the child from the birth mother was wrong,

and paying the birth mother for her labors constituted a complex mix-ture of baby-selling, prostitution, and rape. "In both contract pregnancy and consensual slavery," writes one critic, "fulfilling the agreement . . . violates the ongoing freedom of the individual."[35] Such contracts, adds another, "create a *national traffic* in women exploited for their reproduc-tive faculties and functions . . . They are reproductive purchase orders where women are *procured* as instruments in a system of breeding."[36]

When the surrogate was of a different race than the intended parents, the injustice of the relationship was arguably even more egregious. As one observer put it, "Gestational surrogacy invites the singling out of black women for exploitation not only because a disproportionate number of black women are poor and might possibly turn to leasing their wombs as a means of income, but also because it is incorrectly assumed that black women's skin color can be read as a visual sign of their lack of genetic re-lation to the children they would bear for the white couples who seek to hire them."[37] This was Bilhah all over again, the critics cried, but dressed now in the thin garb of commerce.[38]

Surrogacy and the Law

In many parts of the world, such criticism rapidly made its way into law. Germany and France, for example, banned any form of surrogacy contract, arguing (in the French case) that "the human body, its elements and its products may not be the subject of a contractual agreement."[39] In Australia, the government of Victoria agreed in 1984 that commercial surrogacy was "completely unacceptable as part of an IVF program" and accordingly passed legislation banning surrogacy contracts, agencies, and advertisements.[40] In most parts of Canada, noncommercial surrogacy was quietly allowed, but the law explicitly treated the birth mother in such cases as the child's legal parent, regardless of either her genetic link to the child or any outstanding contract with an intended parent.

In the United Kingdom, the influential 1984 Warnock Report ar-gued that "it is inconsistent with human dignity that a woman should use her uterus for financial profit and treat it as an incubator for some-one else's child."[41] The British government subsequently prohibited commercial surrogacy under the 1985 Surrogacy Arrangements Act but focused primarily on the role of third parties: technically, brokering a surrogacy arrangement was illegal, but entering into one was not.[42]

In the United States, by contrast, the federal government has been comparatively mute: there are no federal laws regarding either gestational or traditional surrogacy, for example, and no federal regulation of their use.[43] Instead, most issues of surrogacy have been determined by state courts and legislatures, many responding directly to the specific cases brought before them.

Initially, for example, the Michigan courts that reviewed Noel Keane's business concluded that commercial surrogacy was directly akin to commercial adoption and thus illegal: "The state's interest," held the court, "is to prevent commercialism from affecting a mother's decision to execute a consent to the adoption of her child."[44] Courts in Kentucky, however, soon found otherwise, ruling in a 1986 case that surrogacy did not constitute baby-selling as long as the contract was entered into *before* conception.[45] Thus what was illegal in Michigan became legal in Kentucky. New Jersey, meanwhile, echoed Michigan; in the infamous Baby M case, the state supreme court invalidated the surrogacy agreement between the Sterns and Mary Beth Whitehead, holding that "this is the sale of a child, or, at the very least, the sale of a mother's right to her child."[46]

As traditional surrogacy gave way to gestational arrangements, some state courts and legislatures continued to rule against commercial surrogacy agreements, defining them—often with reference to adoption law—as illegitimate payment for a child. Other state courts, most notably those in California, explicitly permitted gestational surrogacy and began to carve out an extended set of rights for parents who contracted with a gestational carrier.

In the 1990 case of *Johnson v. Calvert,* for example, a surrogate carrying the contracting couple's genetic child filed for custody of the baby.[47] Because the surrogate in this case was black and not wealthy and the contracting couple was white and well off, the ensuing legal debate ignited a storm of related controversy. (The intended mother was actually Filipino, a fact that was frequently overlooked.) Even protracted opposition, however, did not impress the courts. Instead, both the trial court and the California Supreme Court found for the contracting parents in the *Johnson* case, arguing that, although both "mothers" in this case presented proof of maternity, "she who intended to procreate the child—

that is, she who intended to bring about the birth of a child that she intended to raise as her own—is the natural mother."[48] In California, therefore, the courts explicitly tied "intent" to motherhood, using surrogacy arrangements as a way to determine parenthood when genetic links and labor did not "coincide in the same woman."

This was the distinction that gestational surrogacy allowed, severing the genetic tie from the gestational. And once this split was achieved, it became far easier for courts and other observers to find a role again for contracts, allowing the business of surrogacy to slowly shape the definition of "mother."

Going Global: The International Market for Reproductive Services

In commercial terms, therefore, gestational surrogacy was a godsend. It disaggregated the components of conception, creating a bigger and more profitable market for each. It created considerably more choice for the consumers of reproductive services and reduced the risks and ambiguity that had surrounded traditional surrogacy. These developments then reinforced each other, as greater legal predictability in at least some jurisdictions enhanced both the supply of and demand for surrogacy's basic ingredients.

Not surprisingly, disaggregation of the supply side also allowed the surrogacy market to slowly and surreptitiously go global. By the early 1990s, many regional fertility markets were already pockmarked by inconsistency, the legacy of legislative neglect and widely varying court decisions. In the United States, the market clustered in permissive jurisdictions such as California and Florida. In Europe, reproductive clinics concentrated in the United Kingdom, where noncommercial surrogacy was permitted by law, and in Italy, where the law was silent.[49] Israel also became a familiar site for IVF after 1996, when Parliament passed legislation legalizing gestational surrogacy arrangements.

Well aware of these geographical discrepancies, potential parents from restrictive states frequently sought surrogacy arrangements in other locales, engaging in the kind of "regulatory search" that footloose corporations are often accused of. As technology made it easier for parents to choose all the components of assisted conception—the eggs, the sperm, the womb, the broker, *and* the governing jurisdiction—it was only a small and logical leap to international trade.

One of the first known cases of cross-border surrogacy occurred in 1987, when Alejandra Muñoz, a nineteen-year-old Mexican woman, crossed illegally into the United States to be impregnated with the sperm of her cousin's husband.[50] She was followed in due course by several British parents, including gay and single men, who began in the mid-1990s to hire U.S. surrogates to bear their babies.[51] So did Australians—gay, straight, and single—who were frustrated by their country's combination of advanced fertility treatments and extensive restrictions on surrogacy. Many of these couples made a beeline for California, where the legal environment in the wake of the *Johnson* case provided would-be parents with explicit security.

As this international market developed, niches predictably appeared, frequently spanning racial, regulatory, or economic gaps. Some couples traveled abroad to avail themselves of high-priced services that simply were not available or legal at home: gay Britons, for example, could not easily adopt in the United Kingdom; infertile Australians (or Taiwanese or Kuwaitis) could not legally employ surrogates at home. So they ventured instead to the United States, paying around $75,000 for a child to bring back home.

In other cases, the motives were more directly economic. In 1989, for example, John Stehura, president of a controversial group called the Bionetics Foundation, announced plans to open a surrogacy center in the Philippines that would supply surrogates to couples in the United States for only $2,000.[52] In 1997, a woman from Chandigarh, India, announced that she would carry a child for 50,000 rupees, using the money to procure medical treatment for her paralyzed husband.[53] And in 1995, Polish newspapers quietly solicited women to serve as surrogates for couples in Holland, Belgium, and Germany. The fee was roughly equivalent to two years' average salary in Poland.[54]

If we abstract from the product at hand here, the underlying business model is eminently reasonable. For although eggs and sperm are now widely available in markets like the United States, it is tougher to find wombs. Because wombs come attached to women, who don't have any inherent incentive to endure the physical costs and emotional upheaval attached to pregnancy and labor. Purely in commercial terms, therefore, it makes sense to pay women for undergoing the rigors of pregnancy and thus to seek women for whom paid pregnancy is an economically attractive proposition. Who will these women be? They will be young (to carry a successful pregnancy), they will already have borne children (because parents want surrogates who understand the experience), and they will almost certainly be poorer than those who contract for their services.[55] Some of these poor, young mothers will live in the developed world. But many more, demographically speaking, will live in the poorer nations of the developing world, where opportunities for poor, young women are even scarcer. To put it bluntly, a surrogate earning $20,000 in California is earning only about 40 percent more than a full-time, minimum wage worker.[56] The same surrogate in Mexico, by contrast, would be earning roughly *twenty times as much* as the minimum wage.[57] If we take the market lens, surrogacy should be outsourced, much like garment manufacturing or IT support.

On the surface, of course, this is an outlandish proposition. How can one sanction the rental of foreign wombs to bear domestic babies? How can one allow poor, young women to bear the children of older or wealthier would-be parents? Critics of international surrogacy would certainly describe such arrangements as outrageous examples of exploitation. Janice Raymond, for example, writes that cross-border surrogacy is only a fancy name for reproductive trafficking: "In the First World," she argues, "they call it surrogacy . . . In the Third World, [it's] baby farming."[58] Gena Corea is similarly brusque, describing surrogacy simply as "international traffic in women."[59]

At a gut level, such arguments are difficult to ignore. But a more dispassionate view suggests that at some point the line between domestic and international surrogacy, and between selling eggs and renting wombs, becomes too fine to maintain. If women in California—and England, Israel, Canada, and the Netherlands—can legitimately carry others' offspring, then why is it inherently wrong for women in Mexico or Poland to do the same? If one young woman can legitimately give her eggs to create someone else's child, then why can't another rent her womb? Once we've agreed that the basic practice of surrogacy is acceptable, then preventing international surrogacy makes little sense.

Over the next few decades, a wider trade in wombs is almost certain to emerge. If there is demand in one part of the world (and there is) and lower-priced supply in another (and there is), then the record of both trade in general and reproduction in particular suggests that commerce will proceed. The question is what role governments will play in the regulation of this trade, and how they will approach the potential for exploitation that clearly lurks in surrogacy.

Snowflakes: The Evolving Market for Embryos

In the summer of 2001, Senator Arlen Specter (R-PA) slipped a tiny amendment into the funding bill for the U.S. Department of Health and Human Services. It set aside $1 million to promote "embryo adoption," using the money to fund private groups already involved with the process. The first group to receive this money was a small adoption program called Snowflakes—the same program, in fact, whose director had testified earlier before a congressional subcommittee on stem cell research.

By November 2002, Snowflakes had received $500,000 in federal funds to create public awareness of embryo adoption. It had also received a considerable amount of publicity for its own growing business: matching the leftover embryos of in vitro fertilization with new adoptive parents. The children who resulted from this process weren't really the offspring of surrogacy in the traditional sense, and they weren't adopted through ordinary channels. Instead, they emerged through an intriguing mix of technology, religion, and politics—a strange brew that again altered the perception of "mother" and brought frozen embryos to life.

The Snowflakes story began, oddly enough, with a fairly obscure British law. Under a 1990 statute, all fertility clinics in the United Kingdom were required to destroy frozen embryos after five years in storage. These were embryos created by in vitro fertilization, embryos that had never been transferred and were instead stored by former patients (often now parents) who weren't quite sure what else to do with them. As the number of embryos increased dramatically in the late 1980s, British officials quietly urged clinics either to destroy them or to employ them for research. These entreaties became law in 1990, and the first deadline for destruction occurred on August 1, 1996.*

During that week, publicity around the event was high, and antiabortion foes from around the world were quick to denounce the clinics' actions as "the mass destruction of human life."[60] One of these foes was Ron Stoddart, founder of the California-based Nightlight Christian Adoptions. Stoddart, an energetic former lawyer, already ran a well-respected international adoption service, specializing in placing older Russian children with American families. As he sat listening to radio broadcasts about the British clinics, he was struck, he recalls, by an ironic sense of waste. "There are 50,000 embryos over there," he thought, "and I'm working with families desperate to have babies."[61] Slowly, Stoddart began to play with the idea of embryo adoption, matching prospective families with frozen embryos just as he was already matching prospective families with existing children.

Technically, he was hardly the first to enter this field. Indeed, fertility clinics had discreetly been engaged in embryo transfer for nearly two decades, asking patients to donate extra embryos to other couples unable to conceive. Typically, the fertility doctors handled these arrangements themselves, trying to match the genetic and prospective parents as closely as possible. Nearly all the transfers were conducted anonymously and confidentially, and doctors advised their clients never to reveal the child's genetic origins.

Stoddart, by contrast, had a very different idea. Rather than transfer embryos in secrecy, he imagined a broader and more open process: a process of embryo *adoption*, in which all the parties knew each other, and an outside agency, rather than a doctor, presided over the matching process. By opening the doors to adoption, he reasoned, more people might be willing to make their embryos available to others. The supply, in other words, would expand. And by couching the process in the social language of adoption, he (and presumably others) could manage the

---

*Under the 1990 statute, parents could request that their embryos be stored for a longer period. Embryos were to be destroyed if the parents chose to or if the parents could not be contacted.

market from the outset, applying the same procedures that were already used for more traditional adoption cases.

Thus, when Stoddart began to offer embryo adoption through his existing agency, he treated it much like an open infant adoption. The genetic parents chose and frequently interviewed those who would parent the children their embryos became. The genetic parents formally relinquished all rights to the potential child and often established some system of visitation, or at least a photo exchange. The only real difference was subtle but huge: in embryo adoption, the birth mother—the woman who was bearing another's genetic child—was now legally and socially the "real" mother. The surrogate, in other words, had become the real thing.

The commercial prospects of this shift were intriguing. In 1997, Stoddart launched the Snowflakes program, recruiting potential donors from Christian recipients of IVF treatment. What he presented to them was an escape from the dilemma of "leftover" embryos—a way to employ their frozen conceptions and play some role in determining their future.

On the other side of the equation, Stoddart then quietly searched for couples (no homosexuals allowed) who might prefer an embryo to an egg, a sperm, or an existing (adopted) child. The attractions he described were specific: neither parent would be privileged by being the sole genetic contributor; the couple could learn a great deal about their child's genetic parents; and the mother-to-be could carry the child herself. Using the Snowflakes program, embryo adoption was also considerably less expensive than most alternatives: a $5,500 agency fee, plus $3,000 to $4,000 in medical bills.

For many middle-class couples who couldn't afford the hefty price tags of either IVF or adoption, embryo transfer was an attractive proposition. Moreover, if these couples happened to share Stoddart's antiabortion views, embryo adoption offered an ethically satisfying solution to infertility: they got a baby and saved an unborn child. Or as JoAnn Davidson, director of the Snowflakes program, explained, "If you believe these are children, and we do, they are frozen orphans waiting to be born."[62]

The first "snowflake" was born on New Year's Eve 1998. She was followed in due course by dozens of family matches and a small but growing number of births: nineteen babies by April 2003, thirty-one by

August.[63] Meanwhile, using the $500,000 provided by the Health and Human Services grant, Snowflakes rolled out a series of educational videos describing embryo adoption for three potential audiences: patients, local doctors, and fertility clinics. Like the program itself, the videos subtly targeted a relatively untapped segment of the infertility market: middle-income, strongly religious couples, frequently living outside major urban centers. By 2003, nine thousand embryos were formally available for adoption, and even clinics that did not actively promote embryo donation were reporting dramatically increased interest in the procedure.[64]

Viewed as a market, embryo adoption was still a niche trade at this point. The clients were largely Christian; the total number of births was still small; and the success rates were estimated at only about 21 percent.[65] In addition, even though the total pool of frozen embryos was huge—estimated in 2003 at more than four hundred thousand in the United States alone—the number of people who were likely to donate these embryos remained considerably smaller.[66] As Dr. Mark Sauer of Columbia University notes, "It's unusual for couples to give up embryos. They don't want someone else to have children that they have produced."[67]

Theoretically, though, it's not difficult to imagine the embryo market developing along the trajectory laid out by other fertility treatments. Like artificial insemination before the 1970s and surrogacy before Noel Keane, embryo donation at the turn of the twenty-first century is still in its friends-and-family stage of development, a phase where personal relations count and little money changes hands. Donors clearly are not selling their embryos; they are giving them to other parents and (in the case of Snowflakes at least) retaining some direct link to the families that result. Once this mechanism has been established, however, there is little reason to suspect that more commercial interests won't eventually settle in the field prepared by Snowflakes. Because if people sell eggs and sperm, why not embryos? If prospective parents choose eggs and sperm with regard to their genetic material, why not buy them as a bundle? And if the bundle is actually cheaper and the process less invasive, then embryo transfer should be poised to create a whole new tier of the baby trade, one marked by the same kinds of intermediaries and the same degree of price differentiation that prevail elsewhere in the market.

What makes embryo transfer particularly noteworthy, though, is the extent to which it has been cast in the specific language and legal context of adoption. The Snowflakes program, after all, is about adoption, not transfer or donation. It is painted distinctly as a social process rather than a medical treatment, a way to rescue (unborn) children while creating families. Snowflakes explicitly subjects its prospective parents to the same procedures that govern domestic infant adoption—a home study, parent training sessions, criminal screening, and so forth—and requires all donor couples to sign a formal agreement legally relinquishing all rights to their embryos.

Stoddart modestly denies either a political or a commercial agenda: "I'm not that smart," he insists.[68] But in early 2004, he lobbied the state of California to pass a presumption of parentage statute, which would clarify the transfer of parental rights in the course of embryo adoption. He also planned to request that the $10,000 tax credit given to adoptive parents apply to embryo adoption as well. If any measures along such lines are accepted, adoption agencies will become a logical intermediary for embryo transfer, and the market for this particular fertility option will undoubtedly expand. In the process, embryos will also have been defined, in one state at least, as entities capable of being adopted—entities, in other words, that will be that much harder to destroy.[69]

Who's Your Mama? The Many Meanings of Surrogacy

In many respects, the variants of surrogacy are only part and parcel of the growing array of fertility treatments. Like IVF and its higher-tech cousins, surrogacy has already migrated along the path to a market, moving from personal cases of charity to a distinctly less personal, more commercial realm. Like that of IVF, the surrogacy market now boosts its own specialized cadre of intermediaries, its own legal and medical practitioners, and an emerging international trade. As of 2004, the total price for a gestational surrogate contract was anywhere between $30,000 and $120,000. Eggs were typically sold separately.

Unlike IVF or other fertility treatments, however, commercial surrogacy raises questions that touch upon the very nature of both property and parenting. When couples undergo IVF, the method of conception is new, but the social relations behind that conception remain largely the same: the child is the product of his or her parents. Even when that child is conceived with donor eggs or sperm, the circumstances of birth support the intended link. The child was born of a particular mother; it belongs (socially, legally, emotionally) to that mother.

Surrogacy changes all that. Because with surrogacy, the woman who bears the child is not intended to be its mother. Motherhood, therefore, must be defined by intent rather than presumption. The woman who "intends to procreate" the child, to quote the California Supreme Court—the woman who *arranged* for the child's conception—becomes the mom, replacing centuries of biology with a combination of technology and contract. Note that even if these contracts are not legally enforceable (which is often the case), the principle remains the same. Birth becomes the subject of negotiation, and motherhood is exchanged in the market.

This push into the marketplace has explicitly, and often publicly, raised issues of economic inequity. For when women conceive and bear children unassisted, they are all essentially the same: the queen of the castle endures the same pangs of labor as her handmaid. When one woman bears another's child, however, this fundamental equality is replaced by a more pernicious asymmetry. One woman can bear the child; another cannot. One woman goes home with the child; the other does not. Nature creates this inequity, but then the market reverses and exacerbates it. Because if it is the queen (or Rachel, or the wealthy and well-educated Betsy Stern) who cannot conceive, then she can hire the handmaid (or Bilhah, or Mary Beth Whitehead) to produce what she cannot. It is fundamentally a market relationship, but one that almost always leaves poorer women serving their better-heeled sisters.

Admittedly, this inequity characterizes nearly all aspects of the baby trade: it is wealthy and well-educated couples who have the resources to undergo multiple rounds of high-tech fertility treatments, and wealthy and well-educated couples who can afford $25,000 to cover the costs of a Guatemalan adoption. But in these other areas, the underlying inequities are more neatly disguised. Infertility treatments, after all, are medical procedures conducted in the privacy of a doctor's office. Adoption is a regulated social service, with payments distributed across a hazy array of intermediaries. Only in surrogacy are the inequities laid so bare:

a rich woman pays a poorer one to carry her child. And the shared burden of childbirth—perhaps the only experience that binds women together and separates them categorically from men—is thrust into the marketplace.

In statistical terms, surrogacy is a tiny piece of the baby business. In 2001, there were 571 recorded surrogate contracts in the United States, or less than 0.7 percent of the total attempts at assisted reproduction. Outside the United States, where laws are more restrictive, surrogacy is rarer still. Similarly, although embryo adoption is a growing trend, the absolute numbers are still tiny: only 25 "snowflakes" in 2003. Yet the essence of surrogacy remains in many ways the essence of the baby trade. It employs women to produce children, creating families as well as inequities in the process.

What the surrogacy market lacks, however, is any kind of clear and consistent regulatory framework. Instead it is pockmarked by legal and jurisdictional inconsistencies—by the sharp divisions that linger between states that prohibit payment for surrogacy and those that permit it; states that enforce surrogacy contracts and those that do not; and states that have specific regulations regarding the terms of surrogacy arrangements and those that are mute.

To some extent, this variation may be perfectly acceptable: if the citizens of California are comfortable with surrogacy but those of Michigan are not, then it makes sense for California to enforce surrogacy contracts while Michigan bans or voids them. But inconsistency and variation together carry a steep price. Because they make surrogacy a riskier endeavor than it need be: riskier for the intending parents, who, even in liberal states like California, don't fully know whether their contracts are enforceable; and riskier for the surrogates, who don't have the same kinds of protection that prevail in other endeavors.

Theoretically, these risks could be reduced through federal regulation. Surrogates, for example, could be treated like volunteers in scientific research studies, whose basic rights and health are protected by the U.S. Department of Health and Human Services. Or they could be treated like other paid service providers, with minimum wage requirements and regulations regarding their health and safety at work. In either of these scenarios, individual states would still be free to approach surrogacy as their own citizens see fit. Their specific provisions would be grounded in a minimum of federal regulation, however, and in a system that would clarify when and under what conditions surrogacy would be permitted.

Admittedly, imposing rules on surrogacy will not be easy. Individuals have very strong views on the practice, and the market is not yet large enough to support any kind of commercial lobby. Moreover, in the United States, Congress's power to regulate surrogacy may well face constitutional constraints. It is not clear, for example, whether Congress could use its powers under the commerce clause to regulate the commercial aspects of surrogacy or whether—as has been the case with congressional efforts to criminalize violence against women or guns in school—the Supreme Court would ultimately see such regulation as an unconstitutional intrusion into matters best left to the states.[70]

More centrally, it is also not clear whether the U.S. Constitution could ever be used to protect procreation through surrogacy as a "fundamental right."[71] Under a doctrine known as "substantive due process," the Supreme Court has gradually carved out areas of private activity that are immune from governmental intrusion. Since 1942 and the pivotal case of *Skinner v. Oklahoma*, for example, states have not been able to interfere with an individual's right to procreate.[72] Since 1965, they likewise have been unable to intrude upon a couple's decision to use contraception or, since 1973, to interfere unduly with a woman's ability to obtain an abortion.[73]

For surrogacy, the implication of these rulings is intriguing, but not entirely obvious. On the one hand, the widening scope of activity protected under substantive due process could mean that states like Louisiana or Michigan would be pushed to loosen their limitations on surrogacy, because such limitations could well be found to infringe upon the fundamental rights of privacy and procreation. On the other hand, the same doctrine could also theoretically make it more difficult for states like California to impose any requirements or restrictions—even market-enhancing ones—that do not serve what the courts have defined as a compelling state interest. In other words, the same doctrine could be used to strike down both regulation designed to kill the practice of surrogacy and regulation designed to promote it.

Still, even a narrow extension of rights in this realm would almost certainly help. Like IVF and AI, surrogacy provides a new way of making babies, a new market to match those who want children with those who can help produce them. It remains a market, though, punctuated by inequities and by medical procedures that carry both personal and societal costs. It is a market, therefore, that needs at least a touch of regulation. It needs rules that establish how motherhood is transferred from one woman to another; rules that protect all these mothers along the way; and rules that define whether surrogacy is a privilege, a prerogative, or a prohibited activity.

Ideally, these rules would be established at the national level, creating the same kind of consistency and security that now prevail in areas, such as contraception and abortion, that once also seemed taboo. But if federal action is not forthcoming, then we should settle at least for more certainty at the state level, for local laws and regulations that trace the boundaries of surrogacy and lay a foundation for its commercial exchange. Without these laws, surrogacy risks becoming an ironic remnant of history: an ancient technology that markets embraced but never fully fostered.

CHAPTER 4

Designing Babies

Fixing Flaws and Pursuing Perfection

The proper officers will take the offspring of the good parents to the pen or fold, and there they will deposit them . . . but the offspring of the inferior, or of the better when they chance to be deformed, will be put away in some mysterious, unknown place, as they should be.

—PLATO, *THE REPUBLIC*

THE BABY BUSINESS is littered with thousands of poignant tales. One of the saddest concerns two dying children and the high-tech quest to save them.

Henry Strongin Goldberg and Molly Nash were both born with Fanconi anemia, a debilitating genetic condition that causes bone marrow failure. Most children with Fanconi die by the age of six, usually as a result of leukemia. Occasionally, family members or unrelated donors can save Fanconi sufferers through a bone marrow transplant. To limit the risk of rejection, though, the donated marrow must match precisely with the child's. No one in either the Strongin-Goldberg or the Nash family provided such a match.

In 1995, however, both families learned of a radical technology, one that held at least a sliver of hope for saving their children. Dr. Mark Hughes, a geneticist at Georgetown University's Institute for Molecular and Human Genetics, was pioneering a technique known as preimplantation genetic diagnosis (PGD), in which one cell of a recently formed eight-cell embryo is removed and genetically tested. At this point, his research was largely preventive, used to screen embryos afflicted with Fanconi, Tay-Sachs, or other devastating diseases. However, Dr. John Wagner, a transplant specialist who worked with many Fanconi patients, realized that Hughes's work could also be turned on its head. If he could screen embryos for genetic disease, then presumably he could also screen embryos for genetic markers—for the marrow that would match an already afflicted child. In other words, if Hughes's work were combined with standard IVF techniques, then parents with a Fanconi child could produce a perfect donor; they could conceive one child to save another.

Although they knew that the prospects for rescue were dim, both the Strongin-Goldbergs and the Nashes begged Hughes to work with them. Laurie Strongin and Lisa Nash underwent round after round of IVF treatment, hoping to produce an embryo that matched the marrow of their child. All the while, Henry and Molly were declining, often perilously. Finally, late in 1999, Lisa Nash succeeded. In August 2000, she gave birth to Adam. Blood from his umbilical cord was taken during delivery and used, nine days later, to treat his sister. Within months, Molly began to show signs of recovery. Laurie Strongin, however, had no luck. After nine agonizing cycles, she ended the IVF treatment, giving birth soon after to a healthy child whose marrow didn't match. Henry continued to decline. He died in December 2002, aged seven.

When faced with the prospect of death, nearly all parents would presumably follow the Nashes. They would create a child to save a child, loving the new sibling no less in the process. But the technology of genetic engineering—the microscopic manipulation that created this particular Adam—does not stop at the border of saving lives. For preimplantation genetic diagnosis can already determine whether a child is to be blighted with a wide range of diseases—some fatal, others not. It can distinguish between boys and girls, and between embryos likely to mature into "normal" children and those afflicted with Down syndrome.

With only the slightest bit of tinkering, the technology will soon be able to distinguish other, less devastating traits, such as a lifetime risk of developing breast cancer or a predisposition to obesity.

Almost inevitably, these technological prospects will lead over time to a market. Already, specialists like California's Jeffrey Steinberg have established thriving businesses around PGD, charging would-be parents an additional cost of roughly $3,500 per procedure. The biggest demand comes not from parents like the Nashes or the Strongin-Goldbergs, nor even from families desperate to ensure that their offspring does not suffer from a particular genetic disease. It comes from those who want to select their child's gender.[1] Indeed, at Steinberg's Fertility Institute, fully 70 percent of patients in 2004 were there to choose gender, spending as much as $18,000 for a full course of counseling, diagnosis, and IVF. Currently, Steinberg and his colleagues offer only a relatively limited menu of options: they can screen for genetic illnesses (like Tay-Sachs, sickle-cell anemia, or cystic fibrosis), select boys or girls, and identify those embryos that appear healthiest (an increasingly popular procedure for women who have suffered repeated miscarriages). As the technology evolves, however, Steinberg is confident that his business will grow as well. "We've had e-mails and phone calls requesting [specific traits]," he recounts. "We tell them we're not able to do that. Call back in five or ten years."[2]

One can argue, of course, that a market for PGD—even a market for asthma-free, curly-haired, taller-than-normal offspring—is simply a logical extension of the existing baby business. After all, thousands of clients are using lower-tech methods to pursue essentially similar outcomes. When parents purchase eggs, for example, they are clearly selecting along genetic lines. Why else pay extra for that attractive Ivy League donor? Sperm is also marketed by genes, as evidenced by information regarding the donor's height, weight, and favorite hobbies. Preimplantation genetic diagnosis, in that regard, is only another step forward, a higher-tech means of achieving more accurate results. If parents will pay for smarter eggs and taller sperm, why not pay more to guarantee that the child who results from this high-potential pairing really does carry the optimal set of genes? In economic terms, perfected children make perfect sense.

Yet there is something about designer babies that tugs at most morals. Those who have commented on the practice have thus far been largely negative, arguing, like political scientist Francis Fukuyama, that "when the [genetic] lottery is replaced by choice, we open up a new avenue along which human beings can compete, one that threatens to increase the disparity between the top and bottom of the social hierarchy."[3] Others argue that all forms of PGD are inherently immoral, because they involve both the construction and the destruction of embryos. And more subtle critics take particular issue with cases like those of Henry and Molly—creating one child to save another.

Implicit in nearly all this criticism is a common fear of a very slippery slope. If we screen children for Tay-Sachs and cystic fibrosis, what is to stop us from screening for looks and intelligence? From allowing rich people to construct the children they want, while consigning the poor to the vagaries of chance? Before long, the critics worry, we will be buying and building children of a better breed, tempting nature in the process and tiptoeing toward a science fiction future of multiple expressions of the human race.

In the meantime, however, the early stages of this future have already come to pass. An estimated one thousand children have been born with the assistance of PGD, and more than fifty clinics around the world offer genetic screening of embryos as part of their normal fertility practice.[4] Many of the more recent "patients" at these clinics, moreover, do not suffer from infertility or carry potentially devastating genes. Instead they are choosing PGD as an accessory to conception, paying to get the kind of baby they want.

And they are not alone. According to recent survey data, 25 to 35 percent of prospective parents in the United States say that they would use sex selection techniques if they were available.[5] As these technologies become more commonplace and spawn new kinds of genetic screens, it is hard to imagine that a market for designer babies will not emerge. This market may not become particularly loud or boisterous. It may never encompass those parents who prefer to take their chances the old-fashioned way, or those for whom $18,000 is too steep a price to pay for choice. But there will be some who want to choose, paying not only for a baby but also for the genetic probability of a particular kind of kid.

The Beginnings of Breeding

The pursuit of perfected offspring has a long and largely ignominious past. Part private, part public, this quest stems from an apparently perpetual desire to control that tiny bit of destiny that individuals actually create: their children.

As with many modern medical techniques, the process of human breeding began in ancient Greece, where unwanted babies were routinely left to die and deformed infants were killed at birth. These customary practices reached a social apogee in Sparta, where every newborn was brought before a council of elders and inspected for his likely contribution to the state: if the child seemed weak, it was abandoned to the elements. Plato extolled these policies in the *Republic*, agreeing that "the breed of the guardians . . . [must] be kept pure."[6] He also lauded the Spartans' attempt to encourage marriage and procreation among society's upper classes, arguing, along Spartan lines, that "the best of either sex should be united with the best as often, and the inferior with the inferior as seldom, as possible."[7] Selective breeding for the Greeks, therefore, was a public imposition on private desires, an attempt to mold society through reproduction. By encouraging the "best" individuals to reproduce with one another and eliminating any "inferior" offspring, the state—in theory, at least—could exert some measure of control over its future inhabitants, ensuring, as Plato urged, that "the flock" would be "maintained in first-rate condition."[8]

Such an explicit embrace of breeding faded from the public view over succeeding centuries, replaced by more casual and private practices. "Good" families tried to marry and reproduce among themselves; "bad" infants were quietly left to die or hidden in cloistered institutions. These were purely personal choices, however, with no commercial component or intervention from the state. They prevailed until the latter decades of the nineteenth century, when a man named Francis Galton decided to grab control of heredity.

Born in 1822, Galton was the son of a prosperous banker and first cousin to Charles Darwin. Galton studied math at Cambridge but left after suffering a nervous breakdown that he blamed on hard work. Like other wealthy sons of his generation, he spent time traveling in Africa and the Middle East, dabbling in adventure and scientific study. He came home in 1852, married a daughter of the former master of Harrow, and settled down to nurse a newfound interest in heredity. More specifically, he set out to discover how humans passed certain traits to their offspring and how these traits could be manipulated over time by selective breeding—shaping, as did the Spartans, who should reproduce with whom.

Unlike the Spartans, though, Galton embedded his work in the emerging science of his day, drawing in particular on the evolutionary theories propounded by his famous cousin in *The Origin of Species*. According to Darwin, the evolution of all species was determined by natural selection, a slow-moving process in which only the fittest of a given group survived long enough to reproduce. Other intellectuals had quickly applied Darwin's ideas to the human race, arguing that only the fittest social groups would survive over time.

Galton added math and policy to this mix, drawing two radical conclusions from them: first, that human tendencies could be plotted and understood in a systematic way; and second, that a science of heredity could be used to control human evolution. He stated in his 1869 book, *Hereditary Genius*, "I wish to emphasize the fact that the improvement of the natural gifts of future generations of the human race is largely, though indirectly, under our control . . . As it is easy . . . to obtain by careful selection a permanent breed of dogs or horses gifted with peculiar powers of running, or of doing anything else, so it would be quite practicable to produce a highly-gifted race of men by judicious marriages during consecutive generations."[9]

Galton wrapped his ideas in a new word, *eugenics,* which he defined as "the science which deals with all influences that improve the inborn qualities of a race . . . [and] develop them to the utmost advantage."[10] He embraced statistics as the key to understanding evolution and performed careful analyses of inherited traits, first in sweet pea plants and then in people. With both sets of data, Galton demonstrated striking statistical trends: people as well as pea shoots, it appeared, passed specific characteristics to their offspring. Heavier peas produced heavier pea seeds; taller people produced taller children.

From this data, Galton drew and propounded his eugenic conclusion. To create an improved race, he urged, individuals of "better stock" should be induced to procreate more frequently. "Gifted" families should form early and judicious marriages, facilitated if necessary by state competitions to confirm "merit" and postnatal grants to encourage the production of genetically superior children. Less worthy stock, by contrast, could be gently ushered to monasteries and convents, where possibilities for reproduction would be severely curtailed.[11] In this way, society could preside over a kind of natural selection, enabling the "fittest" to push evolution along.*

For the next thirty years or so, a small but influential band of Galton's followers sustained his quest with relish. Many of these followers were mathematicians, pioneering what would become the study of biometry, the statistical analysis of heredity. Some were social reformers, intent on pursuing the racial perfection that Galton described as an attainable goal. All believed firmly that society could be bettered by applying science to sex.

In England, the eugenics cause was taken up most prominently by Karl Pearson, another one-time mathematician who saw great power in the beauty of numbers. Pearson founded a journal devoted to the statistical study of heredity, published more than a hundred academic papers on heredity and evolution, and gradually extended Galton's theory to include characteristics such as intelligence and emotion. He also became much more vocal in his advocacy, proclaiming that Britain was declining largely as a result of excessive procreation among the "unfit." "No training or education can create [intelligence]," he announced. "You must breed it."[12] As word of his work spread, Pearson eventually was joined in his endeavors by social reformers like Beatrice and Sidney Webb and radicals such as George Bernard Shaw. Some of the country's most prominent feminists also embraced the eugenics cause, linking it to their own fight for contraception.

Similar developments occurred in the United States, where followers of Galton founded a Station for Experimental Evolution in 1904 and a Eugenics Record Office in 1910. Together, these institutions collected vast amounts of information from American household surveys such as

---

*Critically, the mathematical details of Galton's data did not fit his conclusions. Instead, they showed that over time successive generations reverted to the statistical mean. Yet Galton did not retreat from his views or his policy recommendations.

the "Record of Family Traits." They also combed through records held in prisons, hospitals, and institutions for the deaf, blind, and insane. The leader of the U.S. movement, a biologist named Charles Davenport, was particularly interested with abstract human traits, many of which (pauperism, alcoholism, insanity) he classified together as "feeble-mindedness." Between roughly 1910 and 1920, Davenport's work was reflected in a widely held fear that these unfit members of society would eventually drive out the fitter stock. In an infamous 1905 speech, for example, President Theodore Roosevelt warned of the "racial suicide" that would soon befall the United States unless the better of the breed increased their rates of procreation. To forestall this fate, Roosevelt urged "good" mothers to have lots of children and raise them "as they should be."[13]

Others took this cause even further, lobbying for fewer social programs targeted at the unfit and even for prohibition, in some cases, on their reproduction. In 1905, for example, Indiana introduced legislation that prohibited marriage among the mentally deficient, people with "transmissible diseases," and habitual drunkards.[14] It tightened this law just two years later, requiring mandatory sterilization for wards of the state who were deemed to be "criminals, idiots, and imbeciles."[15] Six U.S. states had similar statutes by 1911, and thirty-five had followed suit by 1936.

During the years in which these policies held sway, an estimated sixty thousand "unfit" Americans were forced to undergo state-sponsored sterilization. When one of these subjects, a seventeen-year-old girl named Carrie Buck, appealed her sentence, the Supreme Court demurred, offering a powerful defense of eugenic thought: "It is better for all the world, if instead of waiting to execute degenerate offspring for their crime, or to let them starve for their imbecility, society can prevent those who are manifestly unfit from continuing their kind . . . Three generations of imbeciles are enough."[16]

Similar laws were imposed during this time in Sweden, Denmark, and Finland, based on the same ostensibly scientific rationale established by Galton. There was no demand in this phase of eugenics, no consumers availing themselves of reproductive solutions. Instead there was only the state, using a still-brutal technology to shape how individuals behaved and how—or so it was thought—society evolved.

In Search of Aryans: Eugenics Under the Nazi Regime

By the 1930s, eugenics had become an accepted aspect of state policy. But then the Nazis grabbed eugenics for themselves, pushing the pursuit of perfection to its logical and horrific extreme.

Under the Weimar government (which ruled Germany from 1919 to 1933), eugenics played a relatively minor role. Indeed, German scientists and policy makers during this period looked westward for eugenic advice, seeing the United States as the leading model for race-based policies.[17] In 1933, however, the Nazi party came to power, bolstered by Germany's economic collapse and its citizens' fervent desire to regain their lost glory. Eugenics offered an attractive pathway toward both objectives: it saved money on social programs (better to prevent defective offspring from being born than to support them through life) and promised to rid the German population of any undesirable elements.

Accordingly, the first Nazi eugenics law was passed in 1934. Like the American legislation on which it was modeled, the Law for the Prevention of Hereditary Diseases in Posterity provided for the sterilization of nine classes of "defectives," including manic-depressives, schizophrenics, and alcoholics. Race did not factor in to the law, and all sterilizations had to be reviewed by a special court. "From a legal point of view," proclaimed a leading U.S. eugenics publication, "nothing more could be desired."[18]

The following year, the law was amplified and the number of sterilizations increased to three hundred sixty thousand. Still, outsiders saw little reason for concern. In fact, many foreign observers looked with envy at Germany's policies, seeing them as a laudably efficient means to attain social goals.[19] Quietly, then, the Nazis began to push their policies even further, and American eugenicists continued to applaud. "Thus we have the encouraging example," crowed a contributor to *Eugenical News*, "of a nation that is intelligent enough to see that its first necessity is the biological one of improving its racial quality."[20]

By 1939, however, the sterilization of defectives had become a program for their deaths. It began with euthanasia, described by Hitler as "mercy killing" for "patients who are judged incurable."[21] Under a secret policy known as T4, doctors could opt to kill those patients they considered beyond hope, including homosexuals, alcoholics, and anyone suffering from mental illness. They also began to mark all newborn children with a plus or minus sign, indicating whether they should live or die.

Then the Nazi masterminds extended their policy, and their death chambers, to the larger groups of "defectives" that their physicians had identified. The genocide that occurred—an estimated six million victims—was largely kept silent. But it was also explained almost entirely in eugenics terms. Explicitly and repeatedly, Nazi doctors defined Jews (along with gypsies) as a "diseased race" whose problems could be addressed only through "medical means."[22] The Nazis considered sterilization as an alternative means to their end, but the gas chambers already existed, and they worked.

In the end, it is difficult to pinpoint precisely how eugenics affected Nazi policy. Did decades of scientific study and political acceptance push Nazi leaders toward their final solution? Or did it simply offer a convenient cloak for what they already intended to do? Did respected eugenicists outside Germany help advance the Nazi agenda, or were they irrelevant to it? We may never know. We can, however, trace the intimate threads that linked eugenics, the quest for social perfection, and mass extermination. These are the threads that started in Sparta, ran through Galton, and then led with a horrifying logic to the concentration camps of Europe.

Rebirth: The Science of Genetics

In the wake of Nazi atrocities, the entire field of eugenics slunk deep out of sight. Evolutionary societies that had flourished during the 1920s and 1930s vanished, as did nearly all the scientists working under the now tarnished mantle of selective breeding. State and national laws on mandatory sterilization disappeared as well, or were simply ignored by societies fearful now of what a focus on perfection could produce. In 1942, the U.S. Supreme Court essentially reversed its decision in the *Buck* case, arguing now that mandatory sterilization violated "a sensitive and important area of human rights . . . the right to have offspring."[23]

Meanwhile, although the program of eugenics had been fundamentally tarred by mid-century, the science was quietly advancing. Building on the work of Gregor Mendel—an Augustinian monk who had first experimented with tens of thousands of pea plants in the 1860s—a new crop of scientists began to examine the precise mechanisms of inheritance. With his peas, Mendel had proposed that hereditary factors came in pairs: a light green element from one parent, for example, and a dark green element from the other. Whichever element was stronger, or "dominant," would determine the color of the resulting offspring.

Interestingly, for decades Galton and his followers had overlooked Mendel's work; statisticians at heart, they never really probed the biological drivers of the phenomenon they hoped to control. But biologists had begun to take notice and to build what became the burgeoning field of genetics. The differences in this new science were more than simply semantic. For where the eugenicists had hoped to shape evolution, the geneticists hoped only to understand it. And whereas the eugenicists looked to large-scale data for answers, the geneticists looked instead to the tiniest corners of life: the fabric of cells that passed inherited traits from one generation to the next.[24]

By the turn of the century, researchers had already identified genes and chromosomes, proving in the laboratory what Mendel had hypothesized from his garden. Parents, they showed—be they peas, fruit flies, or humans—carried multiple sets of genes, each embedded with the determinants of specific traits. The genes were arranged on chromosomes, and each parent passed a fixed array of these chromosomes to their offspring. The set of chromosomes that the child inherited, shaped by the power play of dominant and recessive genes, determined who that child would be.

Take, for example, the simplest case of hereditary illness. Suppose that Joe and Alice, a healthy married couple, each carry a recessive gene for Tay-Sachs disease, a rare but devastating condition that typically kills its victims before the age of two. The gene for Tay-Sachs, we now know, is contained on chromosome 15. If both Joe and Alice are carriers, then each of them has a tiny imperfection on this chromosome, an inactive gene that normally directs the body to produce a critical enzyme known as Hex-A.[25] Because Alice and Joe each also have an active Hex-A gene, they are perfectly healthy. But every time they conceive a child, Joe and Alice will each pass one of their two genes to this offspring—either A, the healthy dominant gene, or a, the recessive gene for Tay-Sachs. Mathematically, this combination of genes produces four distinct and equally probable outcomes: AA (a healthy child who doesn't carry the Tay-Sachs gene); Aa and aA (healthy children who carry the Tay-Sachs gene), and aa (a child with Tay-Sachs). The biology, therefore, carries an ineluctable arithmetic. Each time they conceive, Alice and Joe have a 25 percent chance of producing a child who will die in infancy.[26]

The math of Tay-Sachs is particularly stark, as it is with similarly inherited diseases like cystic fibrosis and sickle-cell anemia. In each of these cases, there is a single gene that causes the damage, and a one-in-two probability that any carrier will pass this defective gene to his or her offspring. Other genetic illnesses (and traits) are more complicated— derived from multiple genes, chromosomal abnormalities, or random mutations in a parent's genetic code. Down syndrome, for example, is a genetic condition caused by the presence of an additional twenty-first chromosome; Turner's syndrome occurs when girls receive only a single X chromosome instead of the normal two. In both of these cases, the child's condition is inherited, but the parents are not necessarily carriers, as they are for Tay-Sachs or cystic fibrosis. Likewise, some basic physical traits, such as blue eyes, result from a relatively straightforward pairing of recessive genes, whereas others—such as intelligence, musical ability, and height—emerge from a far more intricate weave of overlapping genes and environmental factors.

By the 1930s, the basic math of genetic combination had been identified. Using probability theory and large-scale data sets, researchers had analyzed patterns of blood type, demonstrating how these types—the now familiar A, B, and O—were passed down through generations and represented in the overall population. They had begun to probe the nature of linkage, examining how the co-appearance of multiple traits (red hair with blue eyes, for example, or certain diseases with certain blood groups) related to their placement on the chromosome. By the 1940s, scientists were able to plot how individual genes controlled specific chemical reactions inside the body.[27]

The DNA Breakthrough

Then in 1953, James D. Watson and Francis Crick, scientists at Cambridge University, discovered the internal structure of genes themselves, the famous "double helix" of DNA (deoxyribonucleic acid) that translates tiny bits of protein into bodily commands.[28] Other researchers then took this breakthrough to its next logical step, identifying the mutations in DNA—often only a single missing or replaced amino acid in the string of DNA—that led to a variety of genetic illnesses.

Initially, the practical implications of these findings were limited. Scientists understood the chemical underpinnings of life; they were unraveling at a molecular level why one child had blue eyes and another brown; but there wasn't much they could *do* with this monumental breakthrough. Indeed, unlike its eugenics cousin, the science of genetics was detached from any political or social implications: researchers strove to understand life, but not necessarily to change it.

As the science advanced, however, this once fine line began to blur. The starting point was "genetic counseling," a small cottage industry that emerged from the medical side of genetics. By the 1950s, several of the doctors who studied genetic deformities among their patients began small sideline businesses in prenatal consulting, helping worried parents determine whether their offspring were at risk for genetic disorders. Most of the people who sought these services had already suffered the birth (or death) of a seriously ill child. Most of the doctors who advised them were the leading geneticists of their time. The science, doctors and parents understood, was still rough. But the specialists who staffed the clinics could at least help explain the basic math of genetics and the likelihood that a given couple would pass a certain disease on to their child. If Joe and Alice had already given birth to a Tay-Sachs baby, for example, a doctor could advise them that any subsequent child would face the same 25 percent chance of affliction. There was nothing that Joe and Alice could do to affect this probability, but the doctor could at least inform them of the odds.

Transcending the Odds

By the 1950s, however, small improvements in science had enabled researchers to test for the presence of some recessive genes, allowing prospective parents to learn whether or not they were carriers of a specific disease. Demand for genetic counseling grew as a result, from parents who had already experienced a tragedy to those who merely suspected some proclivity in their family background.

In 1951, there were ten genetic counseling clinics in the United States, and an estimated three or four in the United Kingdom. Within a decade, the two countries together boasted nearly thirty such clinics, offering an expanded range of services.[29] Over the next twenty years, researchers identified almost nine hundred diseases linked to defects of a single gene, roughly fifty of which could be discovered through prenatal testing. As this roster increased, it understandably drove interest in genetic services. Groups known to be at particularly high risk for certain disorders—African Americans for sickle-cell anemia, Jews for Tay-Sachs—were among the largest users of the tests and the most active proponents for their expansion.

Meanwhile, developments in prenatal medicine had fundamentally changed the nature of genetic counseling. In the late 1960s, doctors had perfected the procedure of amniocentesis, using a long, fine needle to extract amniotic fluid from the womb of a pregnant woman. They subsequently tested the fluid, determining whether the child-to-be suffered from a range of diseases, including chromosomal disorders. Essentially, amniocentesis shifted the locus of examination from the parent to the child, from the carrier worried about inherited defects to the potentially afflicted offspring.

Amniocentesis differed from prenatal screening, however, in two crucial ways. First, whereas the screening gave only probabilities, amniocentesis gave facts. And whereas screening gave parents few options, amniocentesis presented them with a single, harsh choice: to keep the afflicted fetus or abort it. For by the time amniocentesis had become prevalent, so too had abortion. The United Kingdom permitted abortion under certain circumstances beginning in 1967; the United States followed suit in 1973. Sweden made abortion available upon request in 1973, as did Italy (under more restrictive circumstances) in 1978. For the first time in these countries, therefore, parents had both the medical and the legal means to exercise some measure of control over their genetic destiny. They could choose not to have an afflicted child.

By 1974, the number of genetic counseling centers in the United States had surged to four hundred. Within two years, these centers were conducting twenty thousand genetic diagnoses a year, up dramatically from the total of five thousand diagnoses performed prior to 1976.[30] Not all these diagnoses contained bad news, presumably, and not all parents who received bad news chose to act upon it. Yet the combination of better information and more options clearly changed the landscape of pregnancy. For the first time, parents could now choose not only whether to have a child and with whom (the focus of eugenics) but also whether to give birth to a *specific* child, one blessed or cursed by a revealed genetic fate. If eugenics had grasped for control over parents, then genetics gave power to the parents, allowing them to decide which child to produce.

The Effects of Ultrasound

Further steps toward prenatal detection occurred with the emergence of ultrasound, a technology first used to detect submarines during World War I. After the war, researchers slowly began to experiment with other applications, gradually discovering its usefulness in revealing even early-stage fetuses. Realizing, as one put it, that "there wasn't much difference between a fetus *in utero* and a submarine at sea," they eventually focused on prenatal diagnosis, using the sound waves of ultrasound to produce high-resolution pictures (known as sonograms) directly through the mother's abdomen.[31] Because the technology was both powerful and painless, it quickly caught the attention of obstetricians and hospitals. By the mid-1990s sonograms had become a standard element of prenatal care, employed in roughly 70 percent of pregnancies in the United States, and nearly 100 percent in Europe.[32]

Typically, the technology was used simply as an additional diagnostic tool: obstetricians could view the fetus *in utero* and confirm that development was proceeding normally. Occasionally, though, they also spotted visible evidence of future problems—a particular fold of the neck skin that often signaled Down syndrome, for example, or the open spine that could indicate spina bifida. In these cases, parents were left with the same crushing choice as that wrought by amniocentesis: to continue with the pregnancy or abort a damaged child. Most of them chose the latter.[33] In other, quieter cases, parents have clearly used ultrasound-plus-abortion as a relatively inexpensive way of selecting the sex of their child. Indeed, in countries such as India and China, ultrasound and amniocentesis have spawned a whole business of prenatal discovery, allowing parents to learn the gender of their child in time to abort.[34]

Against the broader background of the baby trade, sonograms and genetic counseling seem nearly quaint. Genetic counseling, after all, is simply knowledge applied to pregnancy, advising couples of the risk that their child could be born with a specific, often fatal disease. Sonograms (and amniocentesis) extend this knowledge into the pregnancy and ultimately to the child. Unlike eugenics, which was explicitly directed at social control of individual choice, these higher-tech genetic tools thrust power back into parental hands, giving individuals the ability—and, by implication, the right—to determine at least some aspects of their offspring's fate.

As technology has widened this realm of private choice, however, it has also pressed elements of this choice into the commercial market. Sonograms, for example, are no longer conducted only in the confines of an obstetrical suite, but instead and increasingly in the market for elective medicine. Commercial "video studios," for example, now conduct sonograms for nonmedical purposes, charging expectant parents anywhere from $100 to $300 for their keepsake fetal videos.[35] Prenatal testing also shows signs of robust commercial competition. In 2004, for example, Baylor College of Medicine announced plans to offer its patients the largest panel of prenatal tests available: $2,000 to screen a fetus for fifty indicators of mental retardation. That same year, Quest Diagnostics, a private provider of medical tests, cited prenatal and genetic tests as one of its fastest areas of growth.[36] According to Charles Strom, medical director of Quest's genetic testing center, the growth came in response to a distinct market demand. "People are going to the doctor," he reported, "and saying, 'I don't want to have a handicapped child, what can you do for me?' "[37]

In such cases, parents are treating detection not as a medical service but as something akin to a luxury good—an accessory to childbirth, rather than a need. More importantly, some small number of them are also using prenatal detection as a path to a new form of private eugenics: choosing, for a price, the children they want to keep and those they want to avoid.

Henry and Molly: The Pursuit of Proactive PGD

In the late 1980s, Mark Hughes was a molecular biologist at Baylor College of Medicine in Houston. An outgoing man with degrees in both biochemistry and medicine, Hughes had spent years researching genetic diseases, focusing primarily on steroid hormone receptors—proteins that help to regulate the development of genes. Because this work took him directly into the core of genetic diagnosis, he also spent a lot of time at Baylor's hospital, advising couples who either knew they carried genetic mutations or had recently given birth to an afflicted child.

It was tough work. "Every time I went into the hospital," Hughes recalled, "I'd see a couple that just had a baby with some horrible genetic disease. Imagine dealing with that. And then I'd have to tell them that every other child they'd ever conceive would also have a high probability—a one-in-four chance, usually—of being born with that same horrible thing."[38]

At around this time, Hughes and others in his field had learned of pioneering work under way at London's Hammersmith Hospital. Robert Winston, a reproductive endocrinologist, and Alan Handyside, an embryologist, were trying to identify the gender of very early stage embryos, hoping to prevent the transmission of specific sex-linked diseases. If, for example, a couple was known to carry the gene for hemophilia, which affects only males, the scientists would try to identify and transfer only female embryos. In this way, they could guarantee the baby's sex before birth and ensure affected couples of a healthy child.

In 1989, the team succeeded: they removed a single cell from embryos that were only three days old and identified each one as either male or female. Although none of these embryos was subsequently implanted, the scientists felt confident in predicting that "human preimplantation embryos can be accurately sexed . . . [and] transferred to the uterine environment on the day of diagnosis."[39] They performed this precise procedure the following year, this time allowing the pregnancies to proceed and the children—two sets of perfectly normal female twins—to be born.[40] A subsequent attempt, however, went badly awry when a misdiagnosis of the tiny embryo produced a child with precisely the same defect that Winston and Handyside had sought to prevent.

Hearing this news, Hughes had a breakthrough thought: the London team members were among the most skilled IVF researchers in the world; they were the first to have extracted a single cell from a days-old embryo and the first to discover how to maintain an embryo in vitro—

in the petri dish—for as long as four days. But Winston and Handyside were not geneticists. They didn't really know how to analyze that single cell with the kind of massive precision that their work demanded. Hughes figured that his research might help fill the gap. If he could get to London, he could help identify the genetic composition of that tiny single cell.

Several months later, Continental Airlines provided a set of complimentary tickets and Hughes began his trans-Atlantic shuttle, timing his trips to coincide with the menstrual cycles of the London patients. The expanded team then began to work at what they recognized was a surreal task: "We all knew," Hughes recounted, "that this would be either totally crazy or a milestone."[41] Moving beyond sex selection, the team focused on cystic fibrosis, a disease whose genetic marker had been identified in 1989.

On the third attempt, they succeeded. A couple who both carried the gene for cystic fibrosis gave birth to a healthy child, identified from a single cell of an eight-cell embryo. Winston and Handyside published news of their work shortly thereafter, announcing the advent of what became known as preimplantation genetic diagnosis.[42]

The Practice of PGD

Like many other technological breakthroughs, PGD is conceptually straightforward. It takes the basic procedure of IVF—the creation of an embryo outside the body—and then adds a fillip from genetics, testing the embryo in its very earliest stages for the kinds of diseases that otherwise would not be detected until amniocentesis or birth. By combining assisted reproduction with genetics, in other words, PGD pushes the date of detection back to the time of conception. As a result, as Hughes explains, "Couples at high genetic risk . . . do not have to throw the genetic dice."[43]

Technically, however, preimplantation diagnosis is considerably more complex than either genetic testing or in vitro fertilization. The cell that researchers like Hughes evaluate is tiny, crammed with genetic information that is difficult or even impossible to decode. In a standard PGD procedure, technicians approach the embryo at its eight-cell stage, a stage so early that the embryo is formally still considered a preembryo.

They extract a single cell, identical at this point of development to each of the remaining seven. There is no time for error, because the preembryo must be returned to the womb within twenty-four hours. They then subject this tiny cell to a battery of highly specific tests, probing for the particular mutation—usually only a single blip in the entire genetic sequence—that plagues the couple in question. Mastering these highly technical procedures is extremely difficult, based as they are on both physical dexterity and scientific knowledge. As of 2004, only a handful of researchers around the world were able to perform PGD. In the early 1990s, the number was even smaller.

By this point, Hughes had left Texas for Washington, D.C. He became director of Georgetown University's Institute for Molecular and Human Genetics and also served as head of reproductive genetics at the National Institutes of Health's Human Genome Center. In both positions, he continued to plumb the inner intricacies of genetic disease, trying to identify the markers for other fatal conditions and then fashion the tests that would enable early detection.

Meanwhile, Handyside and a small band of colleagues worked to perfect the clinical mechanics of PGD, offering it to couples who were known to carry a significant genetic risk: parents of Tay-Sachs children, for example, or families marked by Huntington's disease. Between 1990 and 2000, more than one thousand children were born as a result of PGD, free from the outset of whatever genetic disease beset their family. For many of these cases, Hughes was the invisible genie, the research scientist who enabled the fertility specialists to produce these cutting-edge babies. Yury Verlinsky, a Russian-born scientist based in Chicago, was operating separately along a similar track, working with colleagues at his Reproductive Genetics Institute to quietly push the frontiers of PGD.

From Detection to Selection

Then, in 1994, Hughes received an intriguing phone call. It was from John Wagner, a leading transplant surgeon in Minneapolis. Wagner had a rash of patients he was desperately trying to save, and he thought there was a wild chance that Hughes might be able to help.

Most of these patients were dying of Fanconi anemia, a rare disease of the bone marrow carried by a single mutated gene. Like other classic genetic diseases—Tay-Sachs, sickle-cell anemia, cystic fibrosis—Fanconi erupts when both parents carry the gene and pass it along to their offspring. Any child born to Fanconi carriers has a one-in-four chance of being born with the disease.

Typically, these children die by the age of six, as their bone marrow fails to produce the red blood cells they need. Their only hope lies with a bone marrow transplant, a harrowing, high-risk procedure that extracts the child's entire bone marrow and replaces it with that of a donor. If the donor is a sibling with a closely matched immune system, the child has roughly an 85 percent chance of survival. If the donor does not match as closely, the child's body is likely to reject the foreign marrow and succumb. The odds of survival with a nonrelated transplant are only about 30 percent.[44]

For years, Wagner had been in the business of trying to save Fanconi children by matching them with donors and then subjecting them to this grueling transplant. It was a harsh and painful process. For in most cases, no perfect donor existed and Wagner was forced to watch his patients die. Sometimes, if the parents were lucky, they managed to conceive another child in time, a child who did not carry Fanconi and whose bone marrow could be used to save the dying sibling. Sometimes, parents intervened more directly, testing their fetuses during the tenth week of pregnancy and aborting those likely to suffer from the disease. In a very small number of cases, parents had even aborted a healthy fetus that wasn't a match for their afflicted child.[45] Mostly, though, Fanconi parents just tried and tried, racing to produce another child that might save his or her sibling. Only a few of them succeeded.

Wagner's insight was to wonder whether PGD could accelerate this horrible game of waiting. If PGD could detect whether an embryo was likely to suffer from a disease like Fanconi, couldn't it also detect whether an embryo was likely to save a child from Fanconi? Couldn't detection, in other words, be transformed into selection? Wagner knew of one parent who was trying this technique for a child suffering from another genetic defect. Why not attempt it with Fanconi, too?

Initially, Hughes was reluctant. To begin with, he knew that the genetics of Fanconi were particularly maddening. There are at least seven genes that can cause the disease, and certain parental combinations that are extremely difficult to detect. Moreover, Hughes knew that his work at Georgetown was already hovering on a delicate political precipice. As a Catholic institution, the school was explicitly and devoutly opposed to any kind of fetal research.

Technically, Hughes was OK; his cell clusters were smaller and earlier than embryos, and he wasn't performing any experiments on them. But in the heated politics surrounding embryos, Hughes suspected that his work could easily come under attack. He also was slightly uncomfortable himself, knowing that choosing a healthy embryo was different from choosing a healthy, perfectly matched embryo. So he waited and thought and eventually worked out a compromise of sorts with Wagner. Hughes would screen embryos for the parents of Fanconi sufferers, but only if the parents were young, carried the most common mutation of the Fanconi gene, and had always planned to have more children. Hughes would not create one child simply to save another.

Two Children, Two Outcomes

Once Hughes was on board, Wagner worked with the national Fanconi registry to identify two families who fit his criteria. They were Lisa and John Nash, parents of the then twenty-month-old Molly, and Laurie Strongin and Allen Goldberg, whose son Henry was just five months old. Both mothers were young, both sets of parents had the "right" mutation, and both leaped at the chance of using PGD to raise the probability of conceiving a perfectly matched child. Laurie Strongin, though, had just learned that she was already pregnant with her second son, a healthy boy whose genetic makeup was completely different from Henry's. Lisa Nash, therefore, began IVF almost immediately. Laurie Strongin had to wait.

Over the next few years, both families endured a roller coaster of IVF treatments, PGD tests, and agonizing miscarriages. Lisa Nash went through five cycles of IVF and PGD, reportedly spending more than $100,000 in the process.[46] Laurie Strongin endured nine cycles of IVF, produced 198 eggs, and never became pregnant.

In the midst of this frustration, politics intervened to make it all even worse. In 1997, Hughes was accused of using NIH funds inappropriately, conducting research on embryos despite a congressional ban. Technically, Hughes insisted that no violation had occurred: he wasn't working on embryos and hadn't ever used federal funds to support even his basic work on PGD. But he resigned from Georgetown and NIH in disgust, refusing to stop research that he knew could save lives. He eventually moved to Wayne State University, a school outside Detroit that offered what Georgetown couldn't: a privately funded laboratory to continue his work. In Detroit, Hughes also embraced the commercial side of science. Following directly in the footsteps of the early U.S. IVF pioneers, he had left NIH and rejected the possibility of federal funding in favor of the market, establishing a private laboratory, Genesis Genetics, free from the constraints of government regulation. Under existing guidelines, PGD (like IVF before it) was perfectly legal. It just couldn't be supported by federal funds.

While Hughes was moving, though, Henry and Molly were dying. By 1998, the Nashes, whose genetic combination was particularly difficult to decipher, left Hughes and went instead to Yury Verlinsky's Reproductive Genetics Institute in Chicago. Although no one there had yet attempted what the Nashes had in mind, Verlinsky and his team were willing to try. In December 1999, Lisa Nash produced twenty-four eggs, only one of which was a healthy match for Molly. Nine months later, that egg became Adam, and Molly was saved.[47]

Laurie Strongin, who never managed to conceive with the right kind of egg, was forced to proceed along more conventional channels. Henry underwent a bone marrow transplant in July 2000 but died two and half years later.

The Market for Perfection

As one might expect, the story of Henry and Molly made headline news. Like Louise Brown two decades earlier, these two children became the real-world face of high-technology baby-making, the kids whom science was racing to save. As had been the case with Louise Brown, Henry and Molly also ignited both a firestorm of criticism and the inklings of a market.

The criticism was largely predictable. Opponents such as the ever-present Leon Kass, serving now on President George W. Bush's Council on Bioethics, proclaimed that the birth of children like Adam confirmed earlier fears of a very slippery slope. Already, Kass argued, IVF had blinded society to the dangers inherent in manufactured life. Now PGD was adding another inexorable step, allowing parents not only to manufacture their offspring but also to manipulate them. "Make no mistake," Kass cautioned, "the price to be paid for producing optimum or even genetically sound babies will be the transfer of procreation from the home to the laboratory. Increasing control over the product can only be purchased by the increasing depersonalization of the entire process and its coincident transformation into manufacture. Such an arrangement will be profoundly dehumanizing."[48]

Another prominent critic was Michael Sandel, a political philosopher at Harvard University, who also served on the Council on Bioethics. Like Kass, Sandel had a deep and abiding fear of the slippery slope; he, too, expressed the worry that "what began as an attempt to treat a disease or prevent a genetic disorder" would rapidly escalate into "an instrument of improvement and consumer choice."[49]

But Sandel and other opponents had an additional, more subtle concern, one that made PGD more troubling than IVF—more troubling, indeed, than artificial insemination or surrogacy or nearly any other form of assisted reproduction. The trouble stemmed from PGD's capacity to expand the baby business far beyond infertile couples, genetically at-risk couples, or even couples trying to save an existing child. That's because PGD, inherently, was about perfection. And the market for that was potentially unlimited. Drawing a parallel with growth hormones, for example, Sandel asked, "If hormone treatments need not be limited to those with hormone deficiencies, why should they be available only to very short children? Why shouldn't all shorter-than-average children be able to seek treatment? And what about a child of average height who wants to be taller so that he can make the basketball team?"[50] Once genetic enhancement moved out of the laboratory and into the realm of consumer choice, Sandel and other opponents predicted, the desire to engage in such enhancements would become unstoppable. As one commentator opined, "Selection is the first step to design."[51]

Such fears were not unfounded. Indeed, a market for PGD had emerged nearly as soon as word of Henry and Molly escaped, nearly as fast as other parents could rush to copy the Nashes. As with other breakthroughs in baby-making, the economics were blunt. There were parents who would do anything, pay anything, to acquire a particular kind of baby. There were a handful of scientists and doctors who could provide this baby, or at least some chance of it. And there were governments that either regulated the transaction (in parts of Europe and Australia) or pushed it squarely into the private sector (the United States). Accordingly, the market grew wherever it could. If people wanted PGD badly enough—and they did—they would cross any international border to find it.

The early market for PGD, therefore, looked almost exactly like the early market for IVF or surrogacy. Eager clients raced to the highest-profile locales, to the doctors and researchers who had pioneered this cutting-edge technology. The University of Minnesota, home to John Wagner's transplant department, was an obvious site.[52] So was Hughes's new laboratory and Verlinsky's Reproductive Genetics Institute.

By 2002, the University of Minnesota announced that it had received more than five hundred inquiries about PGD treatment "from America and elsewhere."[53] Verlinsky and his colleagues reported in 2003 that they had performed 378 PGD cycles for fifty-four genetic conditions, including 13 cycles in which the only objective was to preselect those embryos capable of producing a child whose bone marrow could eventually be donated to an existing sick sibling.[54] And Hughes was reviewing genetic data for hundreds of couples, charging them $2,500 for a course of treatment that included counseling, analysis, and the creation of individualized genetic tests. Thanks to the donations of several grateful parents, Hughes also presided over a foundation that provided these same services for couples unable to afford his fees.

Expanding the Market

Meanwhile, though, other players were beginning to enter what was clearly an intriguing market. Joseph Schulman's Genetics & IVF Institute, for example, was already deeply involved with prenatal testing, offering to screen its patients for a full range of genetic diseases. As PGD edged into the mainstream, the Institute began to offer preimplantation analysis as well. So did other elite fertility centers, including the Center for Human Reproduction, with nine clinics across the United States, and the Jones Institute in Virginia.[55] Verlinsky's Reproductive Genetics Institute expanded its practice to include satellite centers in Ukraine,

Russia, Belarus, and Cyprus; and clinics in countries with permissive regulatory regimes began marketing themselves to doctors legally unable to provide PGD.[56]

Brazilian clinics, for example, reportedly charged British families around £4,000 to perform analyses that were still banned in the United Kingdom.[57] And in Spain, a clinic linked to a high-profile London fertility specialist provided both chromosomal and gender analyses for £6,000 to £7,000.[58] By 2002, roughly forty clinics in seventeen countries offered PGD, at a cost of about $2,500–$3,500 per procedure.[59] Most of these clinics offered PGD as a standard add-on to IVF, a way of screening all the embryos created in vitro before deciding which ones to implant.[60]

In these cases, the clinics typically used prefabricated testing kits that enabled them to screen for the kinds of chromosomal abnormalities that manifested themselves in well-defined patterns—the extra twenty-first chromosome of Down syndrome, for example, or the missing X of Turner's. Because the tests were essentially the same for all these chromosomal defects, the tests were relatively inexpensive to offer and simple to administer. As a mass-market product, they made great sense. And as a solace to would-be parents, they proved nearly irresistible.

For more complicated cases, however—cases of Tay-Sachs, cystic fibrosis, or Fanconi—the intricacies of PGD remained frustratingly elusive, both financially and practically. Because the overall number of these cases was still rather small and the genetic profiles still erratic, it didn't make economic sense for the mainline fertility clinics to invest in the specialized knowledge that genetic detection still required. Instead, the clinics that wanted to offer these more specialized screens—or the couples who demanded them—quietly relied on specialists like Hughes or Verlinsky, who provided the backroom genetic analysis for dozens of U.S. clinics. In 2003, for example, Verlinsky's Reproductive Genetics Institute performed more than one thousand PGD procedures for more than ninety external clinics.[61]

Meanwhile, another set of clinics, such as Steinberg's Fertility Institute, also offered to screen for gender, a simple and profitable analysis with potentially huge demand. In these latter cases, the availability of PGD actually drove the market for fertility services, because most of the "patients" did not actually suffer from infertility. By the summer of

2004, Steinberg reported that his clinic was seeing roughly ten patients a week for sex selection. "It's gone absolutely berserk," he said. "People are calling left and right."[62]

The Role of Regulation

This furor, of course, was due at least in part to regulatory gaps. In 2004, PGD was officially legal in many industrialized states. France, Denmark, Belgium, and Norway permitted the procedure; the United Kingdom sometimes even covered it as part of the national health-care system.[63] Western Australia was an exception to this trend, as was Germany, which continued to forbid any intervention with the human embryo.[64] But most countries with high-tech reproductive facilities permitted the use of PGD.

What varied, though—and drove patients to Steinberg—were the *terms* of this use. In the United Kingdom, for example, couples could not use PGD to determine the sex of their child unless that child was at risk of inheriting a disease that was directly linked to gender. In the United States and several Australian states, by contrast, parents could select for sex regardless of disease. Spain was also a favored site for sex selection (even though the process was formally illegal), as was Italy, where the law was silent.[65]

Almost immediately, however, a series of high-profile cases revealed the difficulty of restricting PGD or defining precisely the conditions under which it can be employed. Early in 2002, for example, two couples appealed to Britain's Human Fertilisation and Embryology Authority (HFEA), the agency charged with reviewing any use of PGD that falls beyond the explicit, disease-specific guidelines. The two couples requested nearly identical procedures. Like the Nashes and the Strongin-Goldbergs, they both wanted to produce siblings to save a dying child. One of these children, Zain Hashmi, was suffering from thalassemia, a rare inherited blood disorder; the other, Charlie Whitaker, from a similar blood disorder known as Diamond-Blackfan anemia.

After months of deliberation and extensive media attention, the HFEA returned with a split decision: it allowed the Hashmis to proceed with PGD, but prohibited the Whitakers. The logic? Zain Hashmi's disease was the result of a known genetic mutation, one that could easily be passed to any subsequent sibling; Charlie Whitaker's was not. So PGD in the Hash-mis' case could be described as preventing disease in the new child, whereas for the Whitakers, it would be undertaken solely to save Charlie.

The Whitakers eventually traveled to the United States, where they successfully conceived a son to donate marrow to Charlie.[66] The Hash-mis saw the HFEA decision subsequently reversed by Britain's high court and then reinstated by the court of appeals.[67] In the meantime, they, too, traveled to the United States, spending £25,000 on unsuc-cessful PGD trials before returning to Britain.[68]

In another poignant case, a family whose three-year-old daughter had died of severe burns lost their appeal to use PGD to select a female em-bryo. They traveled to a private clinic in Italy, paid £6,000 for a PGD procedure that produced only a single male embryo (the family already had four sons), and decided to donate it to another couple.[69] In explain-ing the HFEA's decision in this case, the chairwoman was adamant: "It's our duty, however painful, to act for the good of the whole of British so-ciety . . . We have consulted the public and the public doesn't like—and we don't like—the idea of designer babies."[70]

The Diagnosis Dilemma

Therein lies the central quandary of PGD. In the abstract, almost no one wants designer babies. No one wants to live in a brave new world in which parents peruse a catalog of traits and carefully select their perfect child: a clever cellist, perhaps, with hazel eyes, brown hair, and a left-side dimple. No one wants—or at least admits to wanting—a world in which rich parents can purchase genetic enhancements for their offspring, while the poor are left to nature's mercy. And almost no one condones selecting gender simply on the basis of preference.[71]

Yet individually and case-by-case, genetic selection frequently makes sense. Why shouldn't the Nashes use technology to save their daughter? Why should any family produce a child destined to die early from Hunt-ington's? What's wrong with making a 4'10" boy just a little bit taller? Or adding a daughter to a family of five sons?

One can argue, as critics do, that any step toward perfection drags us back to the Nazis and to the eugenic agenda that ended in the gas cham-bers of Auschwitz. But although such arguments carry huge emotional weight, the logic is misleading. The horror of Nazi eugenics—and indeed of its gentler precedents in the United States and elsewhere—came from the connection between social objectives and state power. It came from the state determining the contours of "fitness" and "purity" and then imposing that decision—through persuasion, sterilization, and ultimately murder—upon its citizens.

Preimplantation diagnosis stands that sequence on its head. Instead of placing government at the helm of social choice, it leaves that decision squarely in private hands, with parents making intimate decisions about the offspring they will bear. Most of these parents, presumably, make their decisions with little regard for either society or the state. They care about their child. Yet the sum of these tiny decisions has a much broader potential: to reshape, like the old eugenics, the notion of "fitness" and transform children into perfectible goods.

With PGD and its inevitable successors, therefore, the ultimate fear is of the market. It is the fear that millions of consumers, one by one, will make purchases that change humanity. Or as Robert L. Sinsheimer, an eminent biologist at the California Institute of Technology, predicted as early as 1969, "The old eugenics was limited to a numerical enhancement of the best of our existing gene pool. The horizons of the new eugenics are in principle boundless . . . For the first time in all time, a living creature understands its origin and can undertake to design its future."[72]

Already, we are taking small steps in this direction. Families marked by devastating genetic illnesses are frequent users of PGD, detecting their defective genes before passing them along to the next generation. As a result, almost certainly fewer children are being born with fatal diseases like Tay-Sachs and Fanconi anemia.[73] In some cases, researchers have also begun to screen for diseases that attack later in life, such as breast cancer and early-onset Alzheimer's disease.[74]

If these trends continue, the frequency of inherited mutations—and the prevalence of several major genetic diseases—could decrease dramatically over the course of only a few generations.[75] Lower-tech and less desirable outcomes are also evident in several provinces of India and China, where the pervasive use of ultrasound-plus-abortion has led to a discernible increase in the proportion of male children: in 2000, for example, 117 boys were born in China for every 100 girls.[76] Meanwhile, in the United States and elsewhere, basic PGD—that is, screening for obvious genetic defects—has become nearly routine in IVF; and IVF combined with PGD is the conception method of choice for families marked by genetic disease. We are already choosing our children, therefore, and shaping society in the process.

The question, though, is whether we should. Should parents be allowed to shape their children's genetic destiny? Should they, in the aggregate, be able to shape society's genetic composition? The moral issues behind these questions are enormous, and probably intractable. But the political issues demand resolution. Because if we avoid the politics, then the market and biology will simply take over: those who can choose, and have reason to choose, will almost certainly do so. And their personal choices, mediated by an impersonal market, will slowly shape what we as a race will become.

In policy-making terms, there are several ways to approach this prospect. The first is to use government policy to pull parents off the slippery slope. In other words, if we as a society fear the implications of PGD and related technologies, then we as a society can simply ban them, forbidding parents from engaging in any form of embryonic screening. This is the policy that countries like Germany have already adopted; it is what critics like Kass and Sandel generally advocate. Such a policy would clearly lead to high-profile tragedies, because parents like the Nashes would lose an opportunity to save their children. But arguably it would prevent the broader and more distant tragedies—of degradation, commodification, and social stratification—that the critics fear.

Alternatively, countries like the United States could choose a laissez-faire approach, leaving parents to choose as they desire, and the market to develop as it will. In this vein, one could easily argue that the issues at stake in PGD—a parent's ability to conceive a healthy child—are so personal and intimate as to demand protection from any form of governmental intrusion. Accordingly, the same umbrella of rights that the Supreme Court has extended toward procreation and contraception could also be used to cover PGD and to protect a parent's right to engage in genetic, as well as reproductive, choice.

Policies for PGD, however, need not be confined to the extremes. Yes, we could ban all forms of genetic and embryonic screening, or we could ban nothing. But we could also choose to venture selectively down the slippery slope of designer babies, drawing at least some lines between what is permissible and what is not. For example, although the British decision to permit PGD for one set of parents but not another may strike most Americans as too draconian, it does suggest how lines of instrumentality might be drawn. Theoretically at least, we could differentiate between PGD that selects *against* genetic mutations (for cystic fibrosis, Tay-Sachs, and so forth) from PGD that selects *for* desired genetic traits. We could also choose to cover the former kind of PGD under existing insurance plans, ensuring as a result that its use was not restricted to the wealthy. We could likewise prohibit parents from using PGD or related technologies to choose gender, or we could mandate gender selection only under certain circumstances. Theoretically, any of these policies could be imposed by national legislation, by individual state legislation, or through self-regulation by the clinics and doctors involved.

Admittedly, crafting any policies along these lines would be difficult, especially given the controversy that engulfs any discussion in the United States concerning the human embryo. Admittedly, none of the policies would be watertight, and parents like the Nashes or the Whitakers might well circumvent them in the hope of saving their children. Yet the policies themselves could be put in place. And, with exceptions and time, they could also be enforced.

Like many aspects of the baby trade, genetic selection forces a collision between the public and private spheres of life, between the most intimate decisions that people face and a distant view of how races and societies evolve. When couples like the Strongin-Goldbergs confront the imminent death of their children, they will naturally do whatever it takes to save them. When a mother of four boys contemplates another child, she may understandably want to make that child a girl. These are deeply personal choices, and actions that technology has now made real. The long-term effects of these choices, however, carry social costs. And thus society must have some say in how these choices are made and the extent to which they are left to private preferences and market forces. The only way to exercise this voice is through the political process.

In the end, the politics of PGD may not even be very painful. Despite the vast potential that genetic selection holds; despite fears of social stratification based on genetic manipulation, it's still not clear that even rich parents will want to engage in this manipulation as a matter of course. Instead, parents who can afford to choose may nevertheless decide to let nature take its course, trusting in their own gene pool and the inherent goodness of their offspring.[77] (After all, don't most parents already think that their babies are perfect?) They may decide to decline the market in this case, and to trust instead in what Sandel describes as "an openness to the unbidden."[78] Or they could simply make the more basic decision that Mark Hughes predicts. Given the choice between PGD and nature, he suggests, "most people would rather have sex."[79]

CHAPTER 5

Return to the Forbidden Planet

Issues in Human Cloning

The shroud of the dark side has fallen.
Begun the clone war has.

—STAR WARS: ATTACK OF THE CLONES

BY ANY ESTIMATION, the Raëlians are an eccentric bunch. Launched in France under the leadership of a car-racing former journalist known as Raël, the group tells tales of alien encounters and holds fast to Raël's belief that scientists from another planet used DNA to create life on earth. Members practice ritualized sensual massage and are devoted to cloning, which they argue will ensure immortality by preserving DNA.

After laboring on the absurdist fringe for some time, the group sprang to notoriety in December 2002, when Dr. Brigitte Boisselier, a Raëlian bishop and managing director of Clonaid, the movement's private sector firm, announced the birth of a baby girl cloned directly from one of her mother's skin cells. Despite repeated promises to the contrary, the Raëlians never publicly produced the child.

Dr. Boisselier and her little band may or may not have cloned a human. So too with Severino Antinori, an only slightly less eccentric

Italian fertility specialist who claimed in 2002 that he was well on his way to producing a cloned child. Certainly, though, someone will succeed before very long, shattering what remains of a powerful human taboo.

In scientific terms, cloning is not all that different from other technologies of reproductive medicine. The current method involves taking the DNA from a single cell and implanting it into an egg cell whose own genetic matter has been removed. Although the egg has not been fertilized with sperm, the transfer of DNA, under the right conditions, can "trick" the egg into *believing* it has been fertilized and then growing as if it had been. Technically, the only real difference between cloning and IVF (particularly the more innovative forms of IVF) is the source of the genetic code: from one package of chromosomes rather than two. Conceptually, however, the differences are vast. For in cloning, even the hint of sex disappears, and theoretically individuals can do what has always been impossible. They can reproduce themselves.

Economically, the prospects for commercial cloning are alluring. Why bother, after all, with the guesswork of genetic engineering if you already know what you like? You could re-create your husband, your sister, your great Uncle Max. (Imagine if all the kids in Manhattan named after their great-grandparents really *were* their great-grandparents.) You could reincarnate a pet or a tragically lost child.

Less dramatically, cloning also offers people the chance to re-create vital parts of themselves. Using techniques that are already relatively well developed, future patients could use their own cells to clone genetically identical heart, liver, or lung cells that subsequently could be transplanted back into their own diseased organs. Such production would address the gross imbalance in the current market for transplant organs, where demand vastly outstrips supply.

Already, firms like Massachusetts-based Advanced Cell Technology (ACT) are working on techniques for therapeutic cloning, creating embryonic stem cells that could subsequently be tweaked to produce new, more specific cells or organs. Because the U.S. government has banned all federal support for research into human cloning, ACT relies solely on private funds and presumably hopes for private profits. The company charges $20,000 for cloned milk cows and has announced that its annual earnings could potentially hit more than $10 billion. In Scotland, two groups of prestigious researchers have formed the commercially oriented Scottish Stem Cell Network, backed by funds from the nation's major development agency. And in Korea, Singapore, and China, funds and scientists are pouring into the fields of stem cell research and regenerative medicine.

Like surrogacy, IVF, and genetic selection, the possibility of human cloning raises excruciating moral and philosophical issues. What does it mean to re-create human life? To reproduce without a partner? What defines the identity of people who, genetically speaking, have lived before? We may never resolve these questions, even as technologies for cloning become increasingly common.

Several aspects of cloning, though, are certain. Technological advances will make human cloning possible. These technologies will generate commercial markets.[1] And governments will need to regulate these markets to ensure that the benefits of cloning trump the possible evils.

The Drive to Duplicate

The allure of cloning has long exceeded the technical possibility of doing so. Long before the word *clone* was even coined, long before the science of cloning was remotely possible, people have toyed with the idea of reproducing themselves in full. They have imagined children born not only *from* them, but *as* them as well.

Arguably, the idea of cloning stretches back to Genesis, where Eve emerges, fully formed, from Adam's rib.[2] Eve, to be sure, is not the clone of Adam; she is a separate person of a different sex. But she is born in a decidedly nonsexual fashion, from a single person and without the messy intervention of mating. This image of asexual reproduction, of children born of a single parent, sits at the core of what might be called the cloning fantasy. Sometimes the fantasy involves multiple copies of a particular person. Sometimes, as in the case of Adam and Eve, it more simply centers on reproduction without partners or sex. In all cases, though, the cloning fantasy is appropriately mythical in scope, for it involves a new form of creation and a new way of generating life in the image of the creator. If genetic engineering allows parents to play God, then cloning makes them akin to God, re-creating themselves in the body of their offspring. "Let us make man in our image," declares God in Genesis, "after our likeness."

This desire runs deep. It is the attraction of the well-worn Frankenstein story, of fairy tale rebirths, and of an entire genre of science fiction literature. In *Frankenstein*, after all, a lonely scientist seeks to discover the secret of life by resurrecting the dead. He builds a newborn creature from discarded body parts and animates him with a jolt of electricity. And then Frankenstein lives to see his ruin, as the creature, hopelessly searching for its own origins, embarks upon a series of murders.

A similar motif runs through Aldous Huxley's best-selling *Brave New World*, and even popular movies like *The Boys from Brazil* (in which an evil doctor produces ninety-four clones of Hitler) and *Multiplicity* (in which a busy dad clones himself so that he'll have more time). In all these treatments, there is the seductive pull of sameness: of creating, again and again, the identical likeness of a specific soul. There is the hidden tug of immortality and the obvious attraction of retrieving what was lost, be it a beloved child or one's own receding youth. In the end, however, there is also always the price for these rewards, one that is typically as awesome as the power itself. Frankenstein's "monster" kills his creator's brother, his best friend, and his wife; a Hitler clone sends his Dobermans to maul the evil doctor. At an intimate level, the idea of cloning seems to challenge our expectations about life and death, about our children and ourselves. We want, like God, to reproduce ourselves. But we are desperately afraid of doing so.

Fatherless Tadpoles

For centuries, these fears were purely fictional. Cloning was an ill-defined urge without a word to describe it or the science to make it possible. In the latter years of the nineteenth century, however, as the cellular mechanics of reproduction became more evident, a tiny group of scientists began to contemplate the differences between humans and other species, differences that clustered largely around the practice of mating. Outside the world of mammals, they understood, reproduction is frequently a solitary act: bacteria, for example, simply divide into two identical parts; yeasts create small buds that eventually separate into offspring. Even more complicated animals, like lizards and certain fish, can occasionally reproduce by themselves, through a process known as *parthenogenesis* (from the Greek for "virgin birth"). Yet humans, along with other mammals, depend upon sex: we cannot reproduce by ourselves. We also reproduce in a largely invisible fashion, with both conception and fetal development occurring far beyond the reach of the naked eye.

As described in chapter 2, it took hundreds of years for science to understand the mechanics of reproduction, to move beyond the ancient notion of tiny humans curled up in seeds and to probe instead the process by which egg and sperm combine to form a fetus. Yet as this mysterious process was revealed, it raised an equally mysterious set of questions, many of which still plague modern reproductive medicine. How, for example, does the sperm induce the egg to divide? How does the genetic information of the fertilized egg replicate itself repeatedly? And how does this single set of instructions—and a single ball of cells—ultimately produce a glorious *body* of cells, each with its own separate function?

In pursuit of these puzzles, scientists began to study simpler acts of procreation, hoping in particular to unlock the secret of differentiation, the process by which all-purpose cells develop highly specific functions. To do so, they started generally with frogs and other amphibians, relatively simple animals that typically produce very large numbers of very large eggs.

One of these scientists was Hans Spemann, a German embryologist who would go on to win the Nobel Prize for medicine in 1935. In 1902, Spemann used a strand of hair from his baby son to split a two-celled salamander embryo in half. Each of the halves proceeded to develop naturally, producing two identical salamander embryos and eventually two identical salamanders.

Subsequent experimentation showed that salamanders were almost uniquely versatile, able to regrow several parts of their body. But Spemann was intrigued by the broader possibilities that this splitting had suggested, possibilities that extended far beyond the salamander species. In 1938, he playfully raised these possibilities in a book titled *Embryonic Development and Induction*. If embryonic cells could reproduce themselves and give rise to a complete organism, he wondered, could adult cells somehow do likewise? Could the nucleus of even an advanced cell be prompted to generate something new? From a practical standpoint, Spemann didn't know how to execute this "fantastical experiment." Conceptually, however, he outlined what would have to be done: scientists would need to isolate the nucleus of one cell and then introduce it into the "egg protoplasm" of another. In other words, they would grow an embryo from a single adult cell.[3]

Eleven years after Spemann's death in 1941, two researchers at the Institute for Cancer Research in Philadelphia achieved a startlingly similar result, proving, for the first time, that cloning was physically possible. The scientists—Robert Briggs and Thomas King—were not actually trying to test Spemann's concept or attempt asexual reproduction. They weren't even working in the reproductive field, in fact, but focusing instead on the basic mechanics of gene activation. To understand this process, though, they happened upon precisely the same experiment that Spemann had proposed. They took an unfertilized frog egg, removed its nucleus, and then injected it with the nucleus of a cell taken from another frog's embryo. Then they repeated the same microscopic procedure again and again.

Most of the time, they discovered, the egg "took"—that is, the injection of the foreign nucleus somehow tricked the egg into beginning the process of development. The eggs divided *even though they had not been fertilized* and began to form themselves into embryos. Some of the eggs went through several rounds of division; others became full-fledged embryos that subsequently perished. But some—27 out of 197 attempts—grew into apparently normal tadpoles, genetic replicas of the single cells that had spawned them. King celebrated in a poem he wrote for Briggs:

> It was chubby and plump, a right jolly old tad,
> And we were to it—both Mother and Dad.[4]

For the next several years, other researchers set out to reproduce what Briggs and King had found. They, too, were able to clone tadpoles, but they encountered the same barrier that faced the original team. They could clone the frogs, it appeared, from embryonic frog cells, or from the cells of very young tadpoles. But they couldn't achieve the full intent of Spemann's experiment—using an adult cell to launch the duplicative process. Adult cells seemed to be too old to clone, or too highly specialized.

Clone Dreams

In 1962, however, John Gurdon, a developmental biologist at Oxford University, managed to clone tadpoles from the intestinal cells of fully developed frogs. The results were difficult to interpret, because only a small percentage of Gurdon's transfers developed into tadpoles, and this particular species of frog had intestinal cells that occasionally acted almost like sperm. Yet the possibility of success was bright enough to draw at least a small group of scientists along Gurdon's path, painstakingly trying to coax some kind of adult cells, in some kind of animal, to reproduce themselves in an egg. The purpose of these experiments was to demonstrate that the genetic map of an individual—be it a frog, a mouse, or a human—was not irreversibly altered in the course of cellular differentiation. It was to demonstrate, in other words, that cloning was at least theoretically possible. But for more than twenty years, the scientists had virtually no success.

Ironically, though, just as the science was bogging down, public interest awoke. In 1963, J. B. S. Haldane, one of the world's most eminent biologists, devoted a public speech to Gurdon's frogs. Using the word *clone* for the first time, Haldane waxed rhapsodic about the technology's future. With advanced cloning techniques, he prophesied, "persons of attested ability" could reproduce themselves asexually, "rais[ing] the possibilities of human achievement" in the process.[5]

Although none of these outcomes was even remotely possible at the time, Haldane's enthusiasm, together with his prestige, attracted considerable attention from the world outside biology. The *New York Times* reported his predictions, and an editorial in the *Wall Street Journal* blasted them, arguing that Haldane could well be accused of "preaching racism."[6] Alvin Toffler speculated about cloning's prospects in *Future Shock*, a best-seller published in 1970, and Woody Allen riffed memorably on the theme in his 1973 film *Sleeper*, in which a group of scientists attempt to clone their nation's leader from cells in his nose. Already, cloning was both seductive and scary, the stuff of comedy and nightmare. Yet only tadpoles had been cloned by this point, not very frequently or with any real measure of success.

For the next two decades, cloning remained a public preoccupation and an apparent scientific dead end. Novels like *The Boys from Brazil* and *Do Androids Dream of Electric Sheep?* (the inspiration for the cult movie *Blade Runner*) explored the human implications of cloning, and a growing band of bioethicists began to probe the philosophy. But progress in the laboratory was slim, and mainstream biology concentrated its attention elsewhere. The debate over cloning remained largely abstract, playing out in science fiction and philosophy rather than markets and laboratories. We may have wanted to clone ourselves, but we simply could not.

Dolly: The Short, Sad Story of a Sheep

Matters changed abruptly in 1984, when a Danish veterinarian named Steen Willadsen succeeded in cloning three lambs. Like Briggs and King, Willadsen had used embryonic cells rather than adult ones. But he had cloned mammals—an unprecedented feat—and his lambs appeared to be entirely normal. Quietly, Willadsen also revealed the commercial potential of mammalian cloning. He left the British Agricultural Research Council in Cambridge for Granada Biosciences in Texas, where he began to work on cows.

Scientists at other labs had already cottoned to the prospect of animal cloning—not only frogs anymore, and not only to test the biological boundaries of reproduction. Instead, there was a growing sense that if cloning were possible, it would be particularly profitable in the world of livestock, where prize-winning bulls or highly productive cows often fetched exorbitant prices. If one could produce multiple copies of, for example, a superior steer, the financial rewards would be considerable, because single embryos from these animals could sell for as much as $3,000 each.[7] Accordingly, while bioethicists were debating the evils of human cloning and movie directors were weaving scenarios about them, several teams of unknown animal scientists were slaving away at the more mundane task of cloning cows, sheep, and goats.

Willadsen was one of this bunch, a brash and brilliant scientist who had spent the early part of his career learning to freeze sheep embryos. Along the way, he had also reconfirmed Spemann's salamander experiment with mammalian embryos, proving that it was possible to divide early-stage embryos in half, even in quarters, and producing perfectly normal offspring from the divisions.* In 1984, Willadsen took the next logical step with his

---

*This process is now generally referred to as twinning. It can occur naturally as well, producing identical twins.

sheep embryos. Instead of just implanting each division into the uterus of a surrogate sheep, he took a single cell from the embryo and inserted its nucleus into an unfertilized egg. The lambs that eventually resulted were clones, the first mammals born from asexual reproduction.

In the scientific world, Willadsen's breakthrough was big news. He had proven that cloning was possible even in large mammals and that the offspring were not apparently damaged as a result. Commercially, his lambs suggested that more profitable animals could also be cloned, creating a business where returns were literally multiplied. For example, imagine that a prize bull (or racehorse or milk cow) sold for auction at $10,000. Now imagine that this same animal was mated with another to produce a single embryo. With Willadsen's technique, that single embryo could be divided into eight identical embryos, each destined to grow into an equally valuable adult. Or the eight embryos could themselves be divided, producing a total of sixty-four identical embryos with the same final value. And so on and so on.

Because the cells were young, powerful, and still undifferentiated—*totipotent*, in biological terms—in theory they could be prodded to produce a potentially infinite number of offspring. This multiplicity, of course, was precisely the stuff of fictional nightmares like *The Boys from Brazil*. But when the embryos were cows rather than humans, the social concerns were considerably milder.

In fact, news of Willadsen's success barely made it to the public press. These were only lambs, after all, and the science was difficult to convey. Moreover, Willadsen's clones were technically not very different from the split embryos that preceded them. He was still copying a bundle of early-stage cells rather than an adult being.

It took another twelve years before this final hurdle was crossed. And then cloning exploded into both commercial and social consciousness.

Dolly Was a Little Lamb

Once again, the science took place in a sheep: a Finn Dorsett sheep named Dolly, who rapidly became the most famous animal in the world. Like Willadsen's lambs, Dolly was born in the United Kingdom, the product of relatively obscure scientists toiling at the agricultural fringes of their profession.

What catapulted Dolly to prominence was the final completion of Spemann's "fantastical experiment." Unlike the lambs—or the frogs or the salamanders—Dolly was produced from a single *adult* cell, in this case a mammary cell from a fully mature sheep. For years, Dolly's creators—Ian Wilmut and Keith Campbell of Scotland's Roslin Institute—had been struggling to find a way to reprogram adult cells, to get mature and highly differentiated cells to revert somehow to their earlier and more general selves.

Finally, in 1995, they stumbled upon an unusual fountain of youth. They deprived the selected cells of nutrients for five days, culturing them in a medium deprived of the customary growth factors.[8] For reasons that are still not fully understood, the cells responded to their hunger by retreating into an inactive state, shutting down several key functions in the process. As a result, when Wilmut and Campbell injected the cells into the target egg cell, they behaved not like mammary cells but like eggs. They began to divide, igniting the process that eventually led—in one of 277 attempts—to Dolly.[9]

When word of Dolly broke, the press went wild. Suddenly, the sheep's woolly white head was plastered on newspapers and magazines around the world, bearing headlines that vacillated between apocalyptic predictions and very bad puns: "Clone on the Range," for example, "Baaa-ack to the Future," and "The Fall of Man."[10] Wilmut and Campbell became instant celebrities, and biologists and bioethicists briefly dominated the talk show circuit. The actual sheep, of course, was merely a sideline to the frenzy, a silent example of what science had wrought.

Only months after the announcement of Dolly's birth, U.S. President Bill Clinton decried human cloning as "morally unacceptable."[11] The World Health Organization and the American Society for Reproductive Medicine condemned the prospect, as did the United Nations, the Group of Eight, and the pope.[12] Other opponents leaped similarly into the media, declaring, for example, that "the prospect of human cloning . . . is the occasion for deciding whether we shall be slaves of unregulated progress, and ultimately its artifacts, or whether we shall remain free human beings."[13] Supporters were fewer but no less emphatic. "Now there are no boundaries," exulted biologist Lee Silver, in what became a frequently quoted phrase: "Now all of science fiction is true."[14]

Meanwhile, the excitement over Wilmut and Campbell's achievement frequently belied the more prosaic goal that had motivated them. The two men, after all, were not really trying to crack the puzzle of cloning. They had never worked with humans and had no intention of ever doing so. Instead, they were animal researchers working for a pharmaceutical company that hoped to find a way of coaxing sheep into producing insulin. For them, cloning had been just a fairly efficient means to a rather different end. Cloning was a tool, in other words, rather than a scientific Holy Grail. And it had nothing to do with the prospects for human reproduction. "Human cloning," Wilmut later wrote, "is very far from . . . my own thoughts and ambitions, and we would rather that no one ever attempted it."[15] To outside observers, however, this distinction was irrelevant. Wilmut and Campbell had taken a single cell from an adult sheep. They had grown this cell into a fully formed animal, the identical and undeniable offspring of her single, unmated mother. If they could do this in sheep, they—and presumably others—could do it in humans as well.

In 2002, scientists at Roslin sadly reported that Dolly was aging prematurely, suffering from an acute form of arthritis that typically affected only much older sheep.[16] On February 14, 2003, only six and a half years after her birth, the team that had created Dolly reluctantly put her to sleep. Her death, however, received considerably less coverage than her birth. Scientists knew that her untimely demise raised serious questions about the biology of cloning; many nonspecialists also suspected as much.[17] But in the post-Dolly world it didn't much matter. The clone wars had begun.

The Market for Multiples

If one were to judge cloning solely from the headlines it has raised, one might easily conclude that this is an area of science and ethics, a social debate about how far humans can push science and how far they should. The actual demand for cloning seems stunted by comparison, a small market populated by eccentric millionaires hoping to remake themselves.

In practice, though, the potential market for cloning is both substantially larger and less outlandish. It comes not from people hoping to mass-produce themselves or their children, but rather from those who view cloning as another tool of high-tech baby-making, a way to produce not clones per se, but babies. They are joined in the market by those who clamor for cloning's technological offshoots: for the drugs that might be produced some day by cloned sheep like Dolly, the stem cells that could combat disease, the livestock bred for better traits. In the end, the demand for cloning's most obvious product—multiple copies of a single being—is probably rather small, dwarfed by less dramatic but more commercial opportunities.

Because the obvious product is so controversial, however, the broader process of cloning has been cloaked with the same distrust. There is already a market for several forms of cloning, one that will inevitably grow larger. But it is a quiet market thus far, pushed and shoved and silenced by raucous social concerns. It is entirely possible that these concerns will serve, over time, to squelch the cloning market entirely; investors will shy away from any use of the technology, and scientists will turn to other pursuits. It is also possible, though, that the market will force its opponents to back down. If the demand for cloning's offshoots is large and persistent enough to fuel a profitable industry, then the combination of demand and supply could well do what other controversial but profitable technologies have done in the past. They could yank the market back toward normalcy.

"Pharming": The Market for Pets and Other Animals

The largest current market for cloning reflects the technology's agricultural origins. Although livestock breeders have not managed to produce the perfectly matched, high-quality herds that they envisioned in the early 1980s, the quest for cloned cattle remains strong. So, too, does the goal of using cloned animals to produce drugs intended for humans.

Prior even to the birth of Dolly, a handful of companies—most of them based in the United States, the United Kingdom, Canada, and Australia—were actively working to clone commercial livestock. As described earlier, the attractions in this field were obvious: multiplying the number of high-quality embryos that could be sold for as much as $3,000 apiece, and certifying that each embryo bore a precise array of inherited traits. Because ethical concerns were more limited—few bioethicists worried whether milk cows had souls—the agricultural market developed without much ado.

In the 1990s, four companies dominated the nascent trade. W. R. Grace & Company, a specialty chemicals company, supported a lab at the University of Wisconsin that was devoted to cattle cloning and was responsible for some of cloning's major breakthroughs in the 1980s. In Texas, Granada Biosciences also worked on cloning cow embryos; Genmark, based in Salt Lake City, worked to identify genetic markers for commercial traits such as milk-producing potential and milk fat content.[18] In Scotland, PPL Therapeutics worked to commercialize the work of the Roslin Institute, focusing primarily on using genetically enhanced animals—chicken, sheep, and cows—to produce proteins such as AAT (which treats cystic fibrosis) and insulin.

For about a decade, these firms, along with a handful of smaller rivals, spent serious money in pursuit of "pharmed" livestock. They invested millions of dollars and produced much of the science that would eventually flow to other forms of cloning. But the science of cloning at this point did not square well with the economics. It was simply too expensive to invest in the necessary infrastructure—the scientists, the technicians, the equipment, the livestock—and too difficult to produce a sufficient number of births.[19] In 1992, Granada sold its cloning operations to W. R. Grace. Two years later, W. R. Grace exited the industry as well, spinning off its cloning unit to an outside group of investors.

After the birth of Dolly, however, pharming was reborn. In 1999, researchers at Texas A&M's College of Veterinary Medicine announced that they had successfully cloned a healthy calf from the cells of an adult steer. Several commercial firms then announced their intention of repeating this feat, promising to re-create some of the cattle industry's most prized animals. This time around, the science complied. For example, Infigen, a Wisconsin-based firm, produced a bull cloned from genetically altered fetal cells in March 1997, and then the clone of a champion Holstein in October 2000.[20] The latter quickly fetched $82,000 at the World Dairy Expo.[21] Cyagra, the livestock division of Advanced Cell Technology, offered its cow cloning services to ranchers in 2001, as did ProLinia, a small company spun off by the University of Georgia. By 2001, at least three companies were actively competing in the cloned cattle market, shipping their products—usually extra-large bulls or prodigious milk cows—across the United States. The going price for cloned cows was between $20,000 and $25,000, placing them in the very upper end of the livestock market.[22]

Meanwhile, developments in the agricultural field led rapidly to research in other species. Researchers studied the methods that led to Dolly, adopted and refined and tweaked them, and soon were producing a virtual parade of cloned mammals: rabbits in France, pigs in the United Kingdom and United States, mice in Japan and Hawaii.

Although some of these animals were created simply to prove the possibility, many were the result of a distinct commercial intent. The French rabbits, for example, were bred by two biotechnology firms, both of which specialized in using animals to produce human proteins.[23] The pigs were designed as potential organ donors, equipped with genetic modifications that made their livers, hearts, and kidneys less likely to be rejected by human recipients.[24] Commercial firms were also working on genetically modified cloned chickens, as well as the now commonplace sheep. In all these cases, the intent was commercial: to clone animals either for use or for sale.

An even larger market became evident after 2002, when CC the cat suddenly entered the scene. CC, short for "carbon copy," was produced as part of the "Missyplicity" project, launched in 1997 to produce dog clones—more specifically, the clones of a particular dog named Missy.[25] Missy's owner, a reclusive California millionaire, had convinced a team of researchers at Texas A&M to work on his pet and then backed two associated ventures: BARC (Bio-Arts and Research Corporation) and Genetic Savings and Clone. Other than proving the apparently close connection between cloning and puns, however, Missyplicity hadn't worked. The Texas team succeeded in extracting and renucleating dozen of eggs but never managed to make another Missy.[26]

And so Lou Hawthorne, head of Genetic Savings and Clone, decided to diversify into cats. CC was born after only one failed cat cloning attempt, prompting eager cat lovers to bombard the company with requests.[27] Genetic Savings and Clone reported its intention to invest $3.7 million in the cat cloning business and to charge customers, at least in the early days, a fee "in the low five figures."[28] In the meantime, pet lovers could store their dog's or cat's tissue for only about $1,000—$895 for healthy animals, and $1,395 for dead ones.[29] By 2004, the company had eight customers lined up as part of its "Nine Lives Extravaganza," a

$50,000 package deal that included a cloned cat, a video of the cloning process, and a trip to California.[30]

It was easy, of course, to laugh at Missy and CC, with their eccentric backers and fervent customers. Commentators generally made light of the "carbon kitty" or the desire to re-create a cat. "Why clone a cat?" asked one unimpressed pundit. "Why clone a stupid cat? Why not just get another one?"[31] Animal rights groups were more outraged, but arguing against a kitten—even a cloned kitten—did not prove politically wise.

People might disagree about the desirability of cloning pets, it appeared, and they might refuse to drink milk from a cloned cow. But opposition to these procedures was muted. And thus the market for animal cloning remained relatively unfettered.

The Market for Infertility Treatment

When it came to people, of course, matters were very different. But the distinction was not entirely clear, and concerns over human cloning did not extend so obviously into all of the market prospects. That's because there is an area of human cloning that doesn't look like cloning per se, an area in which the technical process of cloning bumps up against the more traditional market for fertility treatment. In this part of the market, therefore—the part where cloning is just another tool of high-tech reproduction—demand is already stirring.

To understand this overlap, we need to return briefly to the science. In cloning, the nucleus of a single egg cell is destroyed, so that no genetic matter remains.[32] Then the nucleus of another cell is injected into the enucleated egg, replacing the discarded genes with its own. Finally, under carefully controlled conditions, the egg is jolted with a tiny bit of electricity, just enough to ignite a series of intricate chemical reactions and trick the egg into behaving as if it had been fertilized. The embryo that results from these contortions is the child of a single parent: the person (or cell, more precisely) that provided the inserted DNA.

It would seem that this process is unique, a stark departure from sexual reproduction and the ubiquitous mingling of two sets of genes. In practice, however, the difference is more subtle. First, even a true clone is not an identical replica of its parent. Instead, in ways that are not yet completely understood, the developing embryo is affected both by the

womb that nurtures it and by the mitochondria (the self-replicating por-
tions of a cell that process nutrients and provide energy) that remain in the
enucleated egg. CC the cat, for example, did not look exactly like her genetic mother; she was a genetic clone but not, in fact, a carbon copy. So
clones are not necessarily identical replicas, and they may bear some genetic material from a second (mitochondrial) parent. Second, some areas
of assisted reproduction already share technical similarities with cloning,
even if the treatments in these cases are called something different and
even when the parents have no particular interest in copycat production.

Consider, for example, the case of Sharon Saarinen, a thirty-four-
year-old hairdresser desperate to conceive a child. After exhausting the
usual rounds of treatment, she decided in 1998 to try cytoplasmic transfer, an experimental procedure in which the cytoplasm of a younger
woman is injected into an egg from the would-be mother. (Cytoplasm
is the substance that surrounds the nucleus of all human cells.) The procedure worked for Saarinen, and she soon gave birth to a daughter.
Clearly, this little girl was not a clone: she grew from her mother's egg,
fertilized by her father's sperm. But along the way, she also acquired the
DNA of a third person, the anonymous donor who provided the cytoplasm. Saarinen's daughter thus bears the DNA of three people.[33] So,
presumably, do at least some of the thirty other children who were born
in the late 1990s through cytoplasmic transfer.[34]

Similarly, in 1998, doctors at New York University Medical School
began to experiment with nuclear transfer, trying through another route
to rescue the eggs of technically infertile women. In this procedure, instead of transferring fresh cytoplasm into a recalcitrant egg, they took
the nucleus of a fertilized egg and transferred it to a donor egg whose
own nucleus had already been removed. Although the New York doctors stopped their experiments before producing a pregnancy, they subsequently worked with a team of Chinese researchers who, in 2003, did
achieve the first human pregnancy using nuclear transfer. The twins that
resulted from this procedure subsequently died in utero, for reasons that
were not necessarily related to the means of their conception.[35] Had
they lived, however, or if others were to be born through similar means,
then they, too, would be genetic hybrids, created through an unprecedented interlacing of genetic material.

One might argue, of course, that the difference between high-tech IVF and reproductive cloning is substantial. A sperm is still involved in both of the procedures just described, after all, and the genetic mingling of sexual reproduction still occurs. The source of the nucleus in both cases is also a fertilized egg rather than an adult cell, meaning that at least some of the safety concerns that surround reproductive cloning simply don't exist. Moreover, the goal of these transfer procedures is generally to produce *a* child, rather than a child with a particular genetic blueprint.

Yet in practice, both cytoplasmic transfer and the nuclear transfer that occurred in China overlap considerably with the technical side of cloning. Potentially, they also pave the way for other, even more closely related techniques. For example, in cases where the male partner is incapable of producing sperm, theoretically scientists could remove another cell from his body and inject its nucleus into an egg cell from his wife (or other surrogate). If the egg "took," it would eventually produce an embryo, and then a child, who would contain only the male partner's DNA. Less dramatically, couples using traditional IVF but producing only a small number of viable embryos could use cloning techniques to divide these embryos into identical multiples, producing, in effect, artificial twins. This technique, officially called "embryo splitting," would involve only minor modifications to existing practice.[36]

From the perspective of the baby trade, the emergence of such experimental techniques reveals once again the depth of the demand for children. Sharon Saarinen did not choose cytoplasmic transfer because she was curious about trying the new procedure. She chose it because she wanted a child who was genetically related to her and her husband. If cloning can bring children to others like her—would-be parents for whom nothing else works—then both history and economics suggest that a market for reproductive cloning is likely to arise. It may not center, as many predict, on megalomaniacal billionaires or dictators seeking to clone an army. Instead, like most of the baby business, it may come simply from those eager to find some way, any way, to have a genetically related child.

The Market for Re-creation

A similar demand comes from an even sadder segment of the market: parents searching to replace a particular child. This is largely the demand that fuels groups like the Raëlians and drives much of the popular opposition to cloning. In practice, this demand is actually quite small. It remains unrealistic in scientific terms and commercially unattractive. But it is a piece of the cloning market nevertheless, and a demand that is not likely to disappear.

The prototypical case is easy to imagine. A young couple loses their child in a tragic accident. Or a middle-aged couple watches their son, a talented football player or violinist, struck down by illness. Devastated, these parents don't just want another child. They want *their* child back. They retain a lock of the child's hair or freeze his skin cells, and search for a scientist willing and able to clone him.

Such stories, of course, are the stuff of soap operas and science fiction. But they are already quite real. After Dolly's birth, for example, Ian Wilmut was besieged by similar couples, each pleading with him to clone their dead child.[37] So too with Richard Seed, a renegade Chicago scientist who is almost universally disdained by members of the medical mainstream. In 1998, Seed announced that he was prepared to clone humans and that several families had already approached him with requests.[38] Money in these cases is rarely an obstacle.

What appears more problematic is the underlying science. On the one hand, developments in other areas of cloning suggest that human reproductive cloning is well within reach. Sheep and cats, after all, are not biologically very far removed from humans, and they reproduce in fairly similar ways. If we can re-create cats, therefore, then we should eventually be able to re-create humans. But humans, on the other hand, present problems that cats (and sheep and cows) do not. Premature aging in humans, for example, would be more problematic than in cows. So would higher-than-normal rates of birth defects (generally true of animal clones) and attempts that can involve hundreds of eggs and dozens of surrogate wombs.

Moreover, a close look at cloned animals suggests that even successful re-creative cloning does not necessarily "work." CC the cat, for example, was not a carbon copy of the animal from which she was cloned, with visibly different markings in her calico coat. The same was true of Cedric, Cecil, Cyril, and Tuppence, four Dorset rams that Ian Wilmut and his colleagues cloned from cultured embryo cells. Although the animals were genetically identical, their behavior patterns and physical appearances were not.[39] Thus, even if scientists could clone a particular human, there is no guarantee that the clone would resemble the original. And so the deeply felt desire to retrieve a lost child may never be met through cloning.

Nevertheless, scattered reports strongly indicate that a small handful of clients are pursuing re-creative cloning, aided by an even smaller band of maverick scientists. The first of this group was Seed, who bolted into prominence by claiming that he could clone humans and was determined to do so. He spent several years raising money and dodging the FDA but then retired from practice before producing much except controversy. Seed reports, however, that he did have lots of clients, somewhere between two hundred and seven hundred.[40]

Next in line was the flamboyant Severino Antinori, who had become famous in 1994 for helping a sixty-three-year-old woman to bear a child. In 2001, Antinori announced that he expected to produce the world's first human clone within eighteen months. The doctor also reported that he had more than fifteen hundred clients in line, most of whom were trying to resolve infertility problems.[41] Meanwhile, Panayiotis Zavos, a sometime partner of Antinori's, claimed that he, too, was well on his way to producing the first human clone.[42] Like Antinori and Seed, Zavos reported a client list that stretched into the "thousands," along with substantial funds raised from undisclosed sources.[43]

Similar claims have been advanced by the Raëlians, the futuristic cult mentioned earlier. In 2001, the group announced that it had received $500,000 from an American couple who hoped to re-create their dead baby.[44] Then in 2002, the Raëlians proclaimed the birth of Eve, an infant purportedly produced from a skin cell of her mother. Neither claim was ever substantiated, and most scientists refuse to take the Raëlians seriously. "I don't suppose there is a single qualified person with a background in reproductive medicine who believes they have done what they claim," asserted one leading expert. "If Clonaid really has cloned a person, why didn't it put its research out in a scientific journal?"[45] The fact that its founder sports a flowing white tunic and surrounds himself with beautiful women hardly helps the group's credibility, nor does its central belief that humans are themselves clones of an advanced alien race.[46]

But some scientists suspect that the weight of technological advance has made it increasingly likely that even groups like the Raëlians could eventually produce a human clone. "When you look at what would be critically required to clone a human being," says Gregory Stock of UCLA's Program on Medicine, Technology and Society, "surrogates and a large number of eggs are key ingredients, and the Raëlians have those."[47] A similar view comes from Michael Bishop, president of Infigen, the animal cloning firm. "It [human cloning] is being done," he insists. "I have no doubt. It would be stupid and naïve to think it's not."[48]

On scientific grounds, it is difficult to predict whether any researcher—maverick or mainstream—will succeed in producing a human clone. It is hard to know how many people really want to bring loved ones back from the dead, and how many have the financial means to do so. Yet even with these vast uncertainties, a distinct demand for re-creative cloning is slowly emerging, grappling for the science that may eventually create a supply.

The Market for Stem Cells

In the largest current market for cloning, by contrast, the science is considerably more advanced. This market has little to do with babies or fertility or immortality. It is still marginal in purely commercial terms and has attracted a vast amount of political controversy. But when this market takes off—and it will—the business it generates and the politics it affects are likely to drive developments across the entire spectrum of cloning.

This market, of course, is for embryonic stem cells, the all-powerful, undifferentiated cells that launch the beginnings of life. These are the cells that compose the embryo before it reaches roughly the sixty-four-cell stage—the cells that subsequently transform themselves into the body's full array of complex organs: blood, brain, liver, heart.

Because embryonic stem cells have the power to become virtually anything, they also hold the promise—in theory at least—of treating some of society's most devastating illnesses. A child with diabetes, for example, could be injected with embryonic stem cells converted into beta cells, the critical blood-sugar regulators that diabetes patients lack. A patient suffering from Parkinson's disease could receive nerve cells that produce dopamine, the chemical whose absence causes Parkinson's.

Although such treatments are still far from being developed, much less tested, their scientific potential is enormous. So, too, is their potential market: in 2002, for example, Americans spent $132 billion on treatments for diabetes, and an estimated $25 billion on costs related to Parkinson's.[49] If even some portion of that expenditure were replaced by stem cell technologies, the proceeds would be significant—larger, most likely, than those arising from any other modern medical breakthrough.[50]

Of course, the direct uses of stem cells have little to do with reproduction; they are about treating illness or regenerating tissue rather than producing offspring. Yet the link between these two areas is scientifically intense, and the business and politics that surround stem cells inevitably will affect, and be affected by, the baby trade.

Again, we need to return briefly to the science. Human embryonic stem cells, as the name implies, are derived from human embryos. They are indeed the cells of the embryo itself, captured during the very early stages of embryonic development. Technically, this kind of cell is as old as humankind. But because procreation has historically occurred only inside the human body, access to embryonic cells was impossible, and information scant. With the advent of IVF, however, the human embryo began to have a presence outside the body. Scientists could see the living embryo up close; they could manipulate it and watch it develop. Because some of these scientists were engaged in the fertility trade, they also became expert at embryonic division and creation, prodding the egg and sperm to come together and then divide. In the process, they also began to produce thousands and thousands of embryos. Some of these embryos were transferred to fertility patients, where they became fetuses and later children. Others were surplus, stored in vats of liquid nitrogen for patients who would probably never use them.

In 1998, James Thomson, a researcher at the University of Wisconsin, took one of these embryos, removed its inner cell mass, and then prompted these cells to replicate themselves repeatedly in his laboratory.[51] He created, in other words, what is now known as a stem cell *line*, a group of cells that was essentially immortal. Because these cells were also undifferentiated, theoretically they could be prodded into becoming nearly any cell in the human body.

Thomson's announcement, proving that stem cells could be both harvested and maintained, shook the scientific community. Almost instantly, other researchers began rushing down the same path, trying to replicate Thomson's success and experiment with the vast permutations it made possible.[52] But no sooner had the science begun than it found itself in roiling controversies. For in creating stem cell lines, Thomson and his colleagues had also stepped into two political imbroglios. First, they had destroyed an embryo. And second, they had cloned its cells.

The first of these problems is easier to see: when scientists take the inner mass of a tiny embryo they destroy the embryo itself. Its cells live on, but the embryo does not. Accordingly, those who believe that life begins at conception necessarily viewed Thomson's process as akin to abortion. He had taken an embryo and robbed it of the possibility of independent life.

The second attack was subtler but ultimately more important. By prodding these embryonic cells to reproduce themselves, Thomson had effectively created a virtually infinite supply of identical cells—clones, in fact, created from an embryo that itself would never be born. Even though Thomson himself had no interest in reproductive cloning, and even though the scientists who succeeded him were likewise concerned almost entirely with treating disease rather than conceiving children, the line between reproductive and therapeutic cloning was lost in the debate that followed. Thomson had cloned human cells, and theoretically his techniques could be adapted and deployed for reproductive purposes.*

Commercially, the gap between embryonic stem cells and reproductive cloning is huge. If embryonic stem cells have even a fraction of the medical potential that many scientists believe, they will transform how large segments of medicine are practiced and how certain diseases are attacked.[53] Private sector firms will inevitably rush into this market as the science advances and will begin producing the drugs or treatments made possible as a result. Indeed, as described later, the early stages of this scramble are already under way.

By contrast, the market for reproductive cloning is almost certainly much smaller. Although embryonic stem cell technologies could be ap-

---

*Embryonic stem cells, however, cannot themselves give rise to an embryo, because they lack the ability to make a placenta.

plied to particular cases of infertility, the total number of these cases is likely to be small, and the impact on the baby trade essentially nonexistent. In other words, the advent of stem cell technologies will not have a major impact on either the supply of reproductive cloning services or the demand for them. Yet because public debates over therapeutic and reproductive cloning are tightly linked, the politics of stem cells will inevitably affect the market for high-tech reproduction. And the politics of cloning, in turn, may well drive the commercial development of stem cells.

The Politics of Cloning

As had been the case with Dolly's birth, Thomson's stem cell lines ignited a storm of controversy and a rash of political action. Several years earlier, in December 1994, U.S. President Clinton had issued an executive order that banned researchers from using federal funds to create human embryos. He subsequently reiterated this ban after the birth of Dolly, stating even more emphatically that no federal funds could be used for human cloning.[54] The president did not, however, expand the federal ban to cover animal cloning or cellular DNA. As a result, private firms (or privately funded researchers) could still create stem cell lines, and publicly funded researchers could still use them in their work.[55]

Essentially, therefore, the 1997 ban had endeavored to carve a comfortable black line through a field of gray. Clinton acknowledged the promise of stem cell technologies, and he did not prohibit research in the field; but he moved the federal government away from supporting such research efforts. In effect, the ban paralleled similar restraints imposed decades ago on IVF: the work could proceed, but only in private clinics and without government funds.

Critics, however, were not appeased by the ban, arguing that cloning was dangerous enough to require much stronger restraints. Between 1998, the year Thomson's stem cells were created, and 2000, eleven bills along these lines were proposed in Congress, each offering some scheme for either banning or tightly regulating human cloning.[56] None of them passed.

Then in 2001, the newly elected Bush administration revamped the Clinton-era policy. Arguing that "we should not, as a society, grow life to destroy it," President George W. Bush issued an executive order that barred federally funded scientists from working on any newly created stem cell lines.[57] Instead, they could use federal funds only to research the roughly sixty stem cell lines available on August 9, 2001 (the date of the president's order).

In theory, federally funded stem cell research could proceed under these restrictions. But in fact it was severely limited, especially when it became clear that many of the eligible sixty lines could not actually produce viable replicas. Indeed, the number of lines that could realistically be used was closer to twenty.[58] Only a handful of these lines were in the United States, moreover, most of them at the University of Wisconsin and the University of California at San Francisco.[59] By 2004, samples from these lines were selling for as much as $5,000 apiece, further squeezing the prospects for many would-be researchers.[60]

Meanwhile, the politics of stem cell research were becoming increasingly contentious. In July 2002, the President's Council on Bioethics issued "Human Cloning and Human Dignity," a bipartisan report that was supposed to resolve the ethical issues around cloning. It didn't. Instead, the report carved a complicated path around the controversy, refusing to condemn therapeutic cloning (and thus angering its opponents) while still supporting a four-year research moratorium (and thus angering its advocates).

Frustrated, advocacy groups such as the Coalition for the Advancement of Medical Research (CAMR) sprang into action, arguing that "a moratorium is equally damaging—if not more—than a ban. It stops research cold."[61] Personal activists also joined the fray, including famous conservatives like Nancy Reagan and Senator Orrin Hatch (R–UT), whose own lives had been touched by diseases that stem cell technologies potentially could treat. Around the country, several states passed their own laws bypassing the federal restrictions, whereas others passed even more restrictive legislation.[62] And in the midst of the turmoil, a handful of high-profile scientists announced their own intention to create new stem cell lines. At Harvard University, for example, Douglas Melton, codirector of the university's Stem Cell Initiative, reported in the spring of 2004 that he and his colleagues had used donated IVF embryos to produce seventeen new lines, all of which would be distributed, free, to any qualified researcher.[63]

It wasn't always easy to decipher the cloning debate, because the arguments were often subtle and advocates crossed lines in intriguing ways. For example, some of cloning's most passionate objectors came, as one might expect, from religious conservatives who defined life as beginning at conception. Some of these critics (most of them Roman Catholic) also objected to all forms of in vitro fertilization, but others (including many born-again Christians) supported IVF as a means of family building. As a result, a subset of these critics was actually less opposed to reproductive cloning than to therapeutic. As James Q. Wilson, a leading conservative scholar, wrote, "If cloning is to occur, the central problem is to ensure that it be done only for two-parent families who want a child for their own benefit. If the cloned child is born in the same way as a child resulting from marital congress, can it matter to the parents how it was conceived?"[64] By contrast, many diehard opponents of reproductive cloning supported stem cell technologies, particularly when those technologies were perceived (or presented) as holding the key to potential medical cures.

By 2004, these clashing objectives had thrust stem cell research in the United States into a strange sort of limbo. The federal government had pulled all its funds from embryonic stem cell research but continued to fund investigations into stem cells derived from adult sources. By contrast, several state governments—including, most spectacularly, California—had pledged their own public funds to stem cell research, but only a handful of private firms had ventured into the field.[65] Meanwhile, even though polls suggested that most Americans supported therapeutic cloning, they remained adamantly opposed to reproductive cloning.[66] And because the line between these two fields was blurred in the public perception, there was little political momentum in favor of cloning. The science was emerging, demand was clear, but the market was stalled in its tracks.

Supply-Side Strategies

If the United States had been the only country to develop stem cell technologies, then American political opposition might well have brought the science to a halt. Critics of cloning could have pushed promising researchers into other fields of inquiry and forced potential beneficiaries to search for other fixes. They still might. But two factors suggest that opposition in this field will ultimately bow before science. The first is demand; the second, supply.

The demand side of this equation is obvious. An estimated 4.5 million seniors in the United States suffer from Alzheimer's disease. More than 200,000 children have juvenile diabetes. Roughly 1.5 million people are afflicted with Parkinson's disease, and nearly 200,000 are crippled or paralyzed by spinal cord injuries. If stem cell technologies can help treat even a tiny fraction of these patients, then the demand for stem cell research will be monumental. Moreover, because this demand is so deep seated, it is unlikely to go away or yield over the long term to political critique.

This brings us to the other side of the equation. If demand for stem cell technologies is both strong and widespread, and if scientific knowledge is pushing ever closer toward developing products that might meet this demand, then it is simply naïve to suppose that supply will not emerge. Governments may try to prohibit or constrain this market. They can perhaps push the market underground or overseas, but they will not be able over the long run to stanch a growing flow of supply. Instead, the pressure of latent profits will tempt firms into the market and then, slowly but surely, into the political fray as well. The earliest movers are likely to be renegades—firms or entrepreneurs who enjoy operating along the edge of legality. But as these renegades succeed—if they find, for example, even one promising treatment for a major disease—then other firms, better heeled and well established, will soon follow suit. And if these firms see political obstacles blocking their way to the market, they will exert whatever pressure they can muster to remove these barriers.

Such a progression is already under way, most of it outside the borders of the United States. In China, for example, the national government has poured money into biotechnology, focusing on stem cell technologies and wooing ethnic Chinese scientists back from the West.[67] In South Korea, where scientists generated stem cells from a human clone in February 2004, the Seoul National University has already moved to patent the clone production process.[68] In Singapore, the government announced plans in 2001 for Biopolis, a $300 million cutting-edge science park focused on stem cell technologies.

Most ambitious, perhaps, is the United Kingdom, which decided in 2000 to roll stem cell research into its HFEA (Human Fertilisation and Embryology Authority), the regulatory body responsible for other areas of fertility treatment and research. In 2004, British authorities granted their first license for therapeutic cloning and oversaw the opening of a government-funded stem cell bank.[69] Israel has also signaled its intent to encourage commercial stem cell research, as has the Czech Republic.[70]

In response to these incentives, private firms have begun to cluster. In Scotland, for example (home of Dolly and subject to the HFEA's reach), the number of biotech researchers grew from twenty-five hundred in 1999 to around eight thousand in 2003.[71] China has witnessed an inflow of stem cell researchers and growing interest from venture capitalists, and Singapore has already attracted high-tech players like Australia's National Stem Cell Centre.[72]

Together, these early-stage efforts signal the start of a global stem cell industry. It is an industry, to be sure, that is still in its infancy, an industry that has not yet produced any tangible products. But it is an industry nevertheless, backed in many cases by state funding but looking clearly toward the private market. As this industry develops, it will meet and shape the demand for specific stem cell technologies. It will also continue to cluster in those countries that encourage stem cell research.

As a result, prohibitions imposed by any particular country—even a country with the influence and capital of the United States—are not likely to remain effective for very long. Instead, as the science of stem cells develops and the supply of stem cell technologies grows, a market will inevitably be born. And governments will face one of two choices: they can maintain their bans and simply acknowledge that this high-technology industry will flow to other countries. Or they can relax their restrictions and move to regulate the trade they once banned.

In the United States, history strongly suggests that this second option will prevail. Yes, opposition to stem cell technologies will persist. Yes, there will be critics who see any embryo research as akin to murder and any form of cloning as an unacceptable slide toward chaos. But similar criticisms were hurled at contraception in the 1920s and at IVF in the 1970s. Both of these technologies were painted by their opponents as fundamental affronts to nature; both were denied federal funding and constrained, to some extent, by law.[73]

Yet in both cases, the market eventually trumped morality. Over time, the would-be buyers and sellers of both contraception and IVF managed to bring their respective technologies out of the shadows, transforming them from social taboos into respectable, even desirable, products. Condoms, for example, morphed from embarrassing and illicit goods into vital tools of public health; test-tube babies, from biological monstrosities to the kid next door. As the technologies improved and demand expanded, the purveyors in both of these cases (the condom manufacturers, the IVF clinics) were increasingly able to tackle their public foes and muster popular support for their industries. A similar dynamic is likely to occur for stem cells, hastened in this case by the deep demand that already exists and the eagerness of other countries to make stem cells their own.

Of Markets and Monsters

At the turn of the twenty-first century, it is impossible to describe an overall market for cloning. There are no large-scale firms that would describe themselves as operating in the cloning trade, and no established industry. Instead, there are only linked pockets of demand and technology: the bereaved parents trying to re-create their child; the infertile couple determined to conceive; and the patients of a range of diseases that might be treated with stem cells. Substantively, all these people want very different things. But their hopes depend communally on cloning: reproducing cellular life at its most basic stage.

Because the technology of cloning is so primal—because it seems to defy our fundamental understanding of both identity and reproduction—the science behind it has become political as well. Critics, as noted earlier, have attacked cloning as a monstrous or ungodly temptation—as a "ghoulish enterprise," for example, based on "the creation of nascent human life for the sole purpose of its exploitation and destruction."[74] Such condemnation has been bolstered by legislation that prohibits or restricts certain kinds of cloning, and by widespread public suspicion.

Under these circumstances, it is hardly surprising that the demand for reproductive cloning remains small and subversive, clustered around fringe groups like the Raëlians or a handful of devoted Web sites.[75] At this stage, there are simply not very many people who want to clone themselves or their family members. Moreover, it is entirely possible that such a demand will never emerge, not even if the science is perfected or the law changed. How many people really want an extra copy of themselves? How many would voluntarily replace sexual reproduction with its solitary form?

By contrast, the mainstream baby trade provides a more probable path toward cloning. Already, the highest-tech forms of in vitro fertilization are tottering on the edge of cloning, and in cases of extreme infertility, doctors (and their patients) may well be tempted to employ cloning techniques, particularly those that simply transform a single embryo into artificial twins. IVF, after all, already produces a much higher than normal number of twins. Who could tell if another pair arrived? And who would want to stop the process once it was under way? In this fashion, cloning—albeit of embryos rather than adults—could well slip into mainstream science.

Meanwhile, commercial pressure from other areas of cloning will push in a similar direction. Pharmers, for example, will continue their work in animal breeding, while firms like BARC and PerPETuate will focus on pets. If any of these groups achieves even partial success, the impact will be threefold: laboratory techniques will migrate into the field of human cloning; capital will flow more generally into cloning firms; and the public will see positive evidence of cloning's promise.

Success with stem cell technologies would be even more dramatic, potentially raising billions of dollars in new investment and bringing more adherents to cloning's cause. Clearly, there are vast differences between stem cell technologies and reproductive cloning, between cloning sheep and kittens and cloning humans. As a society, we might well decide that cloning embryos to produce stem cells is OK but that cloning them to produce children is not. We could develop cloning technologies but keep them out of the baby business.

Without explicit legislation along these lines, however, such an outcome is improbable. That's because the techniques used for embryonic cloning are too similar to those of animal cloning for the two methods to be kept wholly separate. If scientists know how to reproduce a human embryo, and if they can do so with a fairly high level of safety and efficiency (admittedly, a big "if"), then some scientist, somewhere, will enter the baby-cloning business and make it work. Meanwhile, some cases of infertility may prove particularly amenable to techniques derived from cloning—the man, for example, who produces no sperm, or the homosexual couple who want a child who is genetically theirs. (Theoretically, stem cells from a homosexual man could be harvested and then prodded into developing into an egg cell.)[76]

If cloning can enable these parents to conceive, then some of them eventually will be tempted to try. As one infertile woman put it, "I know it's not right for everyone. But . . . if the only way for a person to have a child of their own is to do this, and if they are willing to take a chance, then they should be able to."[77] And thus if other areas of the baby business are any indication, the development of cloning technologies will lead over time to a market for these technologies, and eventually to the creation of a product that few can resist: a baby. A cloned baby that doesn't look like a monster or a freak or even, necessarily, like the clone of any other. It will just be a baby, his name plastered across the headlines and his conception supported by those eager to produce more.

Cloning will no longer be science fiction, and the creators won't be mad. Instead, they will be eminently respectable, occupying the highest-tech tier of the modern fertility trade and selling new hope to those who want a child.

CHAPTER **6**

Trading Places

The Practice and Politics of Adoption

Do not be afraid, for I am with you; I will bring your children from the east and gather you from the west.

—ISAIAH 43:4–6

THE HOME PAGE for Rainbow Kids is designed to rip your heart out. When you log on to the site—www.rainbowkids.com—you instantly see color photographs of beautiful, usually somber-looking children. There are some babies, some older kids. Most are toddlers, clasping toys or sporting huge bows in their hair. All these children are available— waiting, you quickly learn, for their "forever families."

As you scroll farther, you learn how to search: by country, gender, age. The toughest one is "date added," which shows, in reverse order, how long some children have been waiting. On a recent visit, for exam- ple, you could find six-year-old Bulat, who had been on the list for three and a half years. "He is described as quiet and gentle," the site reports, "and really enjoys playing sports." Ten-year-old Yamile "likes to write and draw . . . and dreams of being a doctor when she grows up." At pre- cious.org, another adoption photo listing, you can learn about Sofia—

159

"sweet and smart, sparkly and fun, polite and inquisitive"—or Rafael, an "A+ student" who "is dreaming to have a family." All these children, like all the Rainbow Kids, are orphans. And essentially, they are all for sale.

Officially, of course, baby-selling is illegal. The parents who visit Rainbow Kids aren't looking to *buy* their children; they're hoping to adopt them. In practice, though, adoption is indeed a market, particularly in its international dimension. There is a huge and unsatiated demand for children, the same demand that propels would-be parents to seek out fertility clinics and surrogacy brokers. There is a tragically large supply of "waiting" children and a panoply of intermediaries—adoption agencies, social workers, lawyers—that work to match the two sides.

There are prices, too, in the adoption trade, differentiated "fees" that clearly distinguish one child from another. Little Anita from Eastern Europe, for example, is a "sweet, affectionate girl" who suffers from fetal alcohol syndrome. Her adoption fees are reduced. Yi-Wei of Korea, an eleven-year-old boy found abandoned on the street, comes with a $7,500 private grant.

In purely economic terms, Anita and Yi-Wei are only tiny bits of the global baby trade, substitutes for the genetic offspring that would-be parents can't produce through other means. Although some parents choose adoption instead of (or in addition to) old-fashioned reproduction, many wander onto the Rainbow Kids site after they've exhausted all other channels of child production—after, as one mother wrote, "it felt . . . that we could not succeed at becoming parents."[1] In these cases the market for existing children functions as a nearly perfect substitute for the nonexistent ones, for the children who weren't born as a result of AI, IVF, or sex. As with the more mechanical forms of reproduction, adoption carries an often hefty price tag, ranging from virtually nothing—the cost of adopting a teenager from the U.S. foster system—to more than $35,000, the fully loaded cost for a healthy white Russian infant.

What separates adoption from other aspects of the baby trade, however, is the obvious difference in "product." In assisted reproduction, the parent is purchasing the *potential* of a child, the hope that technological intervention will lead to the live birth of a baby. The producers, meanwhile, are selling eggs and sperm, services and promises, along with the probability that their high-tech tinkering will create a child. In adoption, by contrast, the child already exists. He or she is a little person, shorn of parents but fully equipped with the rights, dreams, and memories of a human being. Accordingly, the politics and practices of adoption are even more complex than those that surround the more mechanical forms of reproduction. It's one thing (and bad enough, some would say) to sell a sperm or an egg. It's quite another to sell a child.

As a result of this distinction, normative views on adoption split sharply into two camps. On one side are those who see adoption as a purely social interaction: it is about building families and rescuing children and assuaging the pain of missing people. In this view, there is no overlap at all between adoption and commerce, and no notion of putting prices on children. As Adam Pertman, a well-known adoption advocate, puts it, "Any time we put money and human beings in the same sentence, it is a problem: We denigrate the children and we denigrate the process."[2]

From the other side, however, adoption is not only a market but indeed a market of the worst possible sort. It is a market that sells innocent children, putting a price on their heads without any concern for their well-being or for the toll imposed by being treated as trade. Moreover, opponents also charge that the very possibility of adoption, and particularly of international adoption, raises the stakes for poor, pregnant women. If these women know that they can place their children for adoption, and if they can perhaps receive some payment for their labors, they will be tempted or tricked into choosing adoption—to sell their babies for profit, in the harshest version of this critique, and expand an inherently illicit market.[3] Less dramatically, critics of international adoption also argue that it compromises the human rights of the children involved by thrusting them into a cultural context different from their own.[4]

The debates in this field are passionate, with adoptive families and adoption agencies pitted against those who condemn the process. In the United States, the proponents of adoption have tended to win: U.S. families adopt more than a hundred thousand children each year, roughly 15 percent from abroad and nearly all under the confines of a wide-ranging, state-sanctioned system.[5] Most adoptive families are screened by licensed social workers, the FBI (Federal Bureau of Investigation), and a local court. Their homes are evaluated; their finances are reviewed; their friends are enlisted to write letters of recommendation.

Indeed, adoption in the United States is regulated far more heavily than any other branch of the baby trade. In Europe, where roughly sixteen thousand children were adopted internationally in 2003, adoption is also subject to a plethora of regulatory controls.[6]

In some respects, the debate over adoption is both small and highly personal. Those who paint adoption as an intimate, admirable, noncommercial activity tend to be either adoptive parents or adoption agencies. Those who scorn it as illicit trade are neither. There is little public attention paid to the world of adoption (aside from the occasional fluff piece or horror story) and little policy overlap with other aspects of the baby business. Yet the questions that surround adoption are both fundamental and far-reaching. Because in adoption, as in surrogacy, IVF, and fertility treatments in general, there is an awkward imbalance between market forces and public perception, between what is happening on the ground and how we choose to describe it.

One look at Rainbow Kids, for example, suggests that something close to commerce is indeed taking place. The same can be said of the seminars that adoption agencies regularly hold to describe their trade, and the stories of "available children" profiled in glossy magazines. Yet such hints of trade need not imply that adoption is illicit or immoral, or that children are being treated as commodities. Instead, market forces could be exactly what makes adoption work in many cases, what allows a vast supply of children to be matched with the equally vast demand for them. And if a little more commerce were injected into this field, more of the waiting Yamiles and Bulats might leave the world of Rainbow Kids and finally head for home.

Finding Families: The Evolution of Adoption

As a method of acquiring children, adoption has a long and fairly reputable past.[7] Historically, it was the only means by which infertile couples could obtain children, the way for them to salve unmet desires and preserve social goals. Childless couples in ancient Greece, for example, often adopted heirs; in Rome, even couples with children frequently adopted, sometimes selecting more attractive children to displace their genetic offspring. In both of these cases, the underlying motivation was largely economic: parents needed the right kind of descendant to protect their fortunes and preserve their family name. And if they could not produce these descendants on their own, they simply acquired them elsewhere.

During the Middle Ages, this economic relationship assumed a slightly different hue. Because European authorities gave greater sway to bloodlines than the Romans had, families moved away from a formal process of adoption, choosing instead to "take in" children from unrelated families. These children—poor, illegitimate, or simply more numerous than their parents could handle—were frequently installed, or "put out," with wealthier folk as apprentices or servants. Although some of these wards were treated as children, most assumed a considerably lowlier station, toiling in the stables, workshops, or kitchens of their newfound families. They typically remained in these positions until they reached the age of eighteen or twenty-one, when common law returned them to independence.[8] In some parts of Europe, the putting-out system was vibrant enough to encompass most of society's "surplus" children. Putting out didn't work, however, for some of the toughest cases: the infant children of unwed mothers, the bastards of illicit love, or the orphans of famine or war. Many of these children were quietly killed or abandoned.

Across the Atlantic, meanwhile, economic necessity meant that orphans and other "excess" children were regularly assigned either to their extended families or to unrelated families that could use their labor. As early as 1627, for example, fourteen hundred poor or orphaned children were apprenticed directly to the Virginia Company; in 1740, one wealthy Georgia planter took in sixty-one orphans to join his "family" and work his fields.[9] On a smaller scale, individual families simply assumed the care of their orphaned relatives, sometimes using them as economic assets, sometimes treating them as sons or daughters of their own.[10]

This situation—a haphazard combination of economic necessity and informal family ties—prevailed until the middle decades of the nineteenth century, when adoption slowly became more of an arm's-length transaction. The early signs of this transition were subtle. First, adoption cases began cropping up in state courts, usually involving issues of contested inheritance. In 1858, for example, the nieces and nephews of a recently deceased Louisiana man sued to inherit his property, arguing that his adopted daughter had no legal rights to his estate. The state court disagreed, however, and turned to *Webster's Dictionary* to define adoption as "tak[ing] one who is not a child and treat[ing] him as one, giving him a title to the privileges and rights of a child."[11] Accordingly, the court ruled in favor of the adopted daughter and turned her cousins away. Similar language was used in Pennsylvania statutes at around this same time, clarifying the status of an adopted child as a full and lawful heir.[12]

Second, as adoption became an issue of legal concern, state governments began quietly to envelop it in more explicit legislation. Massachusetts passed the first comprehensive adoption statute in 1851, followed in rapid succession by twenty-four other states. Although there was some variation among the adoption acts, they all shared a common and unprecedented characteristic: they made adoption a legal act and subjected the adoption process to the scrutiny of the state. In Massachusetts, for example, the state retained the right to determine whether the proposed parents were "of sufficient ability to bring up the child."[13] In Washington, D.C., congressional statute laid out the means by which adopted children gained the right of inheritance and gave local judges the authority to transfer custody.[14]

As a result of these laws, adoption in the United States became increasingly accepted. Families took orphaned children into their homes and raised them as their own. Children assumed new sets of parents, and the state put contractual relationships—a couple's commitment to raise a particular child—alongside genetic ones. Yet in most cases, adoption was still occurring within the boundaries of the extended family: parents were adopting children they already knew and orphans with whom they already felt a familial link.

At the same time, though, social changes rippling across the United States were creating a new class of orphans: children who frequently had no family to support them. These were children born to the immigrants flooding into growing cities like Boston, New York, and Chicago. They were children born into urban poverty, children born out of wedlock or to married parents who succumbed to disease or accident or simply the stress of having too many mouths to feed. In earlier eras, these children had been put out by local authorities or collected into public almshouses. By mid-century, however, the increased concentration of poor urban children had overwhelmed the public houses: most of their charges received minimal care, and many died alone.[15] As word of their plight spread, these public orphans became an obvious focus for mid-century social reformers, a heart-rending example of the ills wrought by immigration, industrialization, and the era's roller-coaster economy.[16]

Early Experiments

Against this dismal backdrop, one might have expected the reformers to embrace adoption as a nearly perfect solution. Thousands of infertile couples, after all, were aching for children and thousands of children were living without homes. Yet the early reformers did not see this match as feasible, because the available children, they felt, were not the "type" who could ever flourish in typical middle-class homes. And so instead of finding homes, they began to construct private children's agencies, philanthropic institutions that would care for orphaned or abandoned children and offer them what the state did not. All the groups that formed these institutions were passionately devoted to the cause of orphaned children. Few, though, saw formal adoption as a viable option.[17]

The most famous of these early advocates was the Children's Aid Society of New York, founded in 1853 by a Protestant minister named Charles Loring Brace. Like others in the reform movement, Brace was appalled by the squalor and poverty he saw expanding from the nation's urban core. He was particularly aghast at New York City's ranks of homeless children—a "society," he wrote, of "irreclaimable little vagabonds"—and firmly convinced that these children could be saved only by removing them from the streets and sending them instead to "God's Reformatory."[18]

To aid in this transformation, Brace established an unprecedented program of orphan trains. For more than fifty years, he and his associates physically took children (orphaned, abandoned, or simply poor) from New York's roughest neighborhoods and loaded them onto trains bound for the Midwest.[19] Upon arrival, the children were doled out to "healthy" Protestant farm families, destined to spend the rest of their childhoods in a status that hovered between adoption and bound servitude.[20]

Brace's trains made very big news. His Children's Aid Society placed an estimated one hundred thousand children and pioneered the practice of long-distance placement.[21] Brace publicized the dire status of many American orphans and turned reform into a large-scale, well-funded activity. To a large extent, Brace's trains proved that children born to "undesirable" parents could grow and even prosper in newfound homes. He proved, in other words, that adoption by strangers could work. And yet his trains also had an unseemly side, one that would haunt American adoption for years to come. Brace, after all, had done little to check the matches that occurred when his charges disembarked. He never embraced the formal side of adoption, or its potential to make families in any way that wasn't purely functional.[22] Critics have also charged that some of Brace's "orphans" weren't orphans at all, but simply poor children, mostly Roman Catholic, who were taken from their homes without consideration of the parents left behind.[23]

Meanwhile, other agencies were clambering after Brace, trying either to emulate his success or to build a better model. Roman Catholic agencies, for example, tried to provide a religious alternative to Brace's devout Protestantism, and Jewish agencies looked after the growing floods of Jewish immigrants. There were agencies devoted to newsboys and "street arabs" and to the steady stream of infants born to unwed mothers.[24] Most of these agencies, however, conformed to the reformers' underlying suspicions about their charges, and thus to the two core solutions that they offered. Either they provided in-house care for the youngest of children, or, like Brace, they strove to rescue older children by putting them out or assigning them to homes in the Midwest.

Few of these children were ever adopted. In fact, during this period most agencies remained opposed to formal adoption, seeing it as an unnatural intrusion into a family built on blood. Adopting one's relatives, they maintained, was perfectly acceptable. So was taking in an extra farmhand or providing temporary foster care to an orphaned toddler. But unrelated children were dangerous baggage, rightful objects of pity, perhaps, but not the stuff of which families were made.[25]

Over time, however, a handful of well-placed intermediaries began to consider more direct options. In large urban centers like New York and Boston, for example, a small circle of upper-class women took it upon themselves to "save" the babies born to unwed mothers.[26] Quietly, they took these children and delivered them to friends or acquaintances looking for a child. These newborns would subsequently be adopted under state law, joining families as if, in common parlance, "they were their own."

Other brokers soon joined the trade as well: hospital nurses, private maternity homes, local court officials. These brokers operated out of commercial interest and beyond the reach of the law.[27] In 1907, a popular women's magazine took this trade one step further, launching a "child rescue campaign" that featured profiles of dependent children and offered them to interested readers. After its very first installment, the magazine received three hundred requests for the two children profiled; it subsequently found homes for nearly two thousand others—"rescued" as one adoptive mother opined, "from miserable lives and disgrace."[28]

The larger agencies, of course, disdained such matches. They fretted about the dangers of hasty or sentimental placements and warned that children born to poor or unmarried women were likely to be scarred for life. As the director of Boston's Bureau of Illegitimacy noted in 1920, "The children of unmarried parents, who doubtless make up a large number of adoptions, may turn out to show an undue proportion of abnormal mentality."[29] The best hope for such children, most agencies insisted, was to educate them outside the family environment and prepare them for a life of labor. But despite the agencies' pleas to this effect, and despite a growing chorus of experts who insisted that heredity did indeed shape destiny, childless couples besieged the few agencies willing to place infants. By 1919 a judge from the Boston probate court publicly announced that "the woods are full of people eager to adopt children— the number appearing to be in the increase."[30]

At this point, therefore, the major child welfare agencies found themselves in a quandary. On the one hand, the agencies truly believed that many of their charges were unsuitable for adoption. They believed that these children needed institutional care and the kind of treatment only professionals were suited to provide. The market, on the other hand, was revealing something very different. Comfortable families wanted these "unadoptable" children so much that they were running to less professional agencies or to shady intermediaries with no standing in the world of child reform. By standing on the sidelines, therefore, the professional agencies were losing ground.

In retrospect, it's difficult to tell whether the agencies' eventual change in attitude was due to shifting mores, better science, or fear of competition from unsavory upstarts. In any case, between roughly 1920 and 1935, most of the country's largest child service organizations began to offer and eventually promote adoption.[31] Although many of the most prominent reformers continued to insist that "bad heredity" put an adopted child at risk, they now reversed this logic, arguing that because adoption was such a risky business, it was best handled by competent professionals—namely, by the social workers who ran and managed the country's child welfare agencies. Accordingly, as these professionals moved into the adoption business, they endorsed, and then helped to enforce, an ostensibly sharp distinction between "licensed" agencies and "independent" providers, between those that were recognized by the state and those that operated apart from its control.

The Evolution of Adoption

Over the next several decades, adoption in the United States became both more regulated and more regular.[32] The U.S. Children's Bureau began to collect and publish statistics regarding adoption practices in the United States, and many states passed adoption statutes of their own, typically focusing on the procedures involved in matching available children with suitable homes. State governments also began to regulate adoption more formally, issuing licenses to approved child-placing agencies and instituting procedures for examining both agencies and parents.[33]

Under Minnesota's 1917 law, for example, prospective parents had to undergo a "social investigation" before being granted custody of a minor child. In Delaware, the law also provided for a two-year probationary period before an adoption could be finalized, and allowed for social workers or other experts to make recommendations to the finalizing court.[34] Note that in both instances—and indeed in nearly all adoption legislation passed during this period—social workers and state-licensed agencies were knit integrally into the adoption process, serving as ostensible guardians for both the child and the state.[35] By contrast, independent practitioners were excluded, relegated to a shadowy area that was generally regarded as baby-selling rather than adoption.

Yet the market, it appears, did not care. Instead, by the 1930s, the soaring demand for babies had bestowed a newfound prominence on independent adoption agencies. Unlike their state-linked peers, these agencies now openly recruited birth mothers, advertised their services to prospective parents, and charged handsomely for their work. They also guaranteed birth mothers that their identities would remain secret, and they often took—and placed—babies who were only weeks old. This relaxed attitude stood in sharp contrast with the rules of most licensed agencies.[36] But it made the private "homes" exceedingly attractive to birth mothers, many of whom wanted to relinquish their infants as quickly and as quietly as they could, and to prospective parents, who wanted children "as young as possible" and generally preferred *not* to know the mother's identity.[37] By offering something to both sides of the equation, therefore, independent providers could charge for their services and turn adoption into a profitable venture. At the upper end, the going price for a privately placed baby—a little girl, ideally, with blonde hair and blue eyes—was an estimated $1,000 in the 1930s, rising to $5,000 by the 1940s.[38]

Repeatedly, the licensed adoption agencies railed against this trade, arguing that "baby farms" and baby-selling rings harmed the children they served and exploited the parents involved. This they almost certainly did. At one Montreal home, for example, the proprietor regularly took in pregnant women, kept them in squalor, and then transferred their babies—filthy and unfed—to wealthy Americans who were willing to pay.[39] In New York, an attorney named Marcus Siegel placed more than ninety infants for adoption, paying the birth mothers in each case between $1,500 and $2,500 to relinquish their children.[40] Even public reports of such scandals, however, did little to stanch the demand. Instead, as one contemporary article exclaimed, "The baby market is booming . . . We behold an amazing phenomenon: a country-wide scramble on the part of childless couples to adopt a child."[41] Estimates compiled by the Children's Bureau suggested that roughly half of American adoptions in the 1940s occurred outside the purview of licensed adoption agencies.[42]

So again the agencies were caught. They didn't want to replicate such explicitly commercial practices, because their stated purpose was to serve the child. At the same time, though, they realized that their model was under attack. As a 1937 report by the Children's Welfare League of America woefully put it, "The fact that such a large amount of adoption work is going on beyond the reach of the organized social agencies seems to indicate that in some way we have failed to meet the community's need—why has the stream passed us by?"[43]

It took some time for the agencies to respond to this query, but within a decade they had worked through a compromise of sorts, responding to the market without actually joining it.

Publicly, the agencies and their political allies maintained a drumbeat of criticism against the abuses of independent adoption.[44] There were stories in the mainstream media, angry denunciations when scandals broke, and even an eventual congressional investigation. Quietly, however, the agencies also began to change the way they did business. First, they essentially reversed their deep-seated distrust of heredity. Rather than suspect abandoned or illegitimate children of bearing inherently "bad genes," and rather than subject even the tiniest of children to batteries of emotional and intelligence tests, adoption agencies started assuming, for the most part, that their charges were perfectly normal. To some extent, this change in attitude was part of a larger intellectual shift, a movement away from the rigid view of genetic determinism (or "nature") in favor of environment (or "nurture").[45] But it was also deeply strategic. Because if most children were destined to fare well in their adoptive homes, then agencies no longer had to worry about finding the perfect child for a given couple; they didn't need to place "average" or "inferior" babies only in "average" or "inferior" homes. In other words, by changing their own theories of adoption, agencies were able to expand the pool of potential matches.[46]

A second change focused on the agencies' relationship with young and unmarried mothers. In earlier decades, most licensed agencies had disdained unwed mothers as criminal, feebleminded, or simply bad. Insofar as they concerned themselves with the mothers' welfare, it was typically to urge these young women to keep the children they bore, either because motherhood would redeem the fallen woman or because the bond between mother and child was considered too precious to sunder.

In the aftermath of World War II, however, out-of-wedlock births soared from 88,000 in 1938 to 201,000 by 1958.[47] Illegitimacy no longer carried quite the stigma it once had, and the development of infant formula meant that women could relinquish even tiny babies without necessarily fearing for their health.[48] As a result, mainstream agencies began to deal more directly with pregnant women, in many instances offering them care and counseling as well as a safe place in which to relinquish their child. Arguably, this change in attitude offered unwed mothers a more compassionate alternative.* It also, though, allowed the agencies to expand their rosters of available children, competing head-on with the baby farms that had long sold their services to "women in need."

Finally, during the postwar period the adoption community began to redefine its notion of the adoptable child. No longer obsessed with genetics, agencies became considerably more open-minded about placing children across religious or cultural lines. They started to place older and handicapped children, and then—slowly and controversially—to encourage adoption across racial lines.[49] As with the agencies' embrace of "bad" genes and unwed mothers, the move to interracial adoption reflected in large part the changing mores of the postwar period: scientists were debunking eugenic theories, middle-class teens were having sex, and racial divisions were finally starting to soften. But they also allowed the licensed adoption agencies to address the threat of independent adoption. For by expanding their definition of adoptable children, by sheltering unwed mothers, and by placing babies across a broader racial spectrum, the agencies were also engaging in a sensible market realignment, expanding the supply of children to meet the soaring demand.[50] Between 1938 and 1965, the number of adoptions in the United States skyrocketed, from 16,000 a year to 142,000.[51]

Supply-Side Shocks and the Global Search

In retrospect, this period soon proved to be the heyday of domestic adoption in the United States. The postwar years brought a new prosperity to the country and a renewed focus on domestic life. As soldiers returned from war and women left the factories they had staffed during the wartime years, Americans embraced a domestic ideal that nearly always included a working husband, a stay-at-home wife, and a couple of kids running

---

*To woo these mothers, increasing numbers of whom came from "good" families, the agencies also began to promise that their identities would be kept secret. It was this move that led, by the 1950s, to the "closing" of most adoption records.

through the suburban yard. Because children were an inherent part of this ideal, childless couples turned to infertility treatments with unprecedented fervor. And when these treatments proved futile or too expensive, they moved rapidly on to adoption.[52] Meanwhile, extramarital relations were also on the rise during this period, leading to more unplanned births and more young women willing to place their children for adoption. For the first time, supply and demand reached a fragile balance, and most infertile couples were eventually able to find children of their own.[53]

In 1955, the U.S. Congress launched its first investigation into the illicit baby trade, eventually finding evidence of an interstate market generating as much as $15 million a year. Aghast, Senator Estes Kefauver (D–TN), who led the investigation, wrote legislation that would make it illegal for any commercial entity to place children across state lines.[54] Only licensed agencies were exempt. But the bill never passed the House of Representatives, in part because several influential representatives knew that their constituents preferred independent adoption.[55]

As a result, U.S. adoption law remained deliberately vague. There were no federal statutes regarding adoption, and no legal distinctions between legitimate and illegitimate practice. Instead, adoption remained almost entirely under the jurisdiction of individual states, most of which maintained a relatively laissez-faire attitude. Adoption was legal in all fifty states; adoptions were finalized before local courts; and prospective parents were generally required to undergo the social investigations imposed in the 1920s. Only a handful of states, however, drew a distinction between licensed adoption agencies and independent practitioners.[56] Elsewhere, a range of intermediaries—lawyers, doctors, brokers—were free to arrange adoptive matches. Baby-selling was explicitly illegal in most states, but few of them bothered to define the limits of associated fees, consulting services, or reimbursement for a mother's pregnancy.[57]

Between roughly 1946 and 1970, therefore, the adoption market in the United States worked relatively well. More than two million children were adopted during this time, through a combination of licensed agencies and independent providers.[58] Although adoption records were increasingly shrouded in secrecy, adoption itself was a fairly public phenomenon, widely accepted as the ideal way of matching children with homes.

Abortion, the Pill, and Adoption

Very quickly, however, this situation dissolved. In 1960, the birth control pill became widely available. Then in 1973, the landmark case of *Roe v. Wade* legalized abortion across the United States. The impact of these events was complicated and sweeping: the liberation of women, the freeing of traditional mores, the separation between procreation and its recreational forms.

But for adoption, the combination of contraception and abortion was disastrous. First, the mechanics of contraception, along with the sexual freedom they entailed, appear to have contributed to a higher incidence of infertility. Women were waiting longer to bear children, and they were increasing their number of sexual partners, a practice that could lead over time to pelvic inflammatory disease and resulting difficulties with conception. More directly, the availability of safe and legal abortion meant a sharp decline in the number of unplanned births, and thus in the number of infants relinquished for adoption.

Between 1970 and 1975, the number of unrelated adoptions in the United States fell precipitously, from more than 89,000 a year to only 50,000.[59] Young women were having abortions in record numbers and relying increasingly on birth control.[60] Women who did choose to give birth were also deciding more frequently to keep their babies, in part because the ease of abortion meant that proceeding with an unwanted pregnancy had become a conscious, public choice. As one manual explained, "If the girl has decided to have the baby rather than having an abortion, there is a sense that she is obligated to care for the child."[61] Before 1973, 20 percent of white unwed mothers relinquished their infants for adoption; by 1982, only 12 percent of these women made the same choice.[62]

For the first time in the postwar period, the supply of available children—particularly healthy white infants—was no longer even close to satisfying the persistent demand. And parents, emboldened now by a generation of relatively easy adoption, were incensed. By 1975, many licensed agencies had stopped accepting applications for healthy white babies, and others informed applicants that the likely waiting time for such a child was three to five years.[63]

As the adoptive market evaporated, frustrated parents began to search for new sources of supply. Some white families pushed to adopt black or biracial children, reigniting a vicious debate about the merits of adoption across racial lines.[64] Some fought for changes in the foster care system, arguing that it kept too many adoptable children in a state of nearly permanent limbo. Most, though, began to look toward the developing world, where the supply of excess children stood sadly undiminished.

Adoptions from Abroad

By this point, a small number of overseas adoptions were already taking place. In the immediate aftermath of World War II, for example, Americans had adopted some of the orphans created by war: some German children, some Greek children, and about fifteen hundred orphaned survivors of Hiroshima and Nagasaki. After these countries stabilized, prospective adopters turned to Korea, where the ravages of civil war had created thousands of orphaned and homeless children.

Between 1953 and 1962, Americans adopted an estimated fifteen thousand children from abroad, creating, for the first time, a considerable population of foreign-born adoptees.[65] They also pushed for subtle changes in the legal structure of adoption, changes that permitted these foreign-born children to enter the United States and eventually become citizens.[66] By 1984, Americans were adopting roughly ninety-five hundred foreign children a year.[67]

The next great wave of international adoptions began in the early 1990s, when the fall of communism opened a vast new supply of available children. In Romania, for example, nearly one hundred thousand babies and toddlers were languishing in horrific orphanages. In China, thousands of infant girls were abandoned each year, left by mothers struggling to comply with their nation's one-child policy.[68] And in Russia, thousands of children were living in state-run baby hospitals or aging children's homes. To their local governments, these children were a political embarrassment, evidence of what communism had not been able to provide. To Western parents, though, they were an odd source of hope—and a new supply of potential adoptees.

The first country to open fully was Romania. In December 1989, the country's brutal dictator, Nicolae Ceauçescu, was executed along with his wife. As camera crews streamed in to film the aftermath, they broadcast haunting pictures of tiny children tied to beds or neglected by their ostensible caregivers.[69] Shocked by these images, international aid agencies rushed into Romania in 1990, followed in short order by parents eager to whisk these children away. Initially, many of these parents were connected to the aid agencies or church groups that had come to volunteer in the country. They hadn't necessarily considered adoption before and were simply responding to the tragedy they saw around them.

As word of their adoptions spread, however, the broader adoption community saw the attractions of Romania: thousands of children in need of homes, fees of only around $2,000, and a legal system that was essentially collapsing. By 1991, a legion of facilitators, brokers, and adoption agencies had descended upon Romania, placing 2,594 children with American families and pushing the cost of a Romanian adoption in some cases to more than $11,000.[70]

At around this time, China and Russia also began to open their orphanages to potential foreign parents. In 1991, China modified laws that had previously forbidden foreigners from adopting; in 1992, Russia established a separate division in its Ministry of Education for foreign adoption and created a database of all potentially adoptable children. With these systems in place, adoption agencies streamed into both countries and children started flowing out. By 1996, Americans alone were adopting more than 2,400 Russian and 3,300 Chinese children each year.[71]

Meanwhile, the agencies that served this global marketplace had also begun to multiply, morphing from the handful of charitable groups that once dominated the field to include a much wider and more diverse set of agencies. By 1999, about eighty U.S. agencies devoted themselves to Russian adoptions, and one hundred fifty had programs in China.[72] Others worked in Vietnam, Guatemala, or Peru; many offered a range of countries from which prospective parents could choose.

All these agencies existed under the hybrid regulatory structure that had grown around international adoption, a structure that essentially vetted parents at both ends of an international transaction. All of them also worked with counterparts in their home countries who handled local regulations and identified available children. Together, these two tiers had come to constitute a vast and growing business in international adoption: in 2003, more than 42,000 children were adopted internationally, 21,616 in the United States alone.[73]

Structure of a Trade

In purely economic terms, adoption is the most rational aspect of the baby trade. There is a vast unmet demand for children and a ready supply of them scattered across the world. By matching demand with supply, adoption would appear to be the ideal solution to infertility, a match of immeasurable value on both sides of the transaction.

Yet the problems with this market are clear. The "buyers" don't *really* want to purchase their babies. The "suppliers" don't want to sell. And governments around the world consistently condemn baby-selling as a crime akin to slavery. But still there are surplus children in the world, and would-be parents who want to adopt them. And so adoption has generated an ersatz market of sorts, a system of structured trades in which the supply of children is channeled to the waiting demand. In this trading system, regulation replaces commerce and prices morph into fees, facilitations, and charity.

Money changes hands in this market-without-a-name, but the money is rarely buying children per se and the system is subject to a labyrinth of formal controls—far more, in fact, than exist in nearly any other sector of the baby business. The system is global and marked by significant national variation, and it sports both a (large) legal sector and a (small) illegal sector. In the United States alone, the adoption system places more than 120,000 children a year, for a cost that typically ranges between zero and $35,000.[74]

These children fall generally into one of three categories: they are older or have special needs, they are healthy newborns, or they are foreign.[75] Although some agencies deal with all three types of adoption, most are increasingly focused on a particular niche.

Domestic Trade

The first of these niches, for older or special-needs kids, resembles most closely the original model of U.S. adoption. The children here are almost entirely the product of the U.S. foster care system; they have been abandoned by their parents or taken from them by law. Sadly, this is the one area of adoption that does not suffer from a lack of supply: on the contrary, there were 534,000 children in the U.S. foster care system as of 2002, roughly 126,000 of whom were formally eligible for adoption.[76] Because these children are legally wards of the state, only state agencies can handle their adoptive placements. And the process typically is exasperating: parental rights must be legally terminated, extended relatives contacted, and, frequently, racial considerations weighed. In the meantime, the children get older and their needs often increase.[77]

Financially, the market for foster adoption is quite different from that for either newborns or foreign children. First, because the children are wards of the state and are placed by the state, adoptive parents pay nothing. Instead, the state pays foster parents a minimal fee to care for these children until they are adopted or reunited with their birth families. In some cases, the foster parents subsequently decide to adopt their charges, getting, in effect, a free adoption. In economic terms, then, foster adoption is both a purely nonprofit venture for the agencies involved and a relative bargain for adoptive parents.

The second distinction, though, is a much harsher one, a distinction that points unambiguously to the variable price of children. Because the children who come out of foster care are simply not deemed as desirable as others: they are older, often scarred by difficult pasts, and frequently children of color. In 2002, 73 percent of the children in U.S. foster care were over the age of five, and 37 percent were African American.[78] Historically, the demand for these children has been stunted, squeezed initially by social workers who refused to place black children with white parents, and then by parents wary of adopting kids whom most would describe as having special needs.[79]

Between the mid-1980s and the mid-1990s, the number of children adopted each year from the U.S. foster system stayed stubbornly in the range of 17,000 to 21,000, accounting for only about 10 percent of the number available in any given year.[80] In 1997, however, Congress passed the Adoption and Safe Families Act, a legislative package designed to move children more quickly from foster care to adoption.[81] As the act's provisions worked their way through the foster system, adoption rates began to rise: roughly 46,000 children were placed in adoptive homes in

2000, 47,000 in 2001, and 53,000 in 2002. These numbers suggest that the demand for foster kids is substantially higher than placement figures once indicated and that the market in this area could well increase over time. For now, however, the placement of older and special-needs kids remains quiet and noncommercial, the province of public agencies that tend only to wards of the state.

The market for newborns, by contrast, is more vigorous and commercial. Currently, an estimated twenty thousand to forty thousand U.S.-born infants are placed each year for adoption; the figures vary widely because there is no central reporting mechanism.[82] Nearly all these adoptions are handled privately, with an estimated two-thirds managed by independent (that is, unlicensed) intermediaries.[83] In a typical domestic adoption, the prospective parents pay an up-front adoption fee (usually between $100 and $500) to the agency of their choice. They then pay between $700 and $3,000 to cover the cost of a home study, the social investigation that determines whether the would-be parents are suitable adopters. If a child is found, the parents then pay a placement fee that varies widely—from $6,500, as indicated in table 6-1, to more than $50,000. They also generally cover the birth mother's medical expenses and her costs of living during the pregnancy.[84]

What complicates the financial picture of infant adoption is the basic calculus of supply: the understandable fear that the dearth of (healthy white) babies means that a given couple will wait months, or even years, before finding their child. For some people—particularly singles, older couples, or homosexuals—the wait could well prove infinite, because many agencies impose criteria that explicitly work against them. As a result, prospective adopters are increasingly trying to beat the odds, usually through procedures with a decidedly commercial cast.

Some parents, for example, place ads directly in newspapers or college magazines, offering upbeat descriptions of their desire to adopt. "Devoted happily married couple wishes very much to adopt white newborn," states one typical ad. "We will give your baby a warm, loving home with strong family values and financial security." Others troll online, visiting sites such as www.adoptionnetwork.com or www.parentprofiles.com, where they join lists of waiting families and broadcast their credentials to potential birth mothers. "We have visions of a life that includes late nights read-

TABLE 6-1

Typical domestic adoption placement fees, 2004

Agency	Adoption fee
Children's Home and Aid Society of Illinois www.chasi.org	15% of income (minimum of $10,000 and maximum of $25,000)
Beacon House Adoption Service (Florida) www.beaconhouseadoption.com	$10,000 placement fee, $2,500 advertising fee
Adoptions from the Heart (New Jersey) www.adoptionsfromtheheart.org	$18,000
Christian Child Placement Services (New Mexico) www.nmcch.org	$12,000
Jewish Family Service, Inc. (Tennessee) www.jewishfamilyservicememphis.org	$15,000
American Adoptions (Kansas) www.americanadoptions.com	$12,000–$19,000 (African American or biracial) $20,000–$25,000 (traditional, Caucasian) $27,000–$35,000 (traditional, expedited)
Family Service Agency (Arizona) www.fsaphoenix.org	20% of gross income; minimum $6,500
Adoption Services (Pennsylvania) www.adoptionservices.org	$40,000–$52,000

Source: Agency Web sites.

ing books," writes one earnest couple, "eating ice cream on hot summer days, finger painting at the kitchen table and snowball fights."

Many couples also work with adoption attorneys or independent brokers, who endeavor to link them directly with birth parents.[85] In a typical case, the couple provides the broker with a file of materials about themselves and their desired child. The broker then presents these materials to a birth mother, allowing her to choose from several prospective families. In the interim, the broker frequently coaches families through the art of presentation, advising them, for example, about what color of paper to use or what kinds of photos to select.[86] Most brokers charge separately for these services, applying an hourly rate of $200 to $350.[87]

Open Adoption

Recently, some brokers and independent adoption agencies have also begun to offer a more radical version of adoption, one that arguably takes the matching of unrelated families to its logical extreme. In "open adoption," the birth mother (and occasionally the birth father) chooses the child's parents in person. Birth parents submit their personal information to a broker who specializes in open services; they review the binders and photographs of potential parents that the broker provides for them; and then they typically meet with the couples they've selected, ensuring that the fit is right. In this process, the historical veil of secrecy is almost completely removed: the adoptive parents know the birth parents, the birth parents actually choose the adoptive parents, and the child is fully informed about the details of his or her origins.

This level of transparency, according to the proponents of open adoption, ensures that the old stigmas of adoption are forever discarded. In theory, the child never has to search for his or her identity, and the birth mother is spared the lifelong burden of wondering what became of her child.[88]

All this may well be true. At a commercial level, however, open adoption also rearranges the fundamental patterns of business. In standard adoption, the adoptive parents are always the "buyers." They are the ones who historically have searched for available children, the ones who pay intermediaries to find and acquire a child. In open adoption, the adoptive parents still pay for the process, but only after the birth parents have found and selected them. It is the birth parents, then, who engage in the initial round of "buying," assuming most of the functions that once belonged solely to the agencies themselves.

In open adoption, in other words, it is the birth parents who select from the dozens of couples clamoring for their child. As a result, the agencies are thrust into a very different role: mediating transactions rather than making them. Not surprisingly, then, the largest players in open adoption are not traditional agencies, but rather a growing hodgepodge of lawyers and well-connected brokers, people who have begun to specialize in the niche of matching, not babies and parents, but birth parents and their adoptive successors.

As of 2004, the typical cost of an infant adoption in the United States ranged between $10,000 and $40,000.[89] In a handful of cases, prices as high as $100,000 were reported.[90]

International Trade

The third major segment of the adoption industry consists of cross-border transactions, the placement of children from one country into families in another. Once a tiny sliver of the baby business, international adoption has rapidly become a major enterprise, accounting for roughly 15 percent of total nonrelative adoptions in the United States.[91]

Three aspects of international adoption differentiate it from its domestic counterpart. First, because the children are moved across international borders, the legal regime is proportionately more complex. International adoptions effectively happen twice: once in the country of the child's origin, and again in his or her new home.

Second, internationally adopted children are by definition more diverse than their counterparts in any single country. They come in many colors, from many cultures, speaking a range of languages. Accordingly, they raise a host of social issues that rarely occur with domestic adoption and create a more differentiated market.

Finally, because these children almost always come from poorer countries, their adoption raises a heightened concern about exploitation and human trade. Some see the flow of foreign-born children as a combination of humanitarianism and family-building. But for others, it is simply trafficking in lives.

Legally, the regime for cross-border adoption is vast and sophisticated. It encompasses the major child-importing and -exporting nations and is embedded in a formal international treaty known as the Hague Convention.[92] Under the convention's terms, both sending and receiving countries are required to establish a central authority governing adoption, an authority that provides protection for the children involved, tracks and reviews prospective parents, and ensures that no baby-selling occurs.[93]

In commercial terms, compliance with the Hague makes international adoption a fairly cumbersome procedure. Would-be parents need to undergo a home study (as they would with domestic adoption), an immigration clearance and FBI background check, and whatever requirements are imposed by authorities in the child's home country. They typically must provide police reports and medical records and then have all the documents notarized and translated. The paperwork is mammoth, as are the opportunities for error.

As a result, the incentives for independent adoption are considerably reduced. Most would-be parents in the United States rely on licensed agencies to handle overseas adoptions, and agencies have considerable leeway in pricing their foreign packages. Typically, they charge an application fee, a home study fee, and a program fee. Overseas charges are figured separately and generally include a set "donation" to the child's orphanage or baby home in addition to fees to the agency's local facilitator, driver, and interpreters. In exchange for these fees, most agencies can provide prospective parents with a child of their choice, usually within a year.

In international adoption, however, the notion of choice is complicated by the variety available. In domestic adoption, after all, supply essentially controls demand: there are so few (healthy white) babies that parents almost never choose among them. In assisted reproduction, choice is a factor of the components available: the egg, sperm, womb, and embryo that will mix together in an unpredictable way. Parents can choose the basic physical characteristics their child is likely to inherit, but they cannot pick a particular kid. With international adoption, however, choice is simultaneously multiplied and made concrete. When parents adopt abroad, they are almost always choosing to adopt a child who is already born.* They are adopting a particular child, in other words, and one who usually is old enough to have displayed both physical characteristics and a certain personality type. In international adoption, therefore, much more so than in domestic infant adoption or assisted reproduction, parents are literally choosing their child.

This process of selection is deeply embedded in the structure of international adoption. To begin with, parents choose the country from which they would like to adopt. For U.S. adopters, this means choosing from thirty-nine possible nations, ranging, as of 2005, from Belarus to Vietnam. All these countries have available children, but the options they offer are different. In China, for example, nearly all the available children are girls, typically between the ages of ten months and seventeen months. In Russia, there are boys and girls, with some infants and a huge supply

---

*There are some exceptions. In Guatemala, for example, parents occasionally identify a pregnant woman and agree to adopt her child.

of older, institutionalized children. In Guatemala, most of the children are very young, subtly classified as either "Latino" or "Mayan."

When parents choose a country, then, they are also choosing a particular type of child. In many cases, they are also choosing a particular price structure, one that implicitly reveals preferences as well. For example, white children are almost always more expensive than black ones; as table 6-2 indicates, the typical cost of adopting a (white) Russian child in 2004 (in addition to travel costs and agency fees) was about $15,000, whereas the cost of a (black) child from Ethiopia was between $6,700 and $8,000. Children of other colors fall somewhere in the middle, ranging from about $6,000 for a Filipino child to about $7,000 for a Chinese and $8,900 for a Colombian.[94] Guatemala stands as a bit of a pricey exception, because children in this heavily Roman Catholic country are frequently placed directly after birth and birth mothers are commonly assumed to be "good girls" forced by cultural constraints to relinquish any child born out of wedlock. Costs also vary sharply by age and degree of handicap. In Russia, for example, the cost of adopting an infant through one prominent agency is $7,000 more than the cost of adopting a school-age child. Handicapped children are frequently offered with some kind of "scholarship" or financial assistance.

At the level of the individual child, meanwhile, international adoption also offers a sometimes shocking array of choices. When parents begin the adoptive process, they usually inform their selected agency of their preferences: whether they want an infant or a younger child, a girl or a boy. They describe the kind of child they feel competent to parent and the kind of family they are hoping to build. Sometimes, the selection ends there. The agency works with its counterpart in the chosen country, identifies a child, and presents him to the prospective parents, usually in the form of a photograph or short video. The parents can choose to accept the child (most do) or wait for a second referral. In other cases, however, parents play a much more active role in the selection process. They actually choose a particular child—from photos or in person—and then begin the process of adopting her.

The most extreme examples of such selection are the online photo listings mentioned earlier. On Web sites like Rainbow Kids or precious.org,

TABLE 6-2

Sample foreign adoption fees, 2004

Agency	Application and agency fees	Program fee: Russia	Program fee: Guatemala	Program fee: China	Program fee: India	Program fee: Ethiopia
Wide Horizons for Children	$5,700	$15,000	$18,240	$7,165	$5,000	$6,700
Holt International	$2,995	NA	$8,690	$9,360	$8,190 (healthy) $5,325 (with health needs)	NA
Angels' Haven	$4,500	$11,000	$17,500	$6,000	NA	$8,000
MAPS International	$2,000	$15,650	$19,000	$12,250	$14,500	NA
Families Thru International Adoption	$4,800	$13,978	$19,000	$3,000	$12,000	NA
Commonwealth Adoptions	$200	$17,000	$26,900	$12,000	$12,000	NA

Sources: Agency Web sites (www.whfc.org; www.holtintl.org; www.angelshaven.org; www.mapsadopt.org; www.ftia.org; www.commonwealthadoption.org) and conversations with author.

agencies regularly list their available charges, organized by country, gender, or age. At any given time, the lists may contain as many as five hundred kids, all of whom are officially eligible for adoption. Many agencies also have their own online lists of waiting children, complete with photos and brief, often heart-wrenching descriptions. Interested parents are urged to contact the agency for more information and to begin the process that will "bring their child home." Although precise numbers are not available, the director of Rainbow Kids estimates that more than six thousand children have been adopted since 1997 from her site alone.[95] Hundreds more are adopted each year through various summer camps or hosting programs that bring older children to the United States to meet prospective families.

There are several ways of viewing these selective arrangements. On the one hand, photo listings and summer camps provide a crucial matching function. They relay information about some of the world's hardest-to-place children: older kids, sibling groups, and babies born with handicaps. They get this information to a wide group of prospective parents, enabling them to find—or pick—their particular child.[96] On the other hand, critics note that such arrangements operate uncomfortably like global bazaars, with well-heeled customers choosing merchandise from a glossy and sentimental catalog.

This brings us to the third distinguishing facet of cross-border adoption. In families that are forged between the first and third worlds it is consistently the parents who come from the wealthier states and the children who migrate out of poverty. It is the poor states that produce children, and the rich that consume them. In the process, poor parents are left behind, serving only as the initial fabricators of other people's children.

This essential equation has caused critics to cast international adoption in a particularly evil light: as a commercial process that both thrives off global poverty and perpetuates it. As Twila Perry, an American legal scholar, argues, "The imbalance in the circumstances . . . involved in international adoption presents a troubling dilemma: in a sense, the access of affluent white Western women to children of color for adoption is often dependent upon the continued desperate circumstances of women in third world nations."[97] Similarly, feminist critics like Janice Raymond assert that international adoption involves trafficking in *both* women and children; like surrogacy, she writes, adoption "encourages *throw-away women* who are discarded after fulfilling their breeding role."[98]

Such criticism, of course, rankles adoption proponents, who insist that international adoption has nothing to do with exploitation or global inequities.[99] Instead it is humanitarianism of the most intimate sort, humanitarianism that literally transplants some of the world's poorest and most vulnerable inhabitants into the homes and hearts of the most privileged. Through international adoption, supporters insist, surplus children are delivered to parents who want them, and surplus capital (via local fees and donations) flows to impoverished states.[100]

And so they do. Yet the claim that international adoption is a virtuous market does not negate the fact that it is nevertheless a market. Adoption agencies hold regular seminars to describe their trade. They list their children online (in some cases) and profile them in glossy magazines. They also charge clearly differentiated prices. It's hard to argue that this isn't commerce, because it is.

The Black Market

It is in the final tier of the baby market, however, that commerce becomes most explicit and extreme. This is the part of the market in which adoption agencies are replaced by baby brokers and money unabashedly changes hands. This is the unsavory but persistent realm of black market babies, a realm populated by infamous intermediaries like Georgia Tann of the Tennessee Children's Home Society, who placed more than one thousand children between 1930 and 1950 and personally reaped more than $1 million in profit. Or Ron Silverton, a California attorney indicted in 1974 for arranging unauthorized adoptions and attempting to sell a person.[101]

It is a world that has recently gone global, too, as evidenced by well-publicized stories of brokers who place attractive children with eager parents and profit handsomely from the exchange.[102] It is difficult to estimate how large this illicit market is or how deeply it affects the broader flow of adoption. In 1975, a congressional hearing estimated that more than five thousand babies were sold each year in the United States, for prices that ranged between $10,000 and $15,000.[103] Today, industry experts estimate that less than 1 percent of domestic adoptions go through implicitly illegal channels, as do perhaps 5 percent of international adoptions.[104] Accusations vary widely across exporting countries, with a handful—Cambodia, Vietnam, India, Guatemala—accounting for the bulk of alleged illegal activity.

Defining this black market, though, is tricky, because nearly all adoptions (aside from those in the foster care system) involve some transfer of money. Indeed, it is this very transfer of money that makes adoption's critics quick to deride it. But black market adoptions have a distinctive set of characteristics, a pattern of trade and behavior that sets them sharply, if subtly, apart.

First, black market adoptions occur by definition outside the boundaries of licensed trade. They are conducted by independent brokers or unlicensed intermediaries who cater exclusively to parents' demands and don't perform the home studies required by state law. The prices involved are often secretive, and key documents are frequently forged. Legitimate adoption is a hugely transparent procedure, involving social workers, judges, and local recording clerks. Black market adoption, by contrast, is quiet and covert, which helps to explain its persistent appeal.

Second, in black market adoption, the prohibition on payment breaks down. Instead of covering only the birth mother's costs for pregnancy and childbirth, baby brokers pay extra, "reimbursing" the mother for relinquishing her child. The monies involved here may be minimal—$180 for a Cambodian infant, according to a 2002 scandal, $20 for an Indian girl—but the principle is key.[105] Under legitimate circumstances, mothers relinquish their children because they cannot, or choose not to, raise them by themselves. These mothers either place their newborns through a court-sanctioned process (the norm in U.S. domestic adoption) or leave them quietly in a baby hospital or public marketplace (the typical route in China). Sometimes, mothers are also judged incapable of parenting and are forced to cede their children to the state. This is a common pattern for children placed in the U.S. foster care system and for many so-called Russian "orphans." Note, however, that none of the relinquishing mothers in these cases was *paid* to place her children. In black market adoption, by contrast, the transaction is explicitly commercial: a mother (or occasionally a father) receives money in exchange for the child.

A third characteristic of black market adoption takes this phenomenon to its logical and egregious extreme. Once children are explicitly purchased and their sale occurs outside formal and transparent channels, it is only a small step toward the outright theft and subsequent resale of children. Thankfully, such cases are rare.[106] But they do occur. In 2001, for example, the United States suspended adoptions from Cambodia, citing allegations of both baby-selling and baby-stealing.[107]

These horrific examples constitute only a tiny fraction of the overall adoptive market. Yet because the extreme end of adoption is so sinister and because even legitimate adoption entails a fair measure of commerce, it is easy to conflate adoption with theft, and for critics to paint all adoptions as thinly veiled versions of baby-selling. As one critic writes, "Adoption in America today is a lucrative industry operating on greed and exploitation, with white babies its precious commodity and prices determined by desperation. Those in the white-baby business are no longer philanthropic individuals . . . but a small group of private entrepreneurs, dealers, and middlemen who have turned a placement into a deal."[108]

What complicates matters even further is that the legal distinction between legitimate and illegitimate adoption is not clear. Following state law, for example, any birth mother can legally arrange for her own child's adoption. In theory, this provision simply allows mothers to decide what is best for their children. In practice, though, it creates a massive loophole: as long as the birth mother agrees, any adoption is technically legal. And any intermediary who "helped" the birth mother or the adoptive parents can reasonably claim to have provided counseling services, legal advice, or any other innocuous service that is difficult to define as illegal. As a result, very few Americans have ever been convicted of baby-selling.[109] Laws are somewhat tighter in Europe, where all the major countries have ratified the Hague Convention and many have laws that explicitly ban baby-selling or child trafficking. Still, even with the toughest legal regime, it remains difficult to determine the provenance of an adopted child or the circumstances that surrounded his or her adoption.[110]

Black market adoption *is* different from legitimate adoption. It occurs furtively and often with forged documents; it involves payment for the child herself; and it occasionally descends into the realm of either kidnapping or theft. But these distinctions are not always obvious, and wily brokers can squeeze rather easily through the loopholes of the law. Moreover, even though legitimate adoption providers despise the black market and the shadow it casts upon all adoption, the legitimate market is itself sharply divided: between public agencies and private, between faith-based nonprofits and independent attorneys. These entities do not like to admit that they are competing among themselves, but they are.

And the terms of competition make it even more difficult to establish any lines. Because if all payment were banished from the world of adoption—a policy often espoused by adoption's foes—then all adoptions would revert to state-run agencies, putting even licensed providers out of business. Similarly, if it were illegal to transport any adopted child across state or national boundaries (another frequent proposal), then scores of intermediaries would lose their commercial niche. In the process, market efficiencies would also vanish, because state-run agencies cannot provide the speed and service of their private counterparts, and state-specific adoption would mean segregating thousands of children far from the parents most likely to adopt them.

This brings us to the central question posed by black market adoption, and indeed by adoption in general. Most people agree that it is inherently wrong to sell a child, that we can never treat babies or the parents who produced them as marketplace commodities.[111] But does this moral prohibition imply that we can never transfer children from one set of parents to another? That we can never allow any form of payment to enter into such a transfer? Does our revulsion for the black market in babies mean that parents can never pay an intermediary to get Yamile or Bulat off the Rainbow Kids list and into their homes? In the contemporary world, adoption undeniably operates as a market. The question is whether this market is necessarily bad.

Selling Souls or Saving Lives? Prospects for the Adoption Market

If one looks at adoption by itself, it's tempting to say yes across the board, to say that money should never enter the relationship between parent and child.[112] It is certainly plausible to suggest that adoption be taken out of private hands and returned fully to governments. It is possible to express deep sympathy for Yamile's and Bulat's plight while still arguing against their adoption. Indeed, on moral grounds, one can argue that the prohibition against selling children is so deep and so crucial that nothing—not even the fate of these children themselves—can violate it.[113]

If one sees adoption as part of a broader baby trade, however, such sweeping pronouncements are more difficult to make. Clearly, profits are being made in other parts of the trade: in infertility treatments, in sperm sales, in surrogacy. By what logic can we argue that the Fertility Institute of Las Vegas can charge its clients $44,800 for a gestational surrogate cycle, but Angels' Haven can't charge $8,000 to place a war orphan from Ethiopia?

Perhaps one can draw a hard and fast line at the child himself, distinguishing between the components of conception and the *product* of that conception. In other words, one can say that from the moment the child is born, he or she can no longer be traded or treated as part of a market transaction. This is a legitimate position. It also, however, often runs contrary to the interests of the child at hand. Because it takes money to bring a little boy from Sierra Leone to Milwaukee; it takes money to care for that little boy in a local orphanage and to ensure that his prospective parents can raise him in an appropriate manner. If this money does not change hands—if, in other words, the market for international adoption were to disappear—that little boy would almost certainly spend his childhood in an institution and without a family.[114] And only a tiny handful of sociologists and child welfare advocates would still maintain that any child is better served by institutional life.[115]

Alternatively, one could allow the transaction to occur but insist that it remain apart from any market influence. Practically, such a position would mean ceding adoption entirely to the state. It would mean expending state resources and replacing market structures with government bureaucracies. This kind of system is eminently possible; indeed, government agencies control the adoption process in most exporting countries (China, Russia, Guatemala, Peru) and several importing ones (the Netherlands, Australia).

In the United States, however, state-based adoption would clash head-on with a deeply seated preference for choice. It would thrust family-making into bureaucratic hands and would likely engender the kinds of delays and inefficiencies that currently cloud the foster system. In the United States, moreover, a state-based adoption system would stand in even sharper contrast with other elements of the baby market. In Australia, after all, adoption sits closer to the state, but so do IVF, egg donation, and surrogacy. If the United States were somehow to bring adoption out of the market entirely, it would mean creating a sharp dichotomy between reproductive options that can be purchased (eggs, embryos, PGD, IVF) and those that cannot. It would mean, in practical terms, allowing the rich to purchase procreation while pushing the poor to adopt.

Such a system is indeed possible, and if we take the moment of conception as a clear dividing line then it may be the best we can do. But taking adoption out of the market would lessen the efficiencies that now exist. It would reduce the number of children available for adoption and increase the amount of time involved. It would also impose older-era guidelines on parenting, leaving government agencies to determine who is suitable to form a family, and how.

Once again, the trade-offs of such a system become most evident when compared to other means of baby-making. At a societal level, adoption almost certainly provides a better option than assisted reproduction. It draws upon the existing supply of children rather than creates new ones. It conserves financial resources that would otherwise be spent on foster care or institutional arrangements, and it avoids the cost of new, higher-tech children.

Admittedly, one wouldn't want childless couples to bear sole responsibility—or indeed any real responsibility—for solving the problem of parentless children.[116] By the same token, though, it also seems foolhardy to put adoption at a relative *disadvantage* to assisted reproduction. If we let people donate eggs and sperm and embryos, how can we insist that infants be handed to the state? If we let an unmarried fifty-two-year-old woman pay $100,000 for the IVF treatment that will provide her with newborn twins, why should we prevent that same woman from paying, say, $25,000 to adopt Sofia or Rafael?[117]

The funny thing about the adoption market is that it works. It doesn't work in every case, of course, and it works better for some kids and parents than others. Yet the history of adoption provides a surprisingly consistent picture of success. Whether they adopt through public agencies or private, through friends or foreign lawyers, and whether they adopt infants who look "just like them" or distant toddlers of a different race, most adoptive parents subsequently assess their experiences in rather glowing terms.[118] They embrace their adopted children as theirs and don't seem to harbor any lingering doubts about the nature of the original transaction. The only prevalent complaints revolve around shortages and bureaucratic delays: too few children, too much red tape.

For adopted children and birth parents, the picture is murkier, but not for reasons that relate directly to commerce. Some limited evidence suggests, for example, that adult adoptees resent the transactions that surrounded their placement.[119] Some studies argue that adoptees bear the lingering pain of their birth mother's "rejection" or that they face a lifelong quest to discover their genetic origins.[120] Most adoption experts currently argue that open adoption is better than closed and that adoptees have a right to know the circumstances of their birth.[121] None of these complaints, however, has anything to do with the *business* of adoption. On the contrary, critics reserve their sharpest bile for the old model of state-based or licensed agency adoption, where all transactions were secret and power rested with a handful of social workers.

Similar complaints are voiced by, or on behalf of, birth mothers, now commonly regarded as the most vulnerable element in the adoption triad. During adoption's heyday in the middle of the twentieth century, birth mothers were routinely denied any say in their child's destiny, or even their own. They were routed into unsavory maternity homes by parents or boyfriends, where their children were frequently taken before they even awoke after the birth. For many birth mothers, placing their child for adoption remains a harrowing memory, a loss from which they never fully recover.[122]

Yet again, the tragedy of adoption in these cases has little or nothing to do with the market. Women didn't relinquish their children in the 1950s and 1960s because they had a financial incentive to do so; they relinquished them because they didn't have the means or social standing to raise them on their own. Circumstances changed somewhat after the advent of birth control and abortion, because the sudden dearth of adoptable infants made brokers more willing to offer enticements, and birth mothers more ready to accept them. A far more important change, though, was that birth mothers began to exercise choice and discretion, deciding whether to place their children and, increasingly, with whom.

Again, therefore, the introduction of market forces actually enhanced the options that birth mothers faced. At the extreme, as noted earlier, market forces have put birth mothers into the buyer's position, enabling them, literally, to select from a catalog of potential parents. Such options do not imply that the decision to relinquish a child has become easy, or that birth mothers see their choices as representing some kind of pleasant parental supermarket. By the same token, though, it is difficult to argue that market forces have worsened the plight of birth parents.

Those who do advance accusations along these lines generally focus on the less-developed world, where, they contend, women are coerced by their own poverty to relinquish children they would prefer to raise.[123]

But again, it is hard to blame the market for *causing* these women's undeniable pain, or to believe that halting cross-border adoption would do anything to alleviate their situation. Instead, the adoption market sends capital flowing in precisely the direction that adoption's opponents desire: from rich countries to poor, from wealthy parents to abandoned, neglected, or relinquished kids.

The market for adoption isn't always pretty. There are children who come from abusive backgrounds and never recover. There are children who yearn for their genetic origins or cultural roots, children who ache for an identity that eludes them. There are children who go to bad homes, and children, like Anita and Yi-Wei, who may never find homes. It is tempting in this market to focus on the nasty underside and on the abusive practices that will always scar adoption's edges.

But setting adoption within the larger baby business presents a starkly different view. For there are children created by IVF who will also grow up to be abused, children born by sperm or egg donation who will also eventually yearn for their own genetic roots. All these children are also created through market transactions, none of which operate under the regulatory apparatus that has long hovered over adoption.

In fact, the U.S. adoption market—clunky and cumbersome as it may be—could even offer a model of how a modified baby business might function. It is a model where money undeniably changes hands, and where some intermediaries profit from transacting in children. Yet it is also a market that combines a relatively small for-profit segment with a much larger nonprofit one. It is a market where government agencies provide oversight and regulation, and private entities compete to provide service. It is a market where parents have to prove that they are suited to parent, but also where most parents—be they gay or straight, single or married, rich or working class—can hope to find "their" child. And it is a market that essentially works.

In September 2005, just before this book went to press, I returned to the Rainbow Kids and precious.org sites to check on the children I had chosen at random some nine months before. Bulat had found his forever family. Yamile, Sofia, and Rafael were still waiting.

CHAPTER 7

Songs of Solomon

Prospects for Building a Better Baby Trade

The real dignity of man consists not in his origin but in what he is and what he may become.

—EDWIN GRANT CONKLIN

SAY THE WORD *market*, and what comes to mind? Financial markets, maybe, or supermarkets. There are markets in real estate; markets in used cars; markets filled with farmers selling pumpkins and cheese. There are markets in odd things like used Pez dispensers, and in highly sophisticated instruments like mortgage-backed securities. But babies? Babies aren't supposed to be sold. Babies aren't supposed to be bought. Babies aren't supposed to have prices fixed on them.

The central contention of this book, however, is that there is a market for babies, a market that stretches across the globe and encompasses hundreds of thousands of people. This market doesn't necessarily work like the market for pumpkins or mortgages. Its prices are more stubborn than supply and demand would suggest; it can never fully provide all the goods that are desired; and the very idea of property rights—the core of most modern markets—remains either ambiguous or contested. This is a market packed with technology but loath to admit it, a market where sellers often cloak their wares in the language of charity.[1]

Yet even with all these oddities, the market for babies—the market for children, really—is still a market. How do we know? It's because there is a deep and persistent demand for reproduction, a demand that often goes far beyond what nature alone can provide. There is supply in this market, too, a wide and steadily increasing supply of ways to produce when procreation fails. There are prices that clearly link supply and demand, and there are businesses that sell their wares in this market, often charging hefty sums along the way.

At a conceptual level, it is easy to bemoan this market, to insist that reproduction—like truth or love or honor—should never be sold. It is also easy to decry the cutting edge of reproductive science, arguing that it breaks the rules of nature or threatens, as Leon Kass once predicted, to lead to "voluntary self-degradation, or willing dehumanization."[2] Such arguments, however, are increasingly unrealistic: the baby business, as this book has shown, is alive, well, and growing. It's hard to imagine that we could ever put this particular genie back in its bottle. Moreover, it's not at all clear that we should. For the baby business—unlike, say, the arms race or the heroin trade—produces a good that is inherently *good*. It produces children, for people who want them. Some paths to these children may be less virtuous than others. Some parents may not deserve the children they get. Yet the underlying dynamic—parents getting children—is certainly not bad.

Parents acquire children all the time, and we generally regard it as a fine thing to do. What differs, of course, is the mode of acquisition in the baby business; it is the entry of commerce into what many regard as an entirely noncommercial affair. This argument, though, does not carry any kind of natural weight. If we think that markets are good and children are good, then it's not obvious why mixing the two is inherently vile. Instead, we can just as easily turn this argument on its head, examining how market mechanisms might help to produce a socially desirable outcome.

To phrase this slightly differently, we have markets in all kinds of things, including health care, child care, and education, and we generally think they work. We have a demand for babies, a supply of babies, and a growing set of intermediaries who serve to bring demand and supply together. Given this situation, we essentially have two choices. We can rue the baby business and call for its demise, or we can accept the market that has arisen and try to make it better.

This book has taken the second path. It argues that there is a market for babies and that this market, despite its flaws and foibles, it not necessarily bad. But how can we make the market work better? How can we harness its power without falling prey to the sins its critics denounce?

There are, it seems, two ways. First, we need to fix the market itself, providing the baby business with the commercial attributes it currently lacks: a semblance of property rights, some common definitions, and a framework that applies across its disparate parts. Second, we need to embed this market in an appropriate political and regulatory context, to impose the rules that will enable the market to produce the goods we want—happy, healthy children—without encouraging the obvious risks.

This second task is harder than the first, because politics, in many ways, is messier than markets. Yet in practice, the resolution between politics and markets is likely to be deeply intertwined. If we can make the baby business work better—if we can match parents and children more consistently, at a lower cost, and with less uncertainty—then political support for the market is likely to grow. And if we clarify the politics, distinguishing what is acceptable from what is not, the market will inevitably work better.

Making Markets Work: The Pursuit of Property Rights

For those who study markets, the importance of property rights has become something of a mantra. Building on the work of Douglass North and Ronald Coase, economists have argued for several decades that property rights are the bedrock of any modern economy, the first step in a long and often arduous trek toward commercial development.[3]

So deep is this belief, and so fervent, that it readily surfaces in disparate political and economic platforms. The World Bank, for example, regularly reviews the state of a country's property rights before granting development assistance. Pharmaceutical companies and movie studios wage massive campaigns to ensure the sanctity of their intellectual property; and politicians, from Margaret Thatcher to George W. Bush, trumpet the advantages of "the ownership society." We accept, nearly at face value, the argument that economic development cannot proceed without a strong foundation of ownership. And why not? The argument itself is perfectly reasonable, in line with both theoretical propositions and empirical support. If societies are to sell, say, wheat, then individuals in that society need to know that the wheat they grow will be theirs to sell. If they are to develop high-tech industries such as software or biotechnology, the firms that invest in these technologies need to know that they can recoup the fruits of their investment, selling products based on what they own. Only property rights can provide this kind of security.[4]

In the baby business, though, such rights are essentially nonexistent. Indeed, this is a $3 billion market without any established framework of ownership.

Consider the following cases. In 2003, a retired firefighter sued a Boston fertility clinic for having implanted embryos in his ex-wife against his objections. In 2000, two couples—one American, the other British— found themselves fighting over the same set of infant twin girls. Both couples had arranged to adopt the girls through a private Internet transaction.[5] And in February 2005, a Chicago couple sued a local clinic for having discarded embryos frozen five years earlier.[6]

Notice what each of these stories has in common: in addition to high-profile drama and dashed hopes, they involve, essentially, a missing set of property rights. The Boston firefighter presumed that the embryos he had helped create—embryos that contained his genetic material—belonged to him. His ex-wife, whose genetic material provided the other half of the embryos, presumed, similarly, that the embryos belonged to her. If the "property" in question had been virtually anything except an embryo, courts in Massachusetts would have been able to resolve their disputes rather easily: the divorced couple could have split a bank account or sold their BMW. They could have divided up the music collection or the wedding china. But an embryo? You can't split it.* More importantly, the court that handled the case didn't even want to deal with it as an issue of property;

---

*Technically, scientists can, under some circumstances, split the embryo at a very early stage into two identical halves. This procedure, in fact, is one potential avenue toward reproductive cloning. For the purposes of the current argument, though, it's irrelevant.

instead, the jury simply found that the clinic should have obtained the father's written consent, and it awarded him compensation for child support.[7]

A parallel logic applies in the case of the discarded embryos. Here, the clinic argued that it had mistakenly destroyed property; the plaintiffs, by contrast, alleged that the clinic had killed their child. Was the embryo property, the courts were asked to decide, or a human being? Should its disposal be treated as the destruction of property, or as murder? It's not clear. The first judge on this case dismissed the couple's claims of wrongful death; a second accepted them; and, as of September 2005, the case was still wending its way through the Illinois legal system.

In the case of the contested twins, two couples found themselves battling over the same set of babies. Again, if the battle had involved a car, a home, or a patent, the courts would at least have had a consistent body of thought on which to rely. For babies, though, the precedent broke down. Clearly, someone made gross errors in this case—most likely the birth mother, as well as the intermediaries involved. Yet the central issue was not whom to blame but rather how to think of the people involved. Were the twins akin to property? Had rights to them been transferred? Did contract law have any role to play? Or were the twins people, over whom property rights held no sway? Moreover, even if they were treated purely as people, and even if their best interests were held to be paramount (the normal procedure in family law cases), then it still wasn't clear who should get them. Both sets of parents wanted them; both sets seemed, initially at least, to be equally capable of parenting.[8] In some respects, therefore, contract law and property rights were actually better suited than family law to resolve this Solomonic standoff.

It is easy to understand why property rights have not been established in the realm of children. To do so would offend the deeply held sensibilities of most people in this field. Adoption professionals, for example, cringe at the thought of treating their charges as property rather than people. Fertility specialists avoid the issue, and many scholars who have examined the baby market reject anything that hints at the commodification of either women or children. One feminist scholar, for example, argues that "life creating substances should be included among those things for which affixing a price tag is inappropriate."[9] Similarly, Michael Sandel, an eminent philosopher, states that "treating children as commodities degrades them as instruments of profit rather than cherishing them as persons worthy of love and care," and legal scholar Margaret Jane Radin has famously claimed that "conceiving of any child in market rhetoric wrongs personhood."[10]

Sandel and Radin are almost certainly right. We don't want to turn children into chattel. We don't want parents treating their offspring as property. But it's not clear that extending property rights into the field of assisted reproduction would have these deleterious effects. Nor is it clear that elements of commodification—paying a price for things of value—is innately wrong or exploitative. Does paying for eggs demean the children who result from such arrangements? Maybe, in some cases. Do surrogate mothers or sperm donors lose dignity in some way that even they themselves can't identify? We simply don't know. Yes, a handful of surrogates have subsequently regretted their experience and rallied against the practice. A tiny group of sperm donors have sought to discover the children they sired.[11] But in the vast majority of cases, surrogates and sperm donors seem either pleased with their contribution or emotionally unaffected.[12] It is difficult to demonstrate empirically, therefore, any inevitably ill effects.

Similarly, although one can argue that any imposition of the marketplace into the realm of reproduction is inherently wrong, again this is an assertion rather than a fact. Empirically, we have no way of knowing whether expensively procured children feel any less cherished than those created for free. We don't know whether their parents, or even other parents, were degraded by the market forces that contributed to their birth.[13] By what right, then, can we claim degradation on their behalf?

The Reality of the Status Quo

Admittedly, one could declare the entire realm of reproduction off-limits to commerce. One could assert that people are free to have children only the old-fashioned way, or to adopt them through charitable organizations attached to the state. One could potentially even extend this view into the field of assisted reproduction, allowing parents to avail themselves of higher-tech services only if they are delivered for free.

The problem with this scenario, however, is that it ignores decades of existing practice. Sperm, for example, are almost never "contributed" for free. Neither are eggs. Instead, they are essentially sold on an open, albeit constrained, market. If countries were to prohibit any kind of financial compensation for either sperm or egg donations, these donations would almost certainly plummet. Indeed, this is exactly what has happened in places like the United Kingdom and Canada, where such laws have created massive shortages of eggs and sperm.[14] And without sperm and eggs, many forms of assisted reproduction are simply not possible.

A similar calculus applies to wombs. Some women, we know, will volunteer to serve as unpaid surrogates, usually for relatives or close friends. Most, however, demand some kind of compensation for their services, even if only for the time and inconvenience of pregnancy. Clearly, if paid surrogacy were banned (as it is in many parts of the world), it, too, would disappear as a reproductive option.

Already, therefore, the basic components of reproduction are being widely sold. One could try to weed out this trade or force it into altruistic, purely voluntary channels. But any measure along these lines would probably just drive the reproductive market underground and eliminate many of the benefits—more children, for a wider variety of parents— that it produces. Again, one could argue, as the critics do, that the cost of creating these newfangled children through market forces is simply too high, that it thrusts us into a world where love is commodified and everything is for sale. Perhaps. But because demand in the baby business is so deep, and because the product it supplies—children—is not inherently evil, those who object to this market will need, eventually, to prove that its risks are as high as they insist. We cannot reject the extension of property rights purely on theoretical grounds.[15]

Meanwhile, eliminating the sale of reproductive components would still not alter the need for order elsewhere along the chain. After all, the most contentious cases in the baby business occur after the egg and sperm have merged to form an embryo, or after that embryo has produced a living child. How are we to resolve these cases without some underlying convictions about either ownership or contractual rights? Do parents own the embryos they produce? Do clinics? Or are embryos the property of the state? Do frozen embryos have a right to be born (a right currently denied to other, implanted embryos)? Do they have a right to be used for research? To inherit things?

(In one famous case, a millionaire couple conceived embryos at an Australian clinic and were then killed in a plane crash before the embryos were implanted. Several women applied to carry the embryos, hoping that they would thereby become eligible to inherit the substantial fortune that the couple had left.)[16]

Under the current system, particularly in the United States, we cannot even begin to answer such questions. Some observers (and court decisions) insist that the embryo is fully human, deserving all the rights and protections of a living child. Other observers (and decisions) treat the embryo as a bunch of cells or tissue, an entity that demands legal protection as property. And still others have tried to carve out a middle ground, ceding the embryo a special status that hovers between human tissue and human life.[17] Certainly, clarifying a system of property rights would not resolve the deep moral issues that surround the human embryo. But a concept of property rights could at least provide a framework for discussion, identifying, at a minimum, who has the right to create, dispose of, implant, and exchange embryos. Similar guidelines could easily extend to the component side of the market, clarifying ownership rights regarding eggs, sperm, and wombs.[18]

Obviously, the question of property rights becomes most contentious when it enters the arena of the living child. No one, presumably, wants to own a child in the sense of owning physical property. Few people would want to give parents full and unchallenged control over their offspring. But issues of contestation—of determining *whose* child this is—inevitably arise. Historically, many of these issues have been resolved by referring to a basic tenet of family law: the best interest of the child involved. This guidepost works relatively well in cases of divorce and custody battles. It also works, though painfully, to help courts and social agencies decide when to terminate parental rights.

In cases of high-tech reproduction, however, its usefulness is likely to decline. Because in many of these cases, the essential facts of parenthood get muddied even before the child is born. Does a sperm donor have any rights in the offspring he genetically fathers? Does he have responsibilities? What about an egg donor? Or a surrogate mother? If a tiny infant has three potential mothers (an egg donor, a surrogate carrier, and an intended mother), how can a court rely solely on the child's best interest to determine his fate? The newborn, presumably, will have had no social relationship with any of the mothers who claim him, meaning that his best interest could easily become only a code word for wealthiest or most stable.[19]

A Plea for Transparency

A system of contracts and property rights, even a crude one, could help bring a measure of clarity to this confusion. It could delineate who has rights to what forms of genetic or social offspring, and under what conditions these rights can be effectively extended. It could legally establish who has not necessarily *ownership* of a particular child, but rather the right or responsibility to parent.

For example, establishing a property rights regime for sperm should be relatively easy. Laws could establish whether men have any lingering rights to the children created by their sperm, and whether (or under what conditions) these children could uncover their genetic heritage. Similar rules could also be extended to eggs and, with somewhat more difficulty, to wombs. In these cases, egg donors (or surrogates) would agree at the outset to the kind of relationship that would extend between them and an eventual child. They would know, explicitly, what kinds of rights they would have with regard to this child, and what kinds of decisions were theirs to make.

Theoretically, such a system could incorporate provisions from the world of adoption, including a mandatory waiting period after the child's birth. During this period, the birth mother (or egg donor) would retain all rights to the child. Once she agreed to relinquish the baby, though, she would simultaneously forfeit any subsequent right to parent him or her.

Critically, a system of property rights could also define the limits of the market, separating those elements that can be sold—sperm, eggs, and wombs, perhaps—from those that cannot.[20] In particular, it could draw a much finer line between the components of babies and the babies themselves, embedding within the system a clear-cut objection to the actual sale of children. Such a line is actually not very difficult to draw. In fact, it simply relies on ensuring that *parents do not profit from relinquishing their children*. Theoretically, parents could still relinquish their children under this kind of system; men could still sell their sperm;

women could receive compensation for reasonable (and documented) pregnancy expenses; and intermediaries could charge fees for managing these exchanges. But although mothers and fathers could renounce their right to parent a particular child, they could not sell this right to others.

Note that in this system, children are not being treated as property per se. They aren't being bargained or sold, and their humanity is never called into question. Instead, property rights are providing a bare minimum of the rules that most economists revere. They are furnishing market participants with a sense of order and predictability, with a set of norms that prescribes behavior and defines the limits of acceptability.[21] Because these norms are transparent, moreover, they allow people to transact more securely and to know what the rules are before they get caught by them.

Critically, creating property rights for the baby business would not, as critics assert, turn children into commodities or mothers into baby machines.[22] It would not tarnish reproduction nor turn intimate relations into financial ones. Instead, property rights would only help to codify a market that already exists, clarifying the terms of ambiguous battles that lead too often to tragedy.

Defining the Market

In the modern economy, most markets are easy to define. The markets for pumpkins and Pez dispensers, after all, are straightforward commercial markets. They have firmly established property rights; prices that shift with supply and demand; and rules that differentiate between commerce and fraud, ownership and theft. These markets are also essentially free, meaning that government intervention is minimal and buyers purchase some combination of what they want and can afford.

Other commonplace markets, by contrast, are more constrained. The insurance and home heating oil markets in the United States, for example, are regulated markets: governments intervene to set prices because the commodities at hand are judged too precious to leave their distribution solely to market forces. In other cases, the commodities are regarded as more precious still—precious enough, in fact, that they must be removed from the market entirely and handed to noncommercial actors.

Heath care fits this description in many parts of the world, as do primary education and clean water. Markets in these cases are replaced by what scholars term "hierarchies," structures of power (rather than structures of commerce) that determine who gets what.[23]

There are no prices in these nonmarkets, and demand often tends to exceed supply. In the United Kingdom and Canada, for example, systems of nationalized health care have removed things like knee replacement surgery from the market. As a result, British and Canadian citizens need not pay to have their knees replaced, but quite frequently they do have to wait, delaying surgery until it's their turn in the queue.

Imperfect Markets

Other markets fall into the broad category of imperfection. These are markets, or quasi-markets, that are destined to disobey the laws of supply and demand. More specifically, they are markets where supply and demand are not likely to produce a high enough level of output.

Consider, for example, lighthouses, the archetypal example of an imperfect market.[24] Presumably, all ships that pass by a rocky spit in Maine want to avail themselves of a nearby lighthouse. They all want the light, and most would probably be willing to pay something for it. But once that lighthouse is constructed, there is no way to force other, nonpaying ships to contribute to its maintenance. So the ships that pay are essentially covering the costs of those that don't. Moreover, because this dynamic is so obvious, shipowners will figure it out early and will refuse as individuals to invest in the lighthouses that, collectively, they all want.

In these imperfect markets, then, investment must come from beyond the individual consumer. It must come from a collective entity—usually, though not always, a government—that recognizes the imperfection and provides what markets on their own do not. All around the world, therefore, governments build lighthouses and roads and electrical grids. They establish land-based phone services and look after public goods like clean air and water. To be sure, there are times when private firms can play a role in these otherwise imperfect markets.[25] Generally, though, they remain the province of noncommercial forces.

Banned Markets

Finally, there are some markets where commerce is deemed fully and completely illegal. Most Western countries, for example, ban the sale of heroin and other mind-altering drugs. They ban the sale of kidneys (always), of blood (usually), and of sex (with some exceptions). In these cases, the market itself is not imperfect; one could, for example, create a perfectly functioning market in either kidneys, blood, or sex. And it's not that a hierarchy coincides with a market, as happens frequently with knee replacement surgery in a nationalized health-care system. Instead, these are markets that society simply deems repugnant. We could sell kidneys, in other words, but we generally choose not to.[26]

What happens in these markets, therefore, is completely predictable: the trade still occurs, but it is fairly limited and explicitly illegal. Prices in this underground or black market are higher than they would be in a legal market (because presumably there are fewer sellers), and demand is constrained.

In Search of Consensus

So which of these markets prevails in the baby trade? It's not clear. One could argue, as many do, that babies and their components fall entirely into the last category—that, like kidneys or blood, they simply should never be exchanged for money. Or one could assert that infertility is a disease and that its treatment should fall naturally into whatever market treats disease in a particular country. Or that infertility is distinctly *not* a disease, that reproduction is not a right, and therefore that the components of baby-making do not deserve any kind of special treatment.

These concerns may seem semantic, but they are actually crucial to any future development of assisted family-building, regardless of whether those families are built through IVF, surrogacy, adoption, genetic intervention, or even cloning. Because until we can categorize these activities in some way—until we can say what they are—we cannot begin to make them work better.

We can start by defining what the baby business is not. Technically, it is not a free market, nor should it be. Most people are repulsed by the very idea of exchanging children for money or of putting a financial price on human heads. Moreover, we don't have well-defined property rights in this arena, nor laws that acknowledge the trade. So the baby business is not like the market for pumpkins or Pez dispensers.

By the same token, though, the baby business is not inherently imperfect. Unlike the situation in lighthouses or roads, where fundamental tensions obstruct the growth of commerce, the components of baby-making are not inimical to trade. We could trade babies if we really wanted to; we are already trading eggs, sperm, and wombs. In purely economic terms, there is nothing that would stop a full-fledged development of the baby trade.

However, acknowledging the possibility of a market is a far cry from establishing its worth. The toughest question of definition, therefore, arises from determining *just what is being traded in this market*. Is it babies, or health, or happiness, or genes? Is it children or families; bits of formless protoplasm or the prospect of a life? In many respects, how one answers this question determines how one considers the entire realm of activity that comprises the baby trade. What makes matters so complex is that people approach this question in fundamentally different ways, defining precisely the same event—egg donation, for example, or online adoption—in vastly different terms.

Yet even amid this confusion, it is not impossible to sketch out some fairly thick lines. For example, we can define virtually all aspects of the baby trade as providing parents with the ability to raise a child of their own. That in the end is what all methods of baby procurement are about: they are technical or social ways for parents to acquire children whom they will subsequently rear and love. Under this definition, using embryos to produce a child is categorically different from using those same embryos for research. And adopting a toddler has no connection to slavery, organ theft, or child prostitution.[27]

More subtly, this definition also defines the baby trade as a service, as the provision of a child rather than the child itself. It indicates that selling a service—providing IVF, carrying a baby to term, completing the paperwork for adoption—is permissible, whereas selling a child is not. In other words, by defining the baby business as the provision of a child to raise, we also begin to define the boundaries between legitimate and illegitimate trade, between those who facilitate a transparent and valued exchange and those who sell what shouldn't be sold.

Fixing Fragmentation

A central theme of this book is the commonality that joins all aspects of the baby trade. Adoption, fertility treatment, surrogacy, even genetic engineering—they are all intimately connected to one another and to the promise they offer of providing children for those who desire them. If the ultimate demand is for a child to raise, then each of the baby markets can be seen as a substitute of sorts, with parents choosing among the types of production they prefer and the kinds of risk they are willing to accept. As individuals, we may believe passionately that certain methods take precedence. Parents may feel that only a genetically related child can be truly theirs; or that it would be reprehensible to engineer a child in a world of waiting orphans; or that traditional surrogacy is somehow more natural than in vitro fertilization.

As a society, however, we need to acknowledge these means as the substitutes they are. Market analogies may be distasteful here, but they cast the light of objectivity on what otherwise becomes colored by passion. If we ban surrogacy but permit IVF, then infertile couples will flock to fertility clinics. If we cover the costs of infertility treatments but not adoption, then IVF doctors will grow rich while children linger longer on waiting lists. If we ban some technologies of reproduction and ignore others, markets will rapidly expand around the poles of neglect. In practical terms, it makes no sense to conceive of the baby business in terms of its component parts. We must regard them, and ultimately regulate them, as one.

Currently, though, the various baby markets exist as almost completely separate entities. Fertility treatments are the province of specialized clinics and medical experts, of endocrinologists and embryologists who are frequently attached to large university hospitals. When prospective parents go to fertility clinics, they present themselves as patients: they have a medical problem and are seeking a medical solution. The fertility specialists then treat them accordingly, doing whatever they can to fix the underlying physical problem and, eventually, to produce a child.

Note, however, that the *child* is not really the focus in this part of the baby trade; instead, it is the would-be parents' infertility. During the course of fertility treatment, therefore, doctors do not typically suggest alternatives to their own form of treatment; they rarely advise their patients to contemplate adoption, foster care, or living without children. Such options simply are not within the confines of their profession: even though they are actually in the business of providing children for parents to raise, they define their role as curing infertility. They are medical experts performing a particular form of health care. As one doctor explains, "We don't sell babies. We sell care of the infertile couple. We sell a process, not an outcome."[28]

Meanwhile, suppliers to the infertility trade function much like suppliers in other, less intimate realms. Hormone producers, for example, are simply pharmaceutical firms, providing highly valued inputs without much downward pressure on price. They invest in R&D, patent their drugs, and sell directly to fertility specialists. They sell products rather than services and have a well-established system of property rights. Egg and sperm "producers" are very different, of course: they are individuals rather than firms and produce only small (for eggs) or limited (for sperm) amounts of product. Yet they are still producers and are essentially treated as such in the market. They aren't medical practitioners; they aren't providing children; they don't directly cure infertility. Instead, like the hormone manufacturers, they produce a tangible product that is subsequently sold into the baby business.

Wombs are more complicated, because they are typically leased rather than sold. Surrogate mothers provide a service instead of a product and retain a more complicated relationship with the children they bear. Unlike egg or sperm donors, surrogates aren't really producers, but neither are they birth mothers in the typical sense of adoption.[29] Specialists who perform PGD are also complicated, because they provide medical services that are linked to infertility but not directly connected to it. Essentially, these doctors produce healthy children rather than fertile parents.

And then there is adoption, which sits oddly apart from the rest of the baby trade. In adoption, the child is much more tangible than in any of the other, related markets. In adoption, the child is real rather than potential, fully formed rather than composed of disparate parts. In adoption, the child has a pre-existing set of parents and a visible or detectable set of traits. Providers in the adoption market, therefore, function very differently from their counterparts in the fertility trade. They are social workers, not doctors, and they are charged, at least in theory, with focusing on the existing child rather than the prospective parent. As a result, they are less overtly commercial and more frequently nonprofit. Most importantly, they are required, often explicitly, to divorce their activities from those of the fertility trade. Although many parents arrive at adoption after suffering from infertility, adoption agencies insist that these parents not see adoption as a "cure" for infertility.[30] They insist, in other words, in splitting adoption from fertility treatment, just as fertility clinics resolutely avoid the topic of adoption.

Yet in reality these two markets are closely linked. Many people pursue fertility treatment because they are wary of adoption. Many others pursue adoption because they have grown weary of or dissatisfied with fertility treatment. Both sides of this market would prefer to believe that they are not substitutes for one another. But in reality, of course, they are. Everyone in the fertility market, everyone in the adoption market, and everyone who purchases eggs, sperm, wombs, and PGD is looking for precisely the same thing: a child to call their own.

Practice in the United States

Typically, markets that sell similar goods are subjected to similar regulatory regimes. Under U.S. law, pumpkins, for example, are treated much like squash or rutabagas. Home heating oil is governed by the same rules as natural gas. And the market for knee replacements works just like the market for hip replacements. In each of these cases, the kind of regulation and the level of regulation don't vary much. So if pumpkin farmers are subject to the basic rules of fair play and safe practice—not to use certain pesticides, for example, nor to employ slave labor—a similar set of rules is likely to apply to farmers producing squash and rutabagas. If prices are capped for home heating oil, they will almost certainly be capped for natural gas as well.

These parallel structures occur because both economists and regulators know that if similar products are governed by disparate rules, the market will simply shift to where prices are lower and rules more lax. If the pumpkin farmer uses slaves, for example, and thus produces cheaper pumpkins, consumers will generally buy pumpkins instead of squash.

And if heating oil prices were capped but natural gas prices were not, consumers would switch to oil-based heat.

These regulatory consistencies are a hallmark of modern economies. Yet in the baby business, they simply do not apply. Instead, as noted earlier, each of the segments in this market functions separately, and each is subject to its own idiosyncratic set of rules.

To understand the depth of these differences, it is useful to consider the examples set out in table 7-1. Sperm, as we see, is subject to only a hint of regulation: under FDA guidelines, sperm banks must be certified by a federal agency and must comply with certain quality control provisions. Eggs, by contrast, are subject to a vaguer set of rules, because it's not entirely clear whether, or under what conditions, the FDA regards them as "reproductive tissues."[31]

At the state level, however, eggs face a crazy quilt of complicated and frequently contradictory regulation. North Dakota, for example, explicitly holds that egg donors have no parental rights to the offspring they might produce. Texas requires written consent from the intended mother and her husband, whereas Florida allows for "reasonable compensation" to the donor. Many other states, meanwhile, remain mute, neither prohibiting egg donation nor regulating it.[32] Surrogacy is even more complicated; it is fully legal in some states, explicitly illegal in others, and largely ignored by federal legislation.[33]

Adding price to this picture makes it even more complicated, because prices vary both in nominal terms and in the amount of reimbursement available. For example, the "price" of pregnancy for most Americans is essentially nothing. Pregnant women receive prenatal care, spend time in the hospital, and deliver their babies—all, usually, without paying the full cost of the services they have received. This isn't, of course, because these services are free—indeed, the typical costs of a normal pregnancy run between $7,000 and $12,000—but because we, as a society, have decided to spread these costs more widely. Thus, most insurance companies are required by law to cover the costs of pregnancy.[34]

Parents pay for their pregnancies, therefore, through their insurance payments, but so do nonparents, former parents, and everyone else who contributes to a particular insurance company. Even women without insurance, meanwhile, can generally experience pregnancy for free.[35] Why

TABLE 7-1

Regulating reproduction

Component	Federal regulation	State regulation				
		Massachusetts	*California*	*Florida*	*North Dakota*
Sperm	Banks subject to FDA regulation as "clinical laboratories"	Donation permitted; consenting husband is legal father	Donation permitted; consenting husband is legal father	Donation permitted; consenting husband is legal father	Donation permitted; consenting husband is legal father
Eggs	Subject, under some conditions, to FDA regulation as "clinical laboratories"	No law; donation permitted	No law; donation permitted	Donation permitted; reasonable compensation allowed	Donation permitted; law says donor is not the parent of the child
IVF	Clinics must report success rates to CDC	Permitted; insurance must cover costs of IVF	Permitted; insurance may exclude costs of IVF	Permitted; insurance must offer *option* of IVF coverage	Permitted; no requirements for insurance coverage
Surrogacy	No law	No law	No law; court decisions in favor of "intended" parents	Law presumes that contracting couple are legal parents; payment prohibited	Contract void; surrogate and her husband are legal parents
PGD	Prohibits use of federal funding	No law	No law	No law	No law
Cloning	Ban on use of federal funds	Prohibits embryo and fetal research	Bans reproductive cloning; allows therapeutic	No law	Bans reproductive and therapeutic cloning
Adoption	Entry of foreign-born children subject to State Department rules; placement of foster children subject to national law	No independent adoption	Independent adoption, advertising, and reimbursement permitted	Independent adoption, advertising, and reimbursement permitted	Independent adoption permitted; advertisement only by state or licensed agency

such generosity? It's because we have decided that healthy pregnancies, like lighthouses, are a public good. And thus we have policies that allow women to bear babies without having to bear the associated financial cost.

This generosity, however, does not extend to assisted reproduction. Instead, as table 7-2 demonstrates, the price of an assisted pregnancy is much higher, even though it arguably leads to precisely the same result: the birth of a child for its parents to raise. What is even more interesting, though, is that the various technical routes to this result are themselves priced so disparately. Eggs run the gamut from $3,000 to $50,000, and surrogates from $10,000 to $75,000. IVF is fully covered in some states, partially covered in others, and left entirely to the free market in most.

The crucial distinction in most cases relates to the market definitions described earlier: if infertility is defined as a medical problem, then its treatment is covered as a medical cost. States decide, in other words, to regulate the market for IVF, just as they regulate home heating oil or hip replacement surgery. But if infertility is seen as fate, a decision, or bad luck, then states stay out of the market and prices flutter upward.

TABLE 7-2

The price of birth

Component	Typical cost	Insurance coverage	Tax credit
Sperm	$300	Varies by state	0
Eggs	$4,500	Varies by state	0
IVF	$12,400 per cycle; $66,667–$114,286 per live birth*	Varies by state	0
Surrogacy	$59,000	None	0
PGD	$3,500	None	0
Cloning	Unknown	None	0
Adoption	$2,500 (foster child) $15,000 (domestic infant) $25,000 (international)	Does not apply	$10,000 (federal)

*From Peter Neumann et al., "The Cost of a Successful Delivery with In Vitro Fertilization," *New England Journal of Medicine* 331, no. 4 (July 28, 1994): 239–243.

One could argue, of course, that such variation is not necessarily bad. There are other markets—think of wine, for example, or land—where prices vary even more and states also impose different regulatory regimes. But babies, obviously, are different. Because as a society we value babies more than wine or land. We treat them, not as rights per se, but at least as something to which all citizens have a nearly identical claim. How, then, can we say that some people can procreate for free, whereas others must pay? And how can we permit such significant variation across state lines and between different versions of assisted procreation?

International Practice

What makes matters even worse is that the baby business doesn't stop at national borders. Instead, prospective parents eagerly and regularly cross international borders, searching for options that are unavailable, illegal, or too expensive at home. Again, we might accept, or at least explain, these searches as the inevitable result of a global market and of comparative advantages that fall naturally across international lines. If sperm is cheaper in Denmark than in Sweden, it makes perfect sense for Swedes to travel to Denmark to acquire Danish sperm. The problem, though, is that it's not only price that's driving Swedes to Denmark—or Britons to Spain, or Australians to the United States. Instead, it is the deep regulatory divides that separate these states and the varying ways they treat reproduction.

For example, as table 7-3 indicates, Israel essentially views assisted reproduction as a national good. Accordingly, it permits most forms of high-tech reproduction, regulates them with a light but transparent hand, and pays for all fertility treatments until a given couple has given birth to two children. In Germany, by contrast, a deep-seated fear of genetic manipulation has manifested itself in explicit and fairly restrictive legislation: no egg transfer, no surrogacy, no PGD.

Such regulatory gaps have already created a growing international market in reproductive tourism. As indicated in chapter 5, British parents who have been deemed ineligible for certain forms of PGD have recently traveled to Spain, Brazil, or the United States to complete the procedure. Italian lesbians (who don't qualify under a 2004 law to receive sperm in their own country) go to the United States or to neighboring European

TABLE 7-3

The international map

Component	United Kingdom	Israel	Egypt	Germany	Denmark	South Africa
Sperm	Donation permitted; compensation illegal	Donation permitted	Donation prohibited	Donation permitted	Donation and sale permitted	Donation and payment in kind permitted
Eggs	Donation permitted; cap on compensation	Donation permitted; no payment beyond expenses	Donation prohibited	Donation prohibited	Donation permitted, but limited	Donation and payment in kind permitted
IVF	Permitted; partially covered by national health plan	Permitted; fully covered under national health plan	Married couples only; no insurance coverage	"Stable" couples only; generally covered under national health plan	"Stable" couples only; fully covered under national health plan	Permitted without restriction; no insurance coverage
Surrogacy	Permitted if couple is married; regulated by HFEA	Permitted, if couple is married and surrogate is single; regulated by Ministry of Health	Prohibited	Prohibited	Prohibited	No relevant statutes
PGD	Permitted; regulated by HFEA	Permitted; subject to local authorities	Permitted	Prohibited	Permitted	No relevant statutes
Cloning	Therapeutic cloning allowed; regulated by HFEA	Prohibited; use of stem cells regulated by Ministry of Health	Prohibited	Prohibited	Prohibited	No relevant statutes
Adoption	Permitted	Permitted	Prohibited	Permitted	Permitted	Permitted

Sources: Howard W. Jones Jr. and Jean Cohen, "IFFS Surveillance," *Fertility and Sterility* 81, no. 5, Supplement 4 (May 2004); Stéphane Viville and Deborah Pergament, "Results of a Survey of the Legal Status and Attitudes Towards Preimplantation Genetic Diagnosis Conducted in 13 Different Countries," *Prenatal Diagnosis* 18 (1998): 1374–1380; Beverly J. Wunderlin, "The Regulation of Medically Assisted Procreation in Europe and Related Nations," PhD dissertation, Department of Sociology, University of North Texas, 2002; Viveca Söderström-Anttila et al., "Oocyte Donation In Infertility Treatment: A Review," *Acta Obstetrica et Gynecologica Scandinavica* 80 (2001): 196; and Julie Selwyn and Wendy Sturgess, *International Overview of Adoption: Policy and Practice* (Bristol, UK: The School for Policy Studies, 2001).

states. And couples from Muslim countries, where sperm and egg donation are either rare or prohibited, quietly venture to Europe, North America, or selected Asian nations. Singapore, for example, has become a leading provider of IVF services, largely on the basis of its international clientele. South Africa has made similar moves in that direction—in some cases, offering low-priced treatments along with a beach vacation—as has Romania.

Again, the market in this context is more than a competition between differential prices and quality of treatment. Instead it is a market composed largely of regulatory differences; of countries that define the same procedures in very different ways and thus attract customers in search of the most conducive environment. When multinational corporations engage in this same kind of search, we call it regulatory arbitrage or, more critically, a race to the bottom. When desperate parents do it, we tend to look the other way.

Yet the logic in both cases, as well as the outcomes, is identical: in a global economy, mobile customers, be they corporations or parents, will flock to the most attractive national locales. They will go where prices are lowest and quality highest, and where regulations are most conducive to their own needs and interests. In the baby business, therefore, national prohibitions on any particular process or technology are not likely to carry much weight. If parents want to conceive with ICSI or a gestational surrogate, if they want to select embryos using PGD or Micro-Sort, they will cross borders to do so. And their home countries are not likely to be either willing or able to stop them. The only constraint in these cases is money.

Seeing the Market Connections

A broad overview of the baby business, therefore, shows a landscape marked by variance. Similar clients find themselves in vastly different markets, depending on where they live and how they choose to pursue a child. Theoretically, these markets can be defined as wholly separate entities: the market for orphaned girls in China, after all, is very different from the market for IVF in Milwaukee. But in practice they are intimately connected, because the little girl in China is at some level a direct substitute for the baby that might be produced via IVF.

We have chosen by default to keep these markets separate, but that is not the only alternative. Indeed, another option—and a far better one—would be to acknowledge the various facets of the baby business as part of a broader whole and then to conceive of the market, and regulate the market, as one.

Models of Regulation

But how? What form of regulation—what kinds of rules—would best suit this highly idiosyncratic trade? Before addressing this question directly, it is useful to consider a brief spectrum of options.

The Luxury Model

One possibility would be to treat the acquisition of children like the purchase of fine jewelry. Children are precious, one could argue, just like jewels, and acquiring them entails a certain degree of luxury. Think, for example, of the fifty-seven-year-old New Yorker who gave birth to twins in 2004, or of celebrities like Joan Lunden, who employed a surrogate to give birth to her second crop of children. Aren't these children essentially luxury goods? If so, then we could choose to regulate their production through the same kind of free market provisions that govern the sale of diamonds, say, or speedboats.

We could ensure that property rights are well defined and that the legal environment ensures the enforcement of baby-making contracts. We could posit, for example, that the presumption of parenthood rests with the intended parents—the individuals, in other words, who contractually arrange for a particular child to be born. And then we could extend this framework to include all forms of assisted reproduction, from IVF to surrogacy, sperm donation, and adoption.

Few observers would want to classify any of these transactions as constructing a luxury market. But they effectively function, and could well be regulated, along those lines. Under this approach, access to the market would not be a cause for public concern, nor would equity among the various participants. This is exactly what one would expect in a high-priced luxury market.

The Cocaine Model

Alternatively, we could think of regulating reproduction as we regulate cocaine or heroin. In other words, we could decide that both assisted reproduction and adoption constitute unnatural interventions in the course of human affairs. We could therefore decide to ban them or to push whatever transactions might still occur into an explicitly black market.

In this model, we wouldn't need to define property rights nor enforce contracts, because the central purpose of regulation would be to ban commercial activity in this sector. Instead, we would prescribe clear-cut laws that forge a neat divide between acceptable modes of child production—the old-fashioned ones, presumably—and any of their newfangled, now illicit, competitors. We could ban adoption as a bad idea or a cultural outrage; halt any external creation of embryos; or even redefine sperm donation as an aberrant act. Although such a framework might seem draconian, it already exists in certain parts of the world: most Islamic nations, for example, prohibit any transfer of genetic material, and many countries explicitly forbid reproductive cloning.

Admittedly, barriers of this type are likely to be porous. As described earlier, determined and wealthy parents can circumvent national restrictions rather easily and venture to more lenient locales. Yet their violation of the rules does not negate the regulatory framework itself. In fact, violations actually underscore the clarity of the rules, confirming what is acceptable and what is not, who is a legitimate provider and who is not.

Let's take an extreme example: suppose that Mr. and Mrs. Mamdouh, living in Cairo, cannot conceive a child by natural means. Their culture and community frown upon adoption, and there are no adoption agencies operating nearby. They cannot procure either eggs or sperm from legitimate commercial entities, and they know that IVF with their own gametes will prove futile. So they go quietly to South Africa, where Mrs. Mamdouh is impregnated with embryos produced from a donor egg and her husband's sperm. The couple returns to Cairo, where, nine months later, they proudly give birth to a baby boy. In this case, the law is clear: the technologies and components they sought were prohibited in Egypt, and anyone who offered to assist the Mamdouhs at home would have been operating illicitly. They therefore did their business abroad, consciously avoiding a restrictive but unambiguous regulatory regime.

The Kidney Model

A third option would be to treat babies, and the components of babies, the way we treat kidneys. In the United States, as in most industrialized nations, it is explicitly illegal to sell a kidney, a liver, or a heart. Indeed, under the terms of the National Organ Transplant Act (NOTA), it is illegal for any person to "acquire, receive, or otherwise transfer any human organ for valuable consideration." People can donate their organs posthumously. They can even donate kidneys while they're still alive.[36] But they cannot sell their organs, because doing so would constitute a federal crime.[37]

There are several obvious advantages to this kind of regulatory model. First, by removing the organ trade from any vestiges of the commercial market, it eliminates any concerns over commodification or the "sale of human flesh." The beauty of NOTA in this regard is its universality: it allows no sale of any organs under any conditions in any U.S. state. Theoretically, one could expand such prohibitions to the reproductive realm.

Second, this regime still allows for organ exchange. Every year, for example, roughly fifteen thousand kidney transplants occur in the United States, along with more than two thousand heart transplants and roughly one thousand lung transplants. Many of the kidneys are donated by friends or relatives of the recipients; the remainder, along with all the hearts and nearly all the lungs, come from anonymous donors, who arrange for their organs to be removed upon their own deaths.[38] So a trade in these organs does occur, and people are willing to cede them without any financial reward. Theoretically, one can imagine a similar voluntary trade in eggs, wombs, or sperm.

A final virtue of the organ donor model is its tilt toward order and safety. Organs are not exchanged in an open market; instead, the transfer is mediated by the nonprofit National Organ Procurement and Transplantation Network in the United States, and by similar organizations abroad. These groups have no financial interest in the exchange and no incentive to do anything that might distort or disrupt the trade that occurs under their auspices. So they try instead to make organ exchange as fair as possible, and as medically sound. As doctors, they also make decisions about organ matches along medical, rather than commercial, lines. Under their watch, patients don't get organs because they are willing or able to pay for them. Instead, they get their heart, liver, or lungs depending on how well they match with a particular donor and how long they have been waiting in the queue. And thus the organ donor model is based on a hierarchy rather than a market; it is a system based on rules rather than money.

The problems with this system, though, are nearly as obvious as the virtues. Because although some people donate their organs without financial compensation, most do not. In the United States alone, more than three thousand people die each year while waiting for kidney transplants. In the crudest of terms, the supply that they yearn for is readily available; each year, about sixty thousand people die in automobile accidents, twelve thousand of whom generally leave organs that are suitable for transplant. Yet most of these people do not leave their organs.

In economic terms, therefore, the market for organs never clears. And in human terms, the toll is exceedingly high. If the baby trade were to move to this kind of model, it would likely face a similar problem of shortages: fewer women willing to donate the right kinds of eggs, fewer surrogate mothers, a smaller supply of sperm. At the same time, the black market for these components would probably grow, much as it already has for kidneys and other vital organs.[39]

Still, organ donation remains a viable model for regulating the reproductive trade. It is clear; it is equitable; and it could easily be applied across the whole range of procreative options. Under this model, parents would likely register with some kind of central authority or information bank. They would state their preferences—a blue-eyed child, an egg from a Jewish woman—and explain their situation. Donors would register at some parallel site, and a disinterested authority—a state board, a medical committee, or a dedicated agency—would determine the matches. Arguably, this is the situation that already prevails in foster adoption and, to some extent, in agency adoption. It is also very similar to the British regulatory system, where a government body—the Human Fertilisation and Embryology Authority (HFEA)—oversees egg donation, regulates the (noncommercial) use of surrogates, and approves all requests for PGD.

The Hip Replacement Model

A fourth and final model might be labeled the hip replacement model. Hips (like fertility treatments) are expensive, and the need for their replacement is distributed more or less randomly: some people have perfectly fine hips that work for the duration of their lives, but others do not. When these hips deteriorate, replacements are rarely critical, because people can live without them. Yet forgoing replacement hips would arguably place those who need them at a distinct and tragic disadvantage: like those who suffer from infertility, they would be forced, through no fault of their own, to live a distinctly less pleasant life. If we left hip replacements to the free market, therefore, the pain of bad hips would be distributed along economic lines. Rich people who needed hip replacements would probably get them, and poorer patients would not.

In most of the industrialized world, however, we have chosen to treat hips quite differently. Rather than leave their replacement to a largely unregulated market, we treat their provision as some form of a social good, something that states should worry about and societies agree to pay for. In Europe and Canada, provision comes generally through a state-sponsored system of national health care. In the United States, it comes through a combination of private insurance and government programs such as Medicaid and Medicare.

The results in both cases are largely the same: after enduring waits, completing paperwork, and clearing administrative hurdles, most people who need replacement hips get them for free. And those with healthy hips have borne the costs, either through taxes (in Europe) or insurance premiums (in the United States). State agencies, meanwhile, oversee this constrained market and impose a mechanism for allocation—some way of determining who gets the hips, and when.

Conceptually, such a model would work equally well in the baby trade. All we would need to do, really, is to define infertility as a medical condition and then subject it to the same kind of coverage now afforded other medical procedures. Indeed, several European nations—Belgium, France, Denmark, the United Kingdom—already operate under this kind of regulatory model, as do several U.S. states.[40] And even where coverage does not exist—where fertility treatments are considered more as a luxury good—the financial costs of making such a shift are relatively small.[41] On purely economic grounds, therefore, it would not be difficult to fold infertility into the health-care system and to treat the baby trade as a niche of modern medicine.

What complicates matters is that the provision of babies is not directly akin to the provision of hips. Presumably, people want hips only when they truly need them—when their own joints have declined to the point where walking becomes painful or impossible. There's not much room for choice in the matter (except, perhaps, for some athletes who arguably accelerate their own physical decline).

With infertility, by contrast, definitions become blurred. Sure, the twenty-eight-year-old woman who's had her ovaries removed due to cancer is technically infertile. So is the thirty-five-year-old man who produces no mobile sperm. But what about the fifty-eight-year-old woman who had children in her thirties and now wants a new set with her second husband? What about the gay man who is technically fertile but wants a surrogate carrier to conceive and bear his child? Or the couple intent on enduring round after round of PGD to produce the infant who might save their existing child? If we choose to treat high-tech baby-making like medicine, then someone, apart from the parents themselves, will need to make these Solomonic choices, determining who gets access to what kind of treatment.

In many European states, societies have grown accustomed to ceding such control to regulatory authorities. Britain's Human Fertilisation and Embryology Authority, for example, oversees all aspects of Britain's reproductive trade. It licenses and monitors all IVF clinics, sets price caps for egg donation, and assesses applications for PGD. Although prospective parents may disagree vehemently with the group's decision in individual cases, its overarching powers are rarely questioned.

In the United States, by contrast, this kind of authority would almost certainly come under greater attack. Compared with their European counterparts, U.S. citizens typically are less willing to give decision-making authority to anonymous regulators or to cede personal matters to unelected bureaucrats. Thus in the United States, there is considerably more support for the luxury model of regulation. As one woman—the mother, in her fifties, of newborn twins—expressed, "I had my babies. I paid for my babies. I could afford my babies. Why is it any more complicated than that?"[42]

Similar (though perhaps more subtle) sentiments are voiced by many practitioners in the fertility industry, who worry that regulation of their trade could rapidly become expensive, unwieldy, and unfair. One prominent specialist, for example, argues that any regulation would slow medical progress in his field: "We have been able," he notes, "to sail under regulatory visibility. If we had been under scrutiny, many steps would have been forbidden."[43]

In the United States, moreover, any regulation of the baby business would undoubtedly encounter the deep-seated politics of abortion. PGD would likely be subject to massive regulatory controls, as would any form of IVF that involved the destruction (and perhaps even the creation) of "excess" embryos. Certain kinds of parents (older women, single women, homosexuals) might be subject to greater regulatory scrutiny, and certain procedures could be constrained or even eliminated. Already, we see this kind of deeply political debate playing out in the field of stem cell research, where antiabortion forces have effectively paralyzed federal funding for the research and have compelled states to adopt a crazy quilt of contradictory policies. We see it, too, in the quiet politicking around embryo transfer, and in efforts, supported by the Bush administration, to consider such transfers as adoption.

Weighing the Options

In the end, however, we may have no choice. Because demand in the baby business is not likely to diminish any time soon. On the contrary, changing demographics and social mores, combined with exploding technological prospects, suggest that increasing numbers of people will want to exert control over conception. They will want to control when they conceive, how they conceive, and even, increasingly, the characteristics of the children they raise as their own. Unless we want this market to explode out of control, we as a society have only four viable options.

The first option is to leave the baby business to the normal course of market forces, allowing supply and demand alone to determine the shape of this trade. Under this structure, supply will flourish but only the rich will enjoy its benefits. At the extreme, such a course leads to the grisly future painted by critics such as Francis Fukuyama, who fears a world populated eventually by two subspecies: the GenRich and the GenPoor.[44]

Following that line of reasoning, we could, alternatively, choose to ban the baby business, deciding that its risks and inherent inequities are simply too great. Yet as this book has demonstrated, prohibition at this point seems futile: demand in the baby business is simply too high and the technologies too good.

And so we could choose a third option, treating high-technology reproduction like organ transplants and removing exchange completely from the market. This alternative is more feasible than the first two and is already, to some extent, the operative model in adoption. Again, though, history suggests that expanding this model to the farther reaches of the baby trade would be exceedingly difficult. The supply (of eggs, sperm, wombs, and embryos) is already available and the players in place.

Which leaves us, really, with only one option. If we don't want the baby business left fully to either the state or the market, we need to find a way of splitting the difference. We need, in other words, to regulate it.

Politics: The Opposite of Sex

Usually, this is the point in any provocative book where the author lays out a road map for reform. Having led readers through hundreds of pages of description and analysis; having criticized others' theories and bemoaned the current state of affairs, the author concludes with a plan, an argument about precisely what should be done to fix the problem at hand.

But this author is not going to do that. Why? Partly, it's because offering a plan at this point would be unreasonable: the baby business is running so quickly and expanding so radically that time is likely to render any detail moot. Policy suggestions made in the fall of 2005, in other words, may be irrelevant a year or two later. The bigger reason, however, is that any individual suggestions would actually run against a central argument of this book: the argument that views markets as political as well as commercial entities. Because if markets are political, and if the market for babies is particularly intimate and controversial and complicated, then any single road map for reform—and indeed any top-down strategy of reform—is certain to fail.

What the market needs, instead, is a *politically determined* strategy, one that emerges from a dedicated and explicit political debate. This debate will not be cordial. Depending on the climate of U.S. politics, it could well move to forestall or eliminate certain aspects of high-tech baby-making. Yet the debate itself is vital. Without it, the baby business will either disintegrate into chaos or fall prey to the narrow interests of particular groups.

As a society, therefore, we need to engage the politics of assisted reproduction. We need to decide what pieces of this emerging technology are acceptable, and for whom. We need to decide how much control parents can exert over their child's conception and genetic makeup, and what part of these conceptions we as a society should pay for. These are not easy decisions. In fact, they are exceedingly difficult decisions, Solomonic choices that force us to wrestle with the very meaning of life and love and parenthood. But at the moment, we are making these choices in a purely ad hoc way, depending on the state, the local court system, and the finances of the individuals involved.

Surely, this is not the best way to deal with such dramatic decisions. Instead, we need to go through what will admittedly be a painful fight, defining at least the basic elements of acceptability: are we willing to allow commercial exchange in any aspect of the baby trade? Are we willing to permit parents and their doctors to manipulate the embryos that will become their offspring? How do we determine which procedures and practitioners push the trade too far? Any one person, this author included, is likely to have strong views on each of these questions. Yet the process here is far more important than any single set of conclusions. We need to debate these questions and subject them to the "pulling and hauling" of politics. [45] Without this process, we will never be able to arrive at a regulatory strategy that sticks.

Instead of recommending a specific set of policies, therefore, this book advocates a *process* of political debate, a process that acknowledges the reality of the baby trade and begins to grope toward some kind of regulatory framework. Admittedly, such a process is daunting. But if we break the debate into more manageable pieces—if we conceive of the baby business in terms of principles rather than problems or technologies—we may find a broader space for consensus, and thus for effective policies.

Matters of Principle: Access to Information

Consider, for example, the basic principle of providing *access to information*. Most Americans view information as a public good, akin to the lighthouse described earlier. They want access to information, they are happy to have the government provide this information for free (or require others to do so), and they don't mind sharing this information more broadly. This set of preferences is particularly strong in matters relating to health or safety, something that explains why we have long had things like warning labels on consumer products and dosage information on drugs.

Carrying this principle to the field of reproductive medicine would be relatively straightforward. It would simply suggest a light-handed regulatory regime in which providers of assisted reproductive services were required to inform potential clients of the costs, benefits, and potential dangers of their services.[46] The government could subsequently decide to aggregate some of this data or to commission additional studies of longer-term risks. In any case, the principle would remain the same: to determine which information is important to the health and safety of the American population, and then to provide it.

Already, we have seen political action supporting this principle. In 1992, Congress passed the Fertility Clinic Success Rate and Certification Act, requiring all fertility clinics to submit basic statistical information to the Centers for Disease Control. In 2004, the President's Council on Bioethics recommended stiffer penalties for clinics that don't report their data as well as longitudinal studies of the children born through assisted reproduction.[47] Should Americans decide that they need more information about the effects of high-tech baby-making—about the impact of hormone treatments, for example, or the costs of labor and delivery for mothers over forty—then those kinds of data could similarly be required.

Equity

A second principle concerns *equity*. Again, this is a concept that most Americans, in theory at least, take seriously. We provide equal education for our children; we guarantee equal standing for all citizens before the law. Although this same principle explicitly does not include health care, we do on many occasions extend the notion of equity into the medical realm: kidneys, as noted earlier, are allocated as equitably as possible, and prenatal care has been extended, by law and regulation, to nearly all American women.[48]

Similar extensions could easily be made for various aspects of the baby trade. We could, for example, determine that infertility (under certain conditions) is a disease and that treatment for this disease must be distributed equitably among its many sufferers. Or we could decide that parenting children is a basic right and that we therefore need to find a way to provide this capability to all who lack it. In either case, the principle of equity gives us at least a common language for policy debate.

Note that the equity principle does not promote a particular policy outcome. It simply provides a yardstick of sorts, a way of framing a messy and complicated debate. What is it about reproduction that we want to distribute fairly? Is it a pregnancy? A genetically related child? Or a chance at parenthood? If it's the first of these options, then implementation would involve providing assisted reproduction services to all kinds of prospective parents, at either a subsidized or a reimbursed cost. If it's the second, then we wouldn't need to cover those forms of reproduction that involve third-party sperm or eggs. And if it's the third, we would probably want policies that promote adoption at the expense of fertility treatments. Yet the logic in each of these cases is precisely the same. First, we need to consider what, if anything, we want to distribute equitably. And then we need to decide how to enact this distribution and cover its inevitable costs.

The Limits of Legality

Meanwhile, of course, we also need to contemplate the *limits of legality*. Although the baby business is full of prospects that don't extend far enough—full, in other words, of parents who don't get the children they crave—it also full of prospects that arguably go too far. It is full of technologies that make many people queasy, and of prospects that we in the end may not want to see realized.

A central question, then, is where to draw the line between legitimate and illegitimate practice; between cutting-edge science and science that pushes too close to that edge. In the abstract, this line always looks blurred. It is slipping and sliding around, drawing us down the slope that proverbially ends in disaster. In practice, though, we can draw lines. We can decide what we want to outlaw, and then—with exceptions, of course, and some bumps along the way—we can make these laws work.

Currently, not many of these laws exist. Instead, the U.S. government has been wary of imposing any limits on high-tech baby-making, preferring to let the courts, the market, or individual state legislatures sort things out. Part of this reluctance may reflect a typical laissez-faire response to emerging markets. Unlike its European counterparts, for example, the U.S. government is notoriously loath to intervene in markets spun off from high-technology sectors or to impose regulatory constraints on high-growth industries. This aloofness holds regardless of the specific sector. The U.S. mobile phone industry, for example, arose in a deregulated market, as did the U.S. Internet industry.

In the baby business, though, the reluctance to regulate stems also from a profound fear of religious or ethical entanglement. Because the abortion debate in the United States has been divisive, politicians have been understandably wary of pursuing any policy agenda that touches, even lightly, on the contested question of abortion. As a result, there are no national policies on in vitro fertilization (which entails creating and often discarding embryos); no national policy on preimplantation genetic diagnosis (which inevitably discards embryos); and no policies that address the issues of genetic engineering.

This state of affairs is not preordained. Indeed, even in a political climate rent by the abortion debate, we could still consider where in the baby business we want to draw the line, where we want to limit either technology or parental choice. Some of these lines already exist. Reproductive cloning, for example, is explicitly banned in the United States. So is cytoplasmic transfer, the process in which donor cytoplasm is used to refresh an older woman's egg. We have laws that prohibit birth mothers from selling their children and rules that define the legitimate boundaries of reimbursement.

These rules may not be perfect. They will certainly be violated from time to time. Yet their very existence confirms that we can, indeed, impose workable limits on the baby trade. We can decide which technologies or arrangements push us as a society beyond where we are willing to go. And then we can ban these procedures under either federal or state law.

The Costs of Reproductive Technology

A fourth principle to consider is *cost*, specifically the cost that even private transactions in the baby-making realm can impose on the rest of society. Consider, for example, the babies born to twenty-five-year-old Teresa Anderson in April 2005. Anderson was a gestational surrogate who, for $15,000, had agreed to carry a child for Enrique Moreno, a thirty-four-year-old landscaper, and his wife, Luisa Gonzalez. To increase the chance of pregnancy, doctors in this case transplanted five embryos into Anderson's womb. They all survived, and Anderson subsequently bore quintuplets for the couple.[49] When the babies arrived, news media carried the happy story, showing the smiling surrogate, the delighted couple, and the five relatively healthy babies.

These babies, however, were extraordinarily expensive: the costs of delivery almost certainly ran to more than $400,000.[50] Gonzelez and Moreno paid to conceive these children, but the rest of us—through insurance fees, hospital costs, possibly even special education as the children mature—are paying as well. According to one recent study, the total cost of delivering a child born through IVF ranges from $69,000 to $85,000. If the child is born to an older woman, the cost rises to $151,000–$223,000.[51] The prospective parents in these cases are paying part of these costs—the IVF, the hormones, the multiple medical visits—but we are paying as well.

Meanwhile, we may also be paying the costs that accumulate as these children grow. Currently, about 35 percent of all births resulting from IVF and ICSI are multiples.[52] Although many of these children are perfectly fine, a significant portion of them arrive prematurely or underweight, conditions that can burden them with problems later in life. Approximately 20 percent of low-birth-weight children experience severe disabilities, for example, and 45 percent need to attend special education programs.[53] If multiples thus have a higher risk of both prematurity and subsequent developmental difficulties (they do) and if assisted reproduction leads more frequently to multiple births (it does), then individual choices about procreation are creating costs for society at large. In making policies about assisted reproduction, we need to consider these costs.[54]

This isn't to say that we should refuse to pay or that we should limit the use of technologies that impose societal costs. Instead, again, the cost principle just shows us how to frame a policy debate. If the cost of delivering quintuplets is exceedingly high, then perhaps we should limit the number of embryos that can be transferred in a single cycle of IVF (most European states already have such limits). If the overall costs of IVF babies are deemed too high, then perhaps we should limit access to the technology, or leave it only for those who can pay. In either case, the cost principle suggests a similar policy procedure: to understand the various costs associated with assisted reproduction; to weigh these costs against their benefit; and then to craft regulatory approaches that balance the benefits against the costs.

The Extent of Parental Choice

A final principle concerns the *extent of parental choice*. Although this topic is closely related to both the limits of legality and the question of cost, it is important enough to consider and debate on its own.

Conceiving a child is a deeply intimate act. Choosing to conceive that child is in some ways more intimate still, because parents must make conscious decisions that run from the prosaic (is this the right time?) to the profound: Should I create a second child in hopes of saving my first? Am I too old? Too sick? Too single?

Since the advent of assisted reproduction, we have shied away from any interference in these choices, believing instead that privacy shields essentially all aspects of procreation from government intervention. As the Supreme Court reasoned in a landmark 1965 decision, "Would we allow the police to search the sacred precincts of marital bedrooms for telltale signs of contraceptives? The very idea is repulsive to the notions of privacy surrounding the marriage relationship."[55]

As we enter the expanded world of assisted reproduction, however, it may be increasingly difficult to maintain such modesty. Unlike traditional reproduction, assisted reproduction has the potential to affect society in fundamental ways. Part of this impact is simply cost: the cost of delivering higher-tech babies; the cost of tending to what could be more expensive educational needs; the cost, perhaps, of caring for children whose parents were ultimately too old to raise them through childhood.

But there are other costs as well, and they are potentially far more profound. What, for example, would happen if gender ratios in the United States were shifted by a generation of parents, each of whom was making the simple, private decision to conceive either a boy or a girl?

What if a subsequent generation of elite parents were able to conceive even more elite children, manipulating their gene pool to be taller, smarter, or more athletic?[56] Or if cloning were to become a realistic reproductive option? At that point, procreative choices would become more than personal. They would affect the very core of how we reproduce ourselves and our society.

Thus, as the technology of procreation evolves, we may well want to revisit the bounds of privacy and parental choice. What kind of control do parents have over the fate of their offspring? And what controls must we deny them? Already, we draw these lines in more mundane realms. Under U.S. law, for example, parents can choose to educate their children at home or to send them to high-priced tutoring services. They cannot choose, however, not to educate their children at all. Similarly, although parents can choose to serve their teenagers beer or give them guns, they cannot let their children purchase beer or carry guns to school. In these cases, society sets clear limits on what parents can do, and where parents' desires for their own children must bow before the broader interests of others.

Drawing these lines in the realm of reproduction will not be easy. It will entail an intense political debate across an intimate and often tragic landscape. But we must have this debate, and we must make these choices. We need to acknowledge the market that reproductive technologies have created and then figure out how to channel this market toward our own best interests. To use the analogies laid out earlier, once we decide to approach the baby business as a market subject to regulation, we can begin to determine which pieces of this market should be treated like kidneys, which like heroin, and which like hip replacements. The remainder can stay as jewels.

In 1938, an influential article in *Fortune* magazine took on the topic of contraception. This was a very big deal at the time, because contraception was still illegal in many U.S. states and was sharply restricted in nearly all of them. Noting that the contraceptive industry was indeed a large and prosperous business, the article argued that the lack of regulation in this field was both hypocritical and dangerous: rich people had access to birth control, poor people were denied, and society at large had no way of distinguishing between products that worked and those that did not.

"The mechanism of conception is the mechanism of life," the article began, " . . . yet man has seen fit to suppress it from his speech, hide it from his young, hold it up to shame, smirk at it, peek at it, and villify it." "Worse," it continued, "he has arranged things so that the well to do can evade the legislation and determine (within the limits of reasonable certainty) whether they shall bear children; whereas the poor cannot." Although taking no stand on the religious and moral issues that suffused any discussion of birth control at the time, the article described a birth control industry that was already flourishing and then suggested, "What birth control needs is preeminently legislation, for the spread between reality and the present national law is wide to the point of absurd."

If one substitutes "reproductive services" into this final sentence, precisely the same argument can be made. In 1938, contraception was, to most people, as notorious and repugnant a subject as surrogate motherhood, fetal research, or genetic engineering are to many critics today. Birth control was seen as an aberration of nature, an ill-fated attempt by humans to interfere in what God had wrought. Ultimately, however, the demand for contraception proved too strong to resist. The technology was available, it worked, and the lure of the market was huge. A similar fate almost certainly awaits the next round of the baby trade.

Men and women, as we've seen, have always wanted to control their reproductive lives; presumably, they always will. What today's round of technology has created, though, is an awe-inspiring range of possibilities. The possibility of deciding not only whether to have children, and when, but also which ones. The ability to choose among genetic combinations and specific traits. To choose the method of conception as well as its likely results.

Such possibilities are admittedly terrifying. They cut to the core of what it means to be human, to live, and to love. But they are also, at some level, rather straightforward: parents need an antibody for their child, and they find someone who can provide one. They can't produce that child by old-fashioned means, so they find enhanced solutions.

It's no use being coy about the baby market or cloaking it in fairy-tale prose. We are making babies now, for better or worse, in a very high-tech way. We are procuring these babies from a wide array of sources, and we are pushing deeper into the components of their birth. We can moralize about these developments if we desire, ruing the gods who pushed nature aside. We can decry the fate of our manipulated offspring, closing our eyes and trying to make them fade back in time. Or we can plunge into the market that desire has created, imagining how we can shape our children and secure our children without destroying ourselves.

Notes

Preface

1. See Dick Lehr, "(Older) Mother's Day," *Boston Globe*, May 10, 1997, C5.

2. Clare Dyer, "All We Wanted Was to Save Our Son," *Guardian*, January 14, 2003, 16.

3. This was after four failed attempts at in vitro fertilization. See Holly Firfer, "How Far Will Couples Go to Conceive?" CNN.com, June 17, 2004, at http://edition.cnn .com/2004/HEALTH/03/12/infertility.treatment/.

4. See Felicia R. Lee, "Driven by Costs, Fertility Clients Head Overseas," *New York Times*, January 25, 2005, A1. Cohen probably spent much less because she lived in Massachusetts, where insurance covers the cost of IVF treatment.

5. Letta Tayler, "Adoption Under Scrutiny," *The Gazette*, November 6, 2003, A23; and Alan Zarembo, "A Place to Call Home: The Anger, Tears and Frustrating Runarounds of a Guatemalan Adoption Case," *Newsweek*, July 15, 2002, 27.

Chapter 1

1. Estimating infertility statistics is notoriously difficult. Ten percent is the figure suggested by the American Society for Reproductive Medicine (available at http:// www.asrm.org/patients/FactSheets/Infertility-Fact.pdf). See also Jeffrey Klein and Mark Sauer, "Assessing Fertility in Women of Advanced Age," *American Journal of Obstetrics and Gynecology* 185, no. 3 (September 2001): 758–770; and Elizabeth Hervey Stephen and Anjani Chandra, "Updated Projections of Infertility in the United States: 1995–2005," *Fertility and Sterility* 70, no. 1 (July 1998): 30–34.

2. Technically, infertility is defined as applying to married couples who are not using contraception and have not become pregnant in the course of twelve months or more of regular intercourse. Impaired fecundity, which includes all women regardless of marital

status, encompasses a broader range of medical issues. For definitions, see Elizabeth Hervey Stephen and Anjani Chandra, "Use of Fertility Services in the United States: 1995," *Family Planning Perspectives* 32, no. 3 (May–June 2000): 132–137. For more recent data, see Anjani Chandra and Elizabeth Hervey Stephen, "Infertility and Medical Care for Infertility: Trends and Differentials in National Self-Reported Data" (presentation at NIH Conference on Health Disparities and Infertility, March 10–11, 2005). Conveyed directly to author.

3. See, for example, Madelyn Cain, *The Childless Revolution* (Cambridge, MA: Perseus Publishing, 2001); and Jeanne Safer, *Beyond Motherhood: Choosing a Life Without Children* (New York: Pocket Books, 1996). For data on the related trend of women postponing childrearing, see Ben J. Wattenberg, "It Will be a Smaller World After All," *New York Times*, March 8, 2003, A17.

4. The results of this particular relationship, though, were less than ideal. When Sarah miraculously gave birth at the age of ninety, Hagar was exiled to the desert along with her son, Ishmael.

5. The literature on ancient fertility rites is voluminous. See, for example, Cynthia Eller, *The Myth of Matriarchal Prehistory* (Boston: Beacon Press, 2000); Lotte Motz, *The Faces of the Goddess* (New York: Oxford University Press, 1997); Sir James George Frazer, *The Golden Bough: A Study in Magic and Religion* (New York: The Macmillan Company, 1922); and Riane Eisler, *The Chalice and the Blade: Our History, Our Future* (New York: HarperCollins, 1987).

6. See Frazer, *The Golden Bough*; Eisler, *The Chalice and the Blade*; Anne Baring and Jules Cashford, *The Myth of the Goddess: Evolution of an Image* (New York: Viking, 1991); and Buffie Johnson, *Lady of the Beasts: Ancient Images of the Goddess and Her Sacred Animals* (San Francisco: Harper & Row, 1988).

7. Marcia C. Inhorn, *Infertility and Patriarchy: The Cultural Politics of Gender and Family Life in Egypt* (Philadelphia: University of Pennsylvania Press, 1996), 1.

8. S. P. Reyna, "Age Differential, Marital Instability and Venereal Disease: Factors Affecting Fertility among the North-West Barma (Chad)," in *Population and Social Organization,* ed. Moni Yag (New Haven, CT: Yale University Press, 1962), 55–73.

9. Samuel L. Siegler, *Fertility in Women: Causes, Diagnosis and Treatment of Impaired Fertility* (Philadelphia: J.B. Lippincott Company, 1944), 5.

10. Ibid., 5.

11. Barbara Ehrenreich and Deirdre English, *Witches, Midwives, and Nurses: A History of Women Healers* (Old Westbury, NY: Feminist Press, 1973), 11.

12. For an overview of the literature on witchcraft, see Alan Charles Kors and Edward Peters, eds., *Witchcraft in Europe, 400–1700: A Documentary History* (Philadelphia: University of Pennsylvania Press, 2001), 1–40; also Thomas Forbes, *The Midwife and the Witch* (New Haven, CT: Yale University Press, 1966); Joseph Klaits, *Servants of Satan: The Age of the Witch Hunts* (Bloomington, IN: Indiana University Press, 1985); Merry Wiesner, *Women and Gender in Early Modern Europe* (Cambridge: Cambridge University Press, 1993); and Deborah Willis, *Malevolent Nurture: Witch-Hunting and Maternal Power*

in Early Modern England (Ithaca, NY: Cornell University Press, 1995). For the connection between midwives and witches, see Sigrid Brauner, *Fearless Wives and Frightened Shrews: The Construction of the Witch in Early Modern Germany* (Amherst, MA: University of Massachusetts Press, 1995). For key excerpts, see Heinrich Kramer and Jacob Sprenger, *Malleus Maleficarum,* reproduced in Kors and Peters, *Witchcraft in Europe,* 180–229.

13. Angus McLaren, *Reproductive Rituals: The Perception of Fertility in England from the Sixteenth Century to the Nineteenth Century* (New York: Methuen, 1984), 45.

14. *Aristotle's Master Piece Compleated,* 1731 edition, quoted in Margaret Marsh and Wanda Ronner, *The Empty Cradle: Infertility in America from Colonial Times to the Present* (Baltimore: Johns Hopkins University Press, 1996), 15.

15. According to one source, it was not until the 1920s or 1930s that contraception was no longer believed to cause permanent infertility. Marsh and Ronner, *The Empty Cradle,* 114.

16. These remedies are described in considerable detail in Jacques Gelis, *History of Childbirth: Fertility, Pregnancy and Birth in Early Modern Europe,* trans. Rosemary Morris (Boston: Northeastern University Press, 1991), 26–33; Louis Portnoy and Jules Saltman, *Fertility in Marriage: A Guide for the Childless* (New York: Farrar, Straus, 1950), 3–4; and Siegler, *Fertility in Women,* 5–10.

17. There are dozens of versions of this text, reissued for more than two hundred years. No version is definitive. See, for example, *Aristotle's Master-Piece* (London: G. Davis, 1830–1839); and the discussion in Roy Porter and Lesley Hall, *The Facts of Life: The Creation of Sexual Knowledge in Britain, 1650–1950* (New Haven, CT: Yale University Press, 1995), 36–37.

18. James McMath, *The Expert Midwife* (Edinburgh: Mosman, 1694), 3, quoted in McLaren, *Reproductive Rituals,* 20.

19. James Walker, *An Inquiry into the Causes of Sterility in Both Sexes; with Its Method of Cure* (Philadelphia: E. Oswald, 1797), 13. So widespread was this view that women who conceived after rape were believed to have been complicit. See also Samuel Farr, *Elements of Medical Jurisprudence,* 2nd ed. (London: Callow, 1815), 46.

20. Howard B. Adelman, *Marcello Malpighi and the Evolution of Embryology,* vol. II (Ithaca, NY: Cornell University Press, 1966), 859–861.

21. For a discussion of these theories, see Elizabeth B. Gasking, *Investigations into Generation 1651–1828* (Baltimore: Johns Hopkins University Press, 1967); Charles W. Bodemer, "Embryological Thought in Seventeenth Century England," in Charles W. Bodemer and Lester S. King, *Medical Investigations in Seventeenth Century England* (Los Angeles: University of California Press, 1968), 1–25; Joseph Needham, *A History of Embryology* (Cambridge: Cambridge University Press, 1934), 115–230; and Peter J. Bowler, "Preformation and Preexistence in the Seventeenth Century," *Journal of the History of Biology* 4 (1971): 96–157.

22. James Graham, *A Lecture on Love: or, Private Advice to Married Ladies and Gentlemen* (London: privately printed, c. 1784), 71, quoted in Marsh and Ronner, *The Empty Cradle,* 21.

23. Graham, *A Lecture on Love,* quoted in Marsh and Ronner, *The Empty Cradle,* 21.

24. See, for example, Rachel Lynn Palmer and Sarah K. Greenberg, *Facts and Frauds in Women's Hygiene: A Medical Guide Against Misleading Claims and Dangerous Products* (New York: Vanguard Press, 1936); Samuel Hopkins Adams, *The Great American Fraud: Articles on the Nostrum Evil and Quacks* (New York: P.F. Collier & Son, 1907); James Cook, *Remedies and Rackets: The Truth About Patent Medicines Today* (New York: W.W. Norton, 1958); and James Harvey Young, *The Toadstool Millionaires: A Social History of Patent Medicines in America Before Federal Regulation* (Princeton, NJ: Princeton University Press, 1961).

25. At the time, van Leeuwenhoek's discovery was taken as proof that life originated in semen, and that the spermatozoa—or "animalcules," as they were called—constituted fully formed humans.

26. P. Morice et al., "History of Infertility," *Human Reproduction Update* 1, no. 5 (1995): 497–504. With the publication of *De Sterilitate,* the term *barrenness* also gave way to the more scientific *sterility.*

27. James Walker, *An Inquiry into the Causes of Sterility in Both Sexes; with Its Method of Cure* (Philadelphia: E. Oswald, 1797), 7–8, quoted in Marsh and Ronner, *The Empty Cradle,* 23.

28. For a history of medical regulation during this period, see Joseph F. Kett, *The Formation of the American Medical Profession: The Role of Institutions, 1780–1860* (New Haven, CT: Yale University Press, 1968); William G. Rothstein, *American Physicians in the Nineteenth Century: From Sects to Science* (Baltimore: The Johns Hopkins University Press, 1972); and Richard Harrison Shyrock, *Medical Licensing in America, 1650–1965* (Baltimore: The Johns Hopkins University Press, 1967). For the declining role of midwives, see Judy Barrett Litoff, *American Midwives: 1860 to the Present* (Westport, CT: Greenwood Press, 1978). For a more explicitly feminist account, see Barbara Ehrenreich and Deirdre English, *Witches, Midwives, and Nurses: A History of Women Healers* (Old Westbury, NY: The Feminist Press, 1973).

29. Nicholas Venette, *Conjugal Love Reveal'd* (London: Hinton, 1720), 125, quoted in Angus McLaren, *Reproductive Rituals: The Perception of Fertility in England from the Sixteenth Century to the Nineteenth Century* (New York: Methuen, 1984), 45. See also Deborah Kuhn McGregor, *From Midwives to Medicine: The Birth of American Gynecology* (New Brunswick, NJ: Rutgers University Press, 1998), 158.

30. See Frederick Hollick, *The Origin of Life: A Popular Treatise on the Philosophy and Physiology of Reproduction, in Plants and Animals, with a Detailed Description of Human Generation* (New York, 1872); and James Reed, *From Private Vice to Public Virtue: The Birth Control Movement and American Society Since 1830* (New York: Basic Books, 1978).

31. McGregor, 153.

32. J. Marion Sims, *The Story of My Life* (New York: D. Appleton and Company, 1885), 243.

33. See Sims, *The Story of My Life*; Deborah Kuhn McGregor, *Sexual Surgery and the Origins of Gynecology: J. Marion Sims, His Hospital, and His Patients* (New York: Garland Publishing, 1989); and Seale Harris, *Woman's Surgeon: The Life Story of J. Marion Sims* (New York: Macmillan, 1950).

34. See the discussion in Marsh and Ronner, *The Empty Cradle,* 48-64; and Harris, *Woman's Surgeon,* 247.

35. See Melvin L. Taymor, *Infertility: A Clinician's Guide to Diagnosis and Treatment* (New York: Plenum Medical Book Company, 1990), 11.

36. The discussion here is vastly simplified. For a more complete description, see ibid., 21–35; Daniel R. Mishell et al., *Infertility, Contraception & Reproductive Endocrinology* (Boston: Blackwell Scientific Publications, 1991); Bernard Gondos and Daniel H. Riddick, *Pathology of Infertility: Clinical Correlations in the Male and Female* (New York: Thieme Medical Publishers, 1987); and Mary G. Hammond and Luther M. Talbert, *Infertility: A Practical Guide for the Physician* (Boston: Blackwell Scientific Publications, 1992).

37. David Lindsay Healy et al., "Female Infertility: Causes and Treatment," *The Lancet* (June 18, 1994): 1539–1544.

38. Ibid., 1539.

39. Sylvia Ann Hewlett, *Creating a Life: Professional Women and the Quest for Children* (New York: Talk Miramax Books, 2002), 216–217. See also Jane Menken et al., "Age and Infertility," *Science* 233, no. 4771 (September 26, 1986): 1389–1394.

40. See, for example, Richard J. Paulson et al., "Pregnancy in the Sixth Decade of Life: Obstetric Outcomes in Women of Advanced Reproductive Age," *Journal of the American Medical Association* 288, no. 18 (November 13, 2002): 2320–2323.

41. Although a teenaged girl has more than 250,000 eggs, they die off rapidly with age. See "They Are the Egg Men," *Economist,* September 3, 1994, 79; and Lewis Krey and Jamie Grifo, "Poor Embryo Quality: The Answer Lies (Mostly) in the Egg," *Fertility and Sterility* 75, no. 3 (March 2001): 466–468.

42. Anne Newman, "The Risks of Racing the Reproductive Clock," *Business Week,* May 5, 1997, 96.

43. See Alice D. Domar, "Infertility and Stress," *Family Building* II, no. 4 (Summer 2003): 4; and Domar, "The Prevalence and Predictability of Depression in Infertile Women," *Fertility and Sterility* 58 (1992): 1158–1163.

44. Quoted in Harbour Fraser Hodder, "The New Fertility: The Promise—and Perils—of Human Reproductive Technologies," *Harvard Magazine,* November–December 1997, 56. For a related discussion of how people perceive their own infertility, see Gay Becker, "Metaphors in Disrupted Lives: Infertility and Cultural Constructions of Continuity," *Medical Anthropology Quarterly* 8, no. 4 (1994): 383–410.

45. Elizabeth Hervey Stephen and Anjani Chandra, "Updated Projections of Infertility in the United States," *Fertility and Sterility* 70, issue 1 (July 1998): 30–34.

46. For more on the role of gonorrhea in changing the treatment of infertility, see Marsh and Ronner, *The Empty Cradle,* 89–96. The first public argument about gonorrhea's effect was in Emil Noeggerath, "Latent Gonorrhea, Especially with Regard to its Influence on Fertility in Women," *Transactions of the American Gynecological Society* 1 (1876), 268–300. Related findings appear in William Goodell, "A Case of Sterility," *American Journal of Obstetrics* 10 (1877): 121–122.

47. For a description of early attempts at artificial insemination, see Marsh and Ronner, *The Empty Cradle,* 93–94; and Walter E. Duka and Alan H. DeCherney, *From*

the Beginning: A History of the American Fertility Society, 1944–1994 (Birmingham, AL: The American Fertility Society, 1994), 51. For early attempts at gynecological surgery, see Alexander J. C. Skene, "The Status of Gynecology in 1876 and 1900," *Transactions of the American Gynecological Society* 25 (1900): 425–438; and Howard Kelly, *Operative Gynecology* (New York: Appleton, 1898). For early (and rough) data concerning success rates, see Max Huhner, *Sterility in the Male and Female* (New York: Rebman, 1913), 56; and Joseph Kammerer, "Review of Literature Pertaining to Diseases of Women," *American Journal of Obstetrics and Diseases of Women and Children* 2 (1870): 546–549.

48. See Robert Tuttle Morris, *Fifty Years a Surgeon* (New York: Dutton, 1935), 218.

49. Such experiments with roosters were among the most influential and important early work on hormones. See George W. Corner, *The Hormones in Human Reproduction* (Princeton, NJ: Princeton University Press, 1947), 228–229.

50. Many of the quacks blended easily with more serious researchers. See, for example, the work of Aleksander V. Poehl, *Rational Organotherapy* (Philadelphia: P. Blakiston's Son & Co., 1906).

51. For more on this discovery and the chain of research that led to it, see Corner, *The Hormones in Human Reproduction,* 79–86; Albert Q. Maisel, *The Hormone Quest* (New York: Random House, 1965); and William P. Graves, *Female Sex Hormonology: A Review* (Philadelphia: W.B. Saunders Company, 1931). Much of this early research was supported by the National Research Council's Committee for Research in Problems of Sex, which itself was supported by the influential Rockefeller Foundation. For more on the committee's work, see Sophie D. Aberle and George W. Corner, *Twenty-Five Years of Sex Research: History of the National Research Council Committee for Research in Problems of Sex, 1922–1947* (Philadelphia: W.B. Saunders Company, 1953).

52. Cited in Maisel, *The Hormone Quest,* 44.

53. For a detailed, albeit uncritical, view of this period, see ibid. Contemporary and more scientific accounts include Corner, *The Hormones in Human Reproduction*; and Graves, *Female Sex Hormonology.*

54. From Rock papers, described in Marsh and Ronner, *The Empty Cradle,* 175. See also Fred A. Simmons, "Human Infertility," *New England Journal of Medicine* (December 13, 1956): 1142. Rock, who went on to become one of the leading developers and proponents of the birth control pill, was also one of the most influential fertility specialists of the twentieth century. See Loretta McLaughlin, *The Pill, John Rock and the Church: The Biography of a Revolution* (Boston: Little, Brown and Company, 1982); and Malcolm Gladwell, "John Rock's Error: What the Co-Inventor of the Pill Didn't Know," *New Yorker,* March 13, 2000.

55. For some of Rock's early experiments, see John Rock et al., "The Detection and Measurement of the Electrical Concomitant of Human Ovulation by Use of the Vacuum-Tube Potentiometer," *New England Journal of Medicine* 217, no. 17 (October 21, 1937): 654–658; and Arthur T. Hertig and John Rock, "Two Human Ova of the Pre-Villous Stage: Having an Ovulation Age of About Eleven and Twelve Days Respectively," *Contributions to Embryology* 184 (1941).

56. J. D. Ratcliff, "Babies by Proxy," *Look* 14, January 31, 1950, 42.

57. Sophia J. Kleegman and Mildred Gilman, "Why Can't You Have a Baby?" *Parents,* December 1947, 31.

58. Duka and DeCherney, *From the Beginning,* 31; and Marsh and Ronner, *The Empty Cradle,* 182.

59. Duka and DeCherney, *From the Beginning,* 69.

60. For evidence that U.S. infertility rose slightly during the Victorian period and then declined toward the middle of the twentieth century, see Marsh and Ronner, *The Empty Cradle,* 92–93, 113–122, 185–187.

61. Joseph Wassersug, "More Help for the Childless," *Hygieia* 25 (November 1947): 835.

62. Cited in Roland Berg, "Childless Couples Can Have Babies," *Look* 21, September 17, 1957, 41–42.

63. Albert Q. Maisel, "The Truth about Sterility," *Parents,* January 1953, 44.

64. Data from this period seem to indicate pregnancy rates of approximately 25 to 36 percent. See, for example, Dorothy Schotton, "The Management of Pregnancy in the Previously Infertile Woman," *Proceedings of the Society for the Study of Sterility* 6 (1954): 1; S. Bender, "End Results in Treatment of Primary Sterility," *Fertility and Sterility* 4, no. 1 (1953): 38–40; and Alan Grant, "Obstetric Abnormalities in the Mother and Child Following Sterility," *Fertility and Sterility* 2, no. 4 (1951): 302–303.

65. He also argued that "only a few dozen" of this group were actually qualified as fertility experts. See Albert Q. Maisel, "Beware the Fertility Racketeers," *Park East,* April 1952, 15.

66. These are average figures. The precise probability varied sharply with age. Author's interview with Dr. Norbert Gleicher, New York City, February 2, 2004. For more specific data on pregnancy rates, see Sanjay K. Agarwal and Richard P. Buyalos, "Clomiphene Citrate with Intrauterine Insemination: Is It Effective Therapy in Women Above the Age of 35 Years?" *Fertility and Sterility* 65, no. 4 (April 1996): 759–763; and Hulusi B. Zeyneloglu et al., "Comparison of Intrauterine Insemination with Timed Intercourse in Superovulated Cycles with Gonadotropins: A Meta-Analysis," *Fertility and Sterility* 69, no. 3 (March 1998): 486–491. For a historical account, see Isabella Taves, "New Advances in Female Fertility," *Look,* May 19, 1964, 90–94.

67. Quoted in Barbara Seaman, "Is This Any Way to Have a Baby?" *Oprah Magazine,* February 2004, 203.

68. Figures communicated from fertility clinics and calculated by author in chapter 2 of this volume. See also "They Are the Egg Men," *Economist,* September 3, 1994, 79; and Centers for Disease Control and Prevention, *Fertility, Family Planning and Women's Health: New Data From the 1995 National Survey of Family Growth* (Hyattsville, MD: National Center for Health Statistics, 1997), 7.

69. See "Fertilization Outside the Womb," *Science Digest* 69, January 1971, 90. For a full history of Edwards and Steptoe's work, see Naomi Pfeffer, *The Stork and the Syringe: A Political History of Reproductive Medicine* (Cambridge: Polity Press, 1993).

70. Quoted in Peter Gwynne, "All About That Baby," *Newsweek,* August 7, 1978, 66.

71. Leon R. Kass, *Toward a More Natural Science: Biology and Human Affairs* (New York: Free Press, 1985), 114.

72. Paul Ramsey, *Fabricated Man: The Ethics of Genetic Control* (New Haven, CT: Yale University Press, 1970), 138.

73. See Dion Farquhar, *The Other Machine: Discourse and Reproductive Technologies* (New York: Routledge, 1996), 140.

74. Jocelynne A. Scutt, *The Baby Machine: Commercialisation of Motherhood* (Carlton, Victoria (Aust.): McCulloch Publishing, 1988), 53, 179.

75. Congregation for the Doctrine of the Faith, *Donum Vitae: Instructions on Respect for Human Life in its Origin and the Dignity of Procreation* (London: Catholic Truth Society, 1987), 27.

76. Cited in Andrew Veitch, "How Dr. Edwards Was Brought out of the Cold," *Guardian,* July 19, 1984, 17.

77. Victor Cohn, "Ethics Board Gives Backing to Test-Tube Baby Research," *Washington Post,* March 17, 1979, A1. For the complete report, see Ethics Advisory Board, Department of Health, Education and Welfare, *HEW Support of Research Involving Human In Vitro Fertilization and Embryo Transfer* (Washington, DC: U.S. Government Printing Office, May 4, 1979).

78. See "Making Babies Is Hard to Do," *Economist,* November 15, 1986, 99; and Jean Seligman, "The Grueling Baby Chase," *Newsweek,* November 30, 1987, 78.

79. See Gina Kolata, "Fertility Inc.: Clinics Race to Lure Clients," *New York Times,* January 1, 2002, F1.

80. See, for example, the description in Liza Mundy, "A Special Kind of Poverty," *Washington Post Magazine,* April 20, 2003, W8.

Chapter 2

1. Anjani Chandra and Elizabeth Hervey Stephen, "Infertility and Medical Care for Infertility: Trends and Differentials in National Self-Reported Data," presented at the NIH Conference on Health Disparities and Infertility, March 10–11, 2005, slide 14. Conveyed directly to author.

2. Chandra and Stephen, "Infertility and Medical Care for Infertility," slide 15. This figure refers to the total number of women in the United States who reported in 2002 that they had ever sought infertility services.

3. There are no formal estimates. The figure of $41 million comes from a representative of the American Society for Reproductive Medicine, conversation with author, January 2005.

4. See Michael Gold, "Franchising Test Tube Babies," *Science* 7, no. 3 (April 1986): 16.

5. This calculation was done using inflation rates in medical care, where prices have risen sharply over the past decade. If one uses the basic rate of inflation, the adjusted price would be only $8,394.

6. Indeed, between 1976 and 2000, prices in the personal computer industry fell an average of 27 percent each year. See Ernst R. Berndt and Neal Rappaport, "Price

and Quality of Desktop and Mobile Personal Computers: A Quarter Century of History," presented at National Bureau of Economic Research Summer Institute, Cambridge, MA, July 31, 2000.

7. In some states, negotiated contracts with insurance companies did exert significant downward pressure on prices. Yet prices still rose on average across the United States.

8. See for example, Kimberly A. Johns, "Reproductive Rights of Women: Construction and Reality in International and United States Law," *Cardozo Women's Law Journal* 5, no. 1 (1998); Berta E. Hernandez, "To Bear or Not to Bear: Reproductive Freedom as an International Human Right," *Brooklyn Journal of International Law* 17, no. 2 (1991); and Meredith Marshall, "United Nations Conference on Population and Development: The Road to a New Reality for Reproductive Health," *Emory International Law Review* 10, no. 1 (1996): 441, 471.

9. Douglass C. North, "Institutions," *Journal of Economic Perspectives* 5, no. 1 (Winter 1991): 97–112.

10. Anne Taylor Fleming, "New Frontiers in Conception," *New York Times Magazine,* July 20, 1980, 14.

11. Ibid., 14.

12. See Aminatta Forna, "Wanted: The Perfect Baby," *Independent,* July 19, 1998, 5; and David Plotz, "The Rise of the Smart Sperm Shopper," *Slate,* April 20, 2001.

13. See U.S. Congress, Office of Technology Assessment, *Artificial Insemination: Practice in the United States: Summary of a 1987 Survey—Background Paper,* OTA-13P-BA-48 (Washington, DC: U.S. Government Printing Office, August 1988), 8, 33.

14. Leslie Milk, "Looking for Mr. Good Genes," *Washingtonian,* May 1999, 65.

15. Pascal Zachary, "Family Planning: Welcome to the Global Sperm Trade," *Wall Street Journal,* January 6, 2000, B1.

16. Interview with author, New York, February 9, 2004.

17. According to Schou, the contribution margin had fallen to 70 percent by 2005. This decline was due to the increased cost of hiring donors.

18. Interview with author, Fairfax, VA, March 2004.

19. See www.gayspermbank.com.

20. Data provided by banks to the author.

21. Conversation with author, February 18, 2005.

22. Naomi Pfeffer, *The Stork and the Syringe: A Political History of Reproductive Medicine* (Cambridge: Polity Press, 1993); "They Are the Egg Men," *Economist,* September 3, 1994, 79.

23. For many years, Serono's best protection was the inherent barriers that potential competitors faced. To produce its drugs, it relied on twice-daily urine collections from one hundred thousand postmenopausal donors. Few other companies were willing to establish a similar base of supply. See Alison Leigh Cowan, "A Swiss Firm Makes Babies Its Bet," *New York Times,* April 19, 1992, section 3, 13.

24. Andrea Adelson, "A Fertility Drug Grows Scarce," *New York Times,* February 26, 1995, 26.

25. Della De Lafuente, "Infertility Drugs Growing Scarce: Shortage Alarms Couples, Jeopardizes Treatments," *Chicago Sun-Times,* February 26, 1995, 6.

26. Quoted in Adelson, "A Fertility Drug Grows Scarce," 26.

27. Interview with author, New York, February, 2004.

28. Alan Trounson et al., "In Vitro Maturation and the Fertilization and Developmental Competence of Oocytes Recovered from Untreated Polycystic Ovarian Patients," *Fertility and Sterility* 62, no. 2 (August 1994): 353–362; and "They Are the Egg Men," *Economist,* September 3, 1994, 79.

29. "Biotech Babies," *Economist,* March 13, 1993, 78.

30. Fiona Fleck, "Switzerland: Profit at Biotech Concern," *New York Times,* February 4, 2004, W1; and Doug Bailey, "Is It Business or Is It Revenge?" *Boston Globe,* May 24, 1992, 29.

31. Quoted in Liat Collins, "A Labor of Love," *Jerusalem Post,* September 14, 2001, 7.

32. For one particularly painful story, see Joan O'C. Hamilton, "What Are the Costs?" *Stanford Magazine,* November–December 2001.

33. For some studies of potential effects, see Roberta B. Ness et al., "Infertility, Fertility Drugs, and Ovarian Cancer: A Pooled Analysis of Case-Control Studies," *American Journal of Epidemiology* 155, no. 3 (February 2002): 217–224; and Louise A. Brinton et al., "Ovulation Induction and Cancer Risk," *Fertility and Sterility* 83, no. 2 (February 2005): 261–274.

34. The sale of human organs is illegal in virtually every country. Iran appears to be the only exception. There is, however, a thriving black market for many organs. For a fascinating report on this market, see Michael Finkel, "Complications," *New York Times Magazine,* May 27, 2001, 26–33, 40, 52, 59. For the black market in cadavers, see John M. Broder et al., "In Science's Name, Lucrative Trade in Body Parts," *New York Times,* March 12, 2004, A1, A19.

35. Because there is no central reporting of donor fees in the United States, no precise data is available. These are estimates provided, via e-mail correspondence, by the ASRM. For confirmation of the $8,000 figure, see also Mark V. Sauer, "Further HFEA Restrictions on Egg Donation in the UK: Two Strikes and You're Out!" *Reproductive Biomedicine Online* 10, no. 4 (2005): 432.

36. See Joan O'C. Hamilton, "What Are the Costs?" and James Herbert, "Donation Dilemmas: Selling of Eggs Gives Birth to Controversy," *San Diego Union-Tribune,* September 3, 2000, E1.

37. See www.tinytreasuresagency.com.

38. Interview with author, Boston, November 2003.

39. The details of this story are true. The names, however, have been changed. From interview with author, Boston, March 2004.

40. Interview with author, March 2005. The names have been changed.

41. Interview with author, March 2005. The names have been changed.

42. Instead, patients—and particularly women—tend to blame themselves for failing to become pregnant.

43. As of 2005, nine U.S. states have laws that require insurance companies to cover infertility treatment. Five states have laws that require insurance companies to offer coverage for infertility treatment. The broader questions surrounding insurance coverage are discussed in chapter 7.

44. Interview with author, Boston, November 2003.

45. Interviews with author, November and December 2003.

46. Interview with author, November 2003. For a story of one clinic's efforts to compete, see Gina Kolata, "Fertility Inc.: Clinics Race to Lure Clients," *New York Times,* January 1, 2002, F1.

47. Similar payment options are described in Ann Wozencraft, "It's a Baby, or It's Your Money Back," *New York Times,* August 25, 1996, section 3, 1; and Joan O'C. Hamilton, "A Pregnant Clause," *BusinessWeek,* March 25, 1996, 46.

48. See http://www.arcfertility.com.

49. Interview with author, November 2003.

50. Quoted in Michael Selz, "Birth Business: Industry Races to Aid Infertile," *Wall Street Journal,* November 26, 1997, B1.

51. The Fertility Clinic Success Rate and Certification Act of 1992 states that "each assisted reproductive technology program shall annually report to the Secretary through the Centers for Disease Control." Critics, however, are quick to note that this law has no teeth, because the Centers for Disease Control (CDC) has no enforcement power, and the only sanction under the 1992 law is for the CDC to publish the names of programs that do not report. See Fertility Clinic Success Rate and Certification Act of 1002, Public Law 102-493 (H.R. 4773); Keith Alan Byers, "Infertility and In Vitro Fertilization: A Growing Need for Consumer-Oriented Regulation of the In Vitro Fertilization Industry," *Journal of Legal Medicine* 18 (1997): 265–313; and Jennifer L. Rosato, "The Children of ART (Assisted Reproductive Technology): Should the Law Protect them from Harm?" *Utah Law Review* 57 (2004): 57–110.

52. Interview with author, February 2004.

53. For more data on cost, see Gary W. DeVane, "Optimal Pregnancy Outcome in a Minimal-Stimulation In Vitro Fertilization Program," *American Journal of Obstetrics and Gynecology* 183, no. 2 (August 2000): 309–315; and Bradley Van Voorhis et al., "Cost-Effectiveness of Infertility Treatments: A Cohort Study," *Fertility and Sterility* 67, no. 5 (May 1997): 830–836.

54. Interviews with author, New Haven, CT, December 2003.

55. According to one recent study, for example, 39 percent of women believe that a woman in her forties can conceive and have a baby as easily as a woman in her twenties. Reported in "Women's Health: Survey Shows Women not Informed on the Latest Feminine Health Information," *Women's Health Weekly,* May 22, 2003, 54. Likewise, a 2001 survey conducted by the American Infertility Association found that nearly 90 percent of women overestimated the period when fertility begins declining by five to ten years. See "Fertility Survey Finds Astonishing Results: Only one of 12,382 Women Answered Correctly," American Infertility Association, reproduced at http://www.americaninfertility

.org/media/aia_survey_results.html. For commentary, see Michael Hanlon, "The Last Egg Race," *Scotsman,* October 24, 2002, 8.

56. 2001 data from the Centers for Disease Control.

57. Centers for Disease Control, *2001 Assisted Reproductive Technology Success Rates,* section 2. Available at www.cdc.gov/reproductivehealth/art.htm.

58. Ibid.

59. See Michele Hansen et al., "The Risk of Major Birth Defects After Intracytoplasmic Sperm Injection and In Vitro Fertilization," *New England Journal of Medicine* 346, no. 10 (March 7, 2002): 725–730. For evidence that suggests a more equitable level of birth defects, see "Test-Tube Kids Develop Normally," *Wall Street Journal,* July 3, 2003, D5; Kerryn Saunders et al., "Growth and Physical Outcome of Children Conceived by In Vitro Fertilisation" *Pediatrics* 97, no. 5 (May 1996): 688–692; and Jennifer R. Bowen et al., "Medical and Developmental Outcome at 1 Year for Children Conceived by Intracytoplasmic Sperm Injection," *Lancet* 351 (May 23, 1998): 1529–1534.

60. See Laura A. Schieve et al., "Low and Very Low Birth Weight in Infants Conceived with the Use of Assisted Reproductive Technology," *New England Journal of Medicine* 346, no. 10 (March 7, 2002): 731–737; Michael R. DeBraun et al., "Association of In Vitro Fertilization with Beckwith-Wiedemann Syndrome and Epigenetic Alterations of LIT1 and H19," *American Journal of Human Genetics* 72 (January 2003): 156–160; and Brian Vastag, "Possible IVF-Birth Defect Link," *Journal of the American Medical Association* 288, no. 23 (December 18, 2002): 2959.

61. See Centers for Disease Control, *1995 Assisted Reproductive Technology Success Rates,* Figure 8B. Nearly identical figures appear in the 2001 Centers for Disease Control report. See also Nanette Elster et al., "Less is More: The Risks of Multiple Births," *Fertility and Sterility* 74, no. 4 (October 2000): 617–632.

62. See "Virginia Clinic is Mum on 'Success' Rate," *Washington Post,* December 4, 2001, F6.

63. ASRM guidelines are periodically published in *Fertility and Sterility.* See, for example, The Practice Committee of the American Society for Reproductive Medicine and The Society for Assisted Reproductive Technology, "Revised Minimum Standards for Practices Offering Assisted Reproductive Technologies," *Fertility and Sterility* 82, supplement 1 (September 2004): S7.

64. According to the director of the NICHHD (National Institute for Child Health and Human Development), the demand for fertility treatments is so pressing that many women choose to undergo therapies that haven't been fully tested by clinical trials. See "NICHD Network Identifies Most Effective of a Series of Infertility Treatments," National Institutes of Health, *NIH News Alert,* January 21, 1999.

65. Interview with author, New Haven, CT, December 10, 2003.

66. Quoted in Gina Kolata, "Harrowing Choices Accompany Advancements in Fertility," *New York Times,* March 10, 1998, F3.

67. Quoted in ibid.

68. For a discussion of this dynamic and its implications, see Ezekiel J. Emanuel, "Eight is Too Many," *New Republic,* January 25, 1999, 8–11.

69. One powerful exception is Ellen Hopkins, "Tales from the Baby Factory," *New York Times Sunday Magazine,* March 15, 1992.

70. Interview with author, December 2003.

71. From a PBS Frontline interview. Accessed at http://www.pbs.org/wgbh/pages/frontline/shows/fertility/interviews/sauer.html.

72. States with either a "mandate to cover" or a "mandate to offer" include Arkansas, California, Connecticut, Hawaii, Illinois, Maryland, Massachusetts, Montana, New Jersey, New York, Ohio, Rhode Island, Texas, and West Virginia. Several of these states cover only specific types of infertility; several others exempt health maintenance organizations from providing coverage. See *States Mandating Insurance Coverage for Infertility and Pregnancy Loss,* International Council on Infertility Information Dissemination, available at http://www.inciid.org/insurance.html. See also Saul Spiegel, "Infertility—Causes, Treatment, Insurance and Disability Status," OLR Research Report, February 3, 2005, available at http://www.cga.ct.gov/2005/rpt/2005-R-0145.htm.

73. In practice, though, older women typically purchase more services, such as assisted hatching and preimplantation genetic diagnosis, and a greater number of additional tests. They are also charged higher fees if they choose to participate in shared risk programs.

74. In a related analysis, Hamilton and McManus find that insurance mandates tend to increase the size of fertility clinics in the given state. See Barton H. Hamilton and Brian McManus, "Infertility Treatment Markets: The Effects of Competition and Policy," mimeo, Washington University at St. Louis, September 2004.

75. For a full analysis of the implications of insurance in Massachusetts, see Martha Griffen and William F. Panak, "The Economic Cost of Infertility-Related Services: An Examination of the Massachusetts Infertility Insurance Mandate," *Fertility and Sterility* 70, issue 1 (July 1998): 22–29.

76. Both California and New York require most insurers to cover infertility treatment. But they explicitly *exclude* IVF from the coverage. For the specific provisions, see National Conference of State Legislatures, "50 State Summary of Laws Related to Insurance Coverage for Infertility Therapy," available at http://www.ncsl.org/programs/health/50infert.htm.

77. Communication with author, May 2005.

78. Bette Harrison, "Focus on In Vitro Fertilization: Frozen-Egg Birth Brings Fame to Doctor," *Atlanta Constitution,* October 18, 1997, 5E; and Elizabeth Heathcote, "Stop the Clock," *Independent,* May 31, 1998, Features, 1.

79. See Aileen Ballantyne, "Egg Timers," *The Times* (London), December 1, 2001.

80. Quoted in Sarah Boseley, "Frozen Egg Baby Hailed as Fertility Milestone," *Guardian,* October 11, 2002, 1.

81. Quoted in Harrison, "Frozen-Egg Birth Brings Fame to Doctor."

82. Quoted in Elizabeth Heathcote, "Stop the Clock." See also Gina Kolata, "Fertility Advances Leave Trail of Ethical Questions," *New York Times,* June 5, 1992, A10.

83. Amy Dockser Marcus, "Fertility Clinic Set to Open First Commercial Egg Bank," *Wall Street Journal,* April 17, 2002, D1.

84. Interview with author, January 2004.

85. Interview with author, January 2004.

86. The egg always contains an X chromosome, the sperm either an X or a Y. It is the sperm's chromosomes, therefore, that determine the sex of a child.

87. See Claudia Kalb, "Brave New Babies," *Newsweek,* January 26, 2004, 45–53; and Meredith Wadman, "So You Want a Girl?" *Fortune,* February 19, 2001, 174–182.

88. Centers for Disease Control, *2002 Assisted Reproductive Technology Success Rates.* Available at www.cdc.gov/reproductivehealth/art.htm.

89. Matthew G. Retzloff and Mark D. Hornstein, "Is Intracytoplasmic Sperm Injection Safe?" *Fertility & Sterility* 80 (2003): 851–858; and "Infertility and Inheritance," *Economist,* June 10, 2000, 87–88.

90. "Infertility and Inheritance," *Economist.*

91. Melissa Healy, "Fertility's New Frontier: Advanced Genetic Screening Could Help Lead to the Birth of a Healthy Baby," *Los Angeles Times,* July 21, 2003, 1; and Cary Goldberg, "Screening of Embryos Helps Avert Miscarriage," *Boston Globe,* June 13, 2003, A1.

92. Anjani Chandra and Elizabeth Hervey Stephen, "Infertility and Medical Care for Infertility: Trends and Differentials in National Self-Reported Data," presented at NIH Conference on Health Disparities and Infertility, March 10–11, 2005, slide 23. Note that the total percentage of married women who suffer from infertility and seek some form of treatment is 36 percent, higher than these numbers indicate. Yet treatment in many of these cases includes only a consultation or some other basic service.

93. Chandra and Stephen, "Infertility and Medical Care for Infertility"; and Chandra et al., "Fertility, Family Planning and Reproductive Health: Data from the 2002 National Survey of Family Growth," *Vital Health Statistics* 23 (forthcoming, 2005). See also Suzanne Wymelenberg, *Science and Babies: Private Decisions, Public Dilemmas* (Washington, DC: National Academy Press, 1990), 14.

94. Chandra and Stephen, "Infertility and Medical Care for Infertility," slide 23.

95. See Martha Griffen and William F. Panak, "The Economic Cost of Infertility-Related Services: An Examination of the Massachusetts Infertility Mandate," *Fertility and Sterility* 70, no. 1 (July 1998): 22–29; Tarun Jain et al., "Insurance Coverage and Outcomes of In Vitro Fertilization," *New England Journal of Medicine* 347, no. 9 (August 29, 2002): 661–666; and John A. Collins, "An International Survey of the Health Economics of IVF and ICSI," *Human Reproduction Update* 8, no. 3 (2002): 265–277.

96. A. Nyboe Anderson et al., "Assisted Reproductive Technology in Europe, 2001: Results Generated from European Registers by ESHRE," *Human Reproduction* 20, no. 5 (2005): 1160.

Chapter 3

1. Quoted in Martha A. Field, *Surrogate Motherhood* (Cambridge, MA: Harvard University Press, 1990), 3.

2. See, for example, the discussion in Barbara Katz Rothman, *The Tentative Pregnancy* (New York: Viking, 1986).

3. As chapter 6 describes in greater detail, birth mothers under some arrangements do receive compensation for their expenses. In rare cases, they are paid to relinquish their children. These latter cases, though, are almost always defined as baby-selling and therefore are treated as illegitimate.

4. For reviews of prevailing legislation, see Field, *Surrogate Motherhood*, 155–182; Amy Garrity, "A Comparative Analysis of Surrogacy Law in the United States and Great Britain: A Proposed Model Statute for Louisiana," *Louisiana Law Review* 60, no. 3: 804; and Beverly Wunderlin, "The Regulation of Medically Assisted Procreation in Europe and Related Nations and the Influence of National Identity, Social Cultural and Demographic Differences" (PhD diss., Department of Sociology, University of North Texas, August 2002). For specific provisions in the United Kingdom, see Ruth Deech, "Legal and Ethical Responsibilities of Gamete Banks," *Human Reproduction* 12, supplement 2 (1998): 80–89.

5. Louisa Lee Moon, "Commercial Surrogacy: A Liberal, Feminist Analysis" (PhD diss., Department of Philosophy, University of California, Irvine, 1994), 1; see also I. Sharpera, *Married Life in an African Tribe* (London: Faber & Faber, 1946), 246.

6. Margaret Marsh and Wanda Ronner, *The Empty Cradle: Infertility in America from Colonial Times to the Present* (Baltimore: Johns Hopkins University Press, 1996), 18–19.

7. Pamela Laufer-Ukeles, "Gestation: Work for Hire or the Essence of Motherhood? A Comparative Legal Analysis," *Duke Journal of Gender Law and Policy* 9, no. 1 (2003): 120.

8. For more on the history of wet nursing, see Janet Golden, *A Social History of Wet Nursing in America* (Columbus: Ohio State University Press, 2001); Avner Giladi, *Infants, Parents and Wet Nurses: Medieval Islamic Views on Breastfeeding and their Social Implications* (Leiden, Netherlands: E.J. Brill, 1999); George Sussman, *Selling Mother's Milk: The Wet-Nursing Business in France, 1715–1914* (Urbana, IL: University of Illinois Press, 1982); and Valerie A. Fildes, *Wet Nursing: A History from Antiquity to the Present* (New York: Basil Blackwell, 1988).

9. Wet nurses frequently were also unwed mothers, many of whom had relinquished their children at birth.

10. Carl Degler, *At Odds: Women and the Family in America from the Revolution to the Present* (Oxford: Oxford University Press, 1980), especially 26–51.

11. For more on historical prohibitions on contraception, see John M. Riddle, *Contraception and Abortion from the Ancient World to the Renaissance* (Cambridge, MA: Harvard University Press, 1992); Andrea Tone, *Devices and Desires: A History of Contraceptives in America* (New York: Hill and Wang, 2001); and Debora Spar and Briana Huntsberger, "Midwives, Witches, and Quacks: The Business of Birth Control in the Pre-Pill Era," working paper 04-049, Harvard Business School, Boston, 2004.

12. For a more formal treatment of supply and demand functions in this market, see Gillian Hewitson, "The Market for Surrogate Mother Contracts," *The Economic Record* 73, no. 222 (September 1997) 212–224.

13. See Noel P. Keane with Dennis L. Breo, *The Surrogate Mother* (New York: Everest House, 1981).

14. For more on the Michigan ruling and its implications, see Carmel Shalev, *Birth Power: The Case for Surrogacy* (New Haven, CT: Yale University Press, 1989), 93–95.

15. See Robert Hanley, "Brokers Play Down Surrogacy Case," *New York Times,* February 5, 1988, B5.

16. See Lori Andrews, *Between Strangers: Surrogate Mothers, Expectant Fathers, and Brave New Babies* (New York: Harper & Row, 1989), 86–87. Levin also backed his agreements, reportedly, with threats, promising surrogates that he would "nail them to the wall" if they reneged.

17. See Carol Krucoff, "The Surrogate Baby Boom," *Washington Post,* January 25, 1983, C5.

18. Quoted in Anne Taylor Fleming, "New Frontiers in Conception," *New York Times Magazine,* July 20, 1980, 24.

19. For the first number, see Krucoff, "The Surrogate Baby Boom," C5. For the second, see Field, *Surrogate Motherhood,* 5; Charles Krauthammer, "The Ethics of Human Manufacture," *New Republic,* May 4, 1987, 17–19; and Deborah L. Ibert, "Encouragement for Infertile Couples," *Bergen (New Jersey) Record,* April 1, 1987, A12.

20. The literature here is voluminous. See, for example, Elizabeth S. Anderson, "Is Women's Labor a Commodity?" *Philosophy & Public Affairs* 19, issue 1 (Winter 1990): 71–92.

21. Ibid., 75–76.

22. Gena Corea, " 'Surrogate' Motherhood as Public Policy Issue," press conference, Washington, DC, August 31, 1987, reprinted in *Reconstructing Babylon: Essays on Women and Technology,* ed. H. Patricia Hynes (Bloomington, IN: Indiana University Press, 1991), 131.

23. Arguments along these lines include Anderson, "Is Women's Labor a Commodity?" Christine Overall, *Ethics and Human Reproduction: A Feminist Analysis* (Boston: Allen and Unwin, 1987); Mary Warnock, *A Question of Life: The Warnock Report on Human Fertilisation and Embryology* (Oxford: Basil Blackwell, 1985); Martha Field, *Surrogate Motherhood: The Legal and Human Issues* (Cambridge: Harvard University Press, 1985); and Gena Corea, *The Mother Machine* (New York: Harper & Row, 1985).

24. The straight free market approach is presented most bluntly by Richard A. Posner. See Posner, *Sex and Reason* (Cambridge, MA: Harvard University Press, 1992); and Posner and Elisabeth M. Landes, "The Economics of the Baby Shortage," *Journal of Legal Studies* 7, no. 2 (1978): 323–348. For arguments that reach a similar, though not identical, conclusion, see Carmel Shalev, *Birthpower* (New Haven, CT: Yale University Press, 1989); and Karen Marie Sly, "Baby-Sitting Consideration: Surrogate Mother's Right to 'Rent her Womb' for a Fee," *Gonzaga Law Review* 18, no. 3 (1982–1983): 539–566.

25. Office of Technology Assessment, *Infertility: Medical and Social Choices* (Washington, DC: U.S. Government Printing Office, 1988), 267–270.

26. *In the matter of Baby M,* 537 A. 2d 1227 (N.J. 1988), 58.

27. Described in Louisa Lee Moon, "Commercial Surrogacy: A Liberal, Feminist Analysis," 24.

28. Andrew H. Malcolm, "Steps to Control Surrogate Births Rekindle Debate," *New York Times,* June 26, 1988, 1.

29. Ibid., and Krucoff, "The Surrogate Baby Boom," C5.

30. Jesse McKinley, "The Egg Woman," *New York Times,* May 17, 1998, section 14, 1.

31. Cited in Field, *Surrogate Motherhood: The Legal and Human Issues,* 5.

32. Centers for Disease Control and Prevention, *2000 Assisted Reproductive Technology Success Rates* (Atlanta: U.S. Department of Health and Human Services, December 2002).

33. Helena Ragoné, "Of Likeness and Difference: How Race Is Being Transfigured by Gestational Surrogacy," in *Ideologies and Technologies of Motherhood,* eds. Ragoné and France Winddance Twine (New York: Routledge, 2000), 65.

34. See, for example, the discussion in George J. Annas, "Fairy Tales Surrogate Mothers Tell," in *Surrogate Motherhood: Politics and Privacy,* ed. Larry Gostin (Bloomington, IN: Indiana University Press, 1988), 350.

35. Mary Lyndon Shanley, " 'Surrogate Mothering' and Women's Freedom: A Critique of Contracts for Human Reproduction," *Signs* 18 (1993): 618–639.

36. Janice G. Raymond, *Women as Wombs: Reproductive Technologies and the Battle over Women's Freedom* (North Melbourne, Australia: Spinifex Press, 1995), xxii. Italics in original.

37. Deborah R. Grayson, "Mediating Intimacy: Black Surrogate Mothers and the Law," *Critical Inquiry* 24 (Winter 1998): 540.

38. Even Elizabeth Anderson, a passionate critic of traditional surrogacy, argued in a 1990 article that "if commercial surrogacy used women only as gestational mothers and not as genetic mothers, and if it was thought that only genetic and not gestational parents could properly claim that a child was 'theirs,' then the child born of a surrogate mother would not be hers to sell in the first place." See Anderson, "Is Women's Labor a Commodity?" 79.

39. Cited in Bernard M. Dickens, "Protecting the Human Body Against the Person: French Laws on the Uses of Bodily Materials," *International Journal of Bioethics* 7, no. 1 (March 1996): 16.

40. See the discussion in Sharyn Roach Anleu, "Surrogacy: For Love but Not for Money?" *Gender and Society* 6, no. 1 (March 1992): 35.

41. Warnock, *A Question of Life,* 45.

42. See the discussion in Gillian Douglas, *Law, Fertility and Reproduction* (London: Sweet and Maxwell, 1991), 151–154.

43. For a discussion of the constitutional implications of surrogacy, see Carol A. Crow, "The Surrogate Child: Legal Issues and Implications for the Future," *Journal of Juvenile Law* 7 (1983): 80–92.

44. Andrews, *Between Strangers*, 30.

45. In 1986, the supreme court of Kentucky ruled that surrogacy did not constitute baby-selling "because of the fundamental differences between the surrogate parenting procedure [and] the buying and selling of babies as prohibited by the [Kentucky statute]." See discussion in Christine L. Kerian, "Surrogacy: A Last Resort Alternative

for Infertile Women or a Commodification of Women's Bodies and Children?" *Wisconsin Women's Law Journal* 12 (Spring 1997): 124.

46. *In the matter of Baby M,* 537 A. 2d 1227 (N.J. 1988), 53. Note, again, that Mrs. Whitehead's parental rights were not terminated and that she was granted visitation rights.

47. *Johnson v. Calvert,* 5 Cal. 4th 84, 851 P.2d 776 (Cal. 1993). See also Beverly Horsburgh, "Jewish Women, Black Women: Guarding Against the Oppression of Surrogacy," *Berkeley Women's Law Journal* 8, no. 29 (1993): 29–62; and Grayson, "Mediating Intimacy," 525–546.

48. Angie Godwin McEwen, "So You're Having Another Woman's Baby: Economics and Exploitation in Gestational Surrogacy," *Vanderbilt Journal of Transnational Law* (January 1999): 281.

49. See Gilda Ferrando, "Artificial Insemination in Italy," in *Creating the Child: The Ethics, Law and Practice of Assisted Procreation,* ed. Donald Evans (Boston: M. Nijhoff Publishers, 1996). Note that matters changed after 2004, when Italy passed legislation that explicitly banned many forms of assisted reproduction.

50. The case subsequently went to court, where Muñoz argued that she had not understood the terms of the contract. See Angie Godwin McEwen, "So You're Having Another Woman's Baby," 288–289.

51. Anecdotes abound. See Lois Rogers and John Harlow, "Childless Britons Use US 'Rent-a-Womb,'" *Sunday Times (London),* January 28, 2001.

52. Margot Cohen, "Cash on Delivery," *Far Eastern Economic Review* (March 23, 1989): 42.

53. Sandhya Srinivasan, "Surrogacy Comes out of the Closet," *Sunday Times of India,* July 6, 1997, 1.

54. Abu Daruvalla, "Poles Hired as Surrogate Mums in Illegal Trade," *Independent,* June 4, 1995, 16, cited in McEwen, "So You're Having Another Woman's Baby," 287. Similar cases are cited in Gena Corea, *The Mother Machine: Reproductive Technologies from Artificial Insemination to Artificial Wombs* (New York: Harper & Row, 1985), 214–215, 245.

55. Philip Parker, "Motivation of Surrogate Mothers: Initial Findings," *American Journal of Psychiatry* 140 (1983): 117–119. More recent data are less stark but still indicate that the bulk of surrogates come from working-class backgrounds and have limited job and educational opportunities. See Helena Ragoné, *Surrogate Motherhood: Conception in the Heart* (Boulder, CO: Westview Press, 1994); Isadore Schmukler and Betsy P. Aigen, "The Terror of Surrogate Motherhood," in *Beyond Infertility: New Paths to Parenthood,* eds. Susan Lewis Cooper and Ellen Sarasohn Glazer (New York: Lexington Books, 1994); and Melinda Hohman and Christine Hagan, "Satisfaction with Surrogate Mothering: A Relational Model," *Journal of Human Behavior in the Social Environment* 4, no. 1 (2001): 63.

56. In 2004, California's minimum wage was $6.75 an hour, or $14,040 a year for a forty-hour workweek.

57. In 2004, the minimum wage in Mexico City was 46 pesos a day, or about $4.20. An annual minimum wage income would thus come to slightly more than $1,000.

58. Janice G. Raymond, *Women as Wombs,* xxii.

59. Gena Corea, *The Mother Machine,* 245.

60. Quoted in "Destruction of Embryos Begins at British Clinics," *USA Today*, August 2, 1996, 13A.

61. Interview with author, January 2004.

62. Twila Decker, "What About the Leftovers?" *St. Petersburg (Florida) Times*, March 29, 2000, 1D.

63. Charles Laurence, "Cara Adopted an Embryo but Gave Birth to a Son," *Sun Herald*, April 6, 2003, 80; Stuart Shepard, "Frozen Embryo Adoption on the Rise," *Family News in Focus*, August 14, 2003.

64. Stuart Shepard, "Frozen Embryo Adoption on the Rise"; Suzanne Smalley, "As Pro-Lifers Adopt Embryos, Critics Raise Questions," *Adoption News*, March 24, 2003.

65. See "Embryo Donation: A Family Building Option," RESOLVE Fact Sheet 61; and Deroy Murdock, "The Adoption Option: Frozen Embryo Adoption Offers Hope to Microscopic Americans," August 27, 2001, www.nationalreviewonline.com.

66. David I. Hoffman et al., "Cryopreserved Embryos in the United States and their Availability for Research," *Fertility and Sterility* 79, no. 5 (May 2003): 1063–1069.

67. Quoted in Rita Rubin, "100,000 Frozen Embryos: One Couple's Surplus can Fill Void of Another," *USA Today*, December 8, 1998, A1.

68. Interview with author, January 2004.

69. As Susan Crockin, a prominent adoption attorney, has argued, "If you can adopt embryos, how can you do stem-cell research on them or discard them?" Quoted in Suzanne Smalley, "As Pro-Lifers Adopt Embryos, Critics Raise Questions."

70. See *United States v. Lopez*, 514 U.S. 549 (1995), and *United States v. Morrison*, 529 U.S. 598 (2000).

71. I am grateful to Constance Bagley, David Han, and an anonymous reviewer for instructing me in the intricacies of substantive due process. For a description, see David Han, "Assessing the Viability of a Substantive Due Process Right to In Vitro Fertilization," *Harvard Law Review* 118 (2005): 2792–2813.

72. *Skinner v. Oklahoma*, 316 U.S. 535 (1942).

73. *Griswold v. Connecticut*, 381 U.S. 479 (1965); and *Roe v. Wade*, 410 U.S. 113 (1973).

Chapter 4

1. Reported on cbsnews.com, "Choose the Sex of Your Baby," April 14, 2004.

2. Ibid.

3. Francis Fukuyama, *Our Posthuman Future: Consequences of the Biotechnology Revolution* (New York: Farrar, Straus and Giroux, 2002), 157.

4. Anver Kuliev and Yury Verlinsky, "Place of Preimplantation Diagnosis in Genetic Practice," *American Journal of Medical Genetics* 134A (2005): 105–110; Jess Buxton, "Embryo Screening," BioNews.org.uk, July 9, 2003; and Ben Harder, "Born to Heal: Screening Embryos to Treat Siblings Raises Hopes, Dilemmas," *Science News*, March 13, 2004.

5. President's Council on Bioethics, "Thinking about Sex Selection: Working Paper 3a," October 17, 2002. Available at www.bioethics.gov/background/background2.html. For similar results, see Dorothy C. Wertz, "Patients' and Professionals' Views on Autonomy,

Disability and 'Discrimination,' " in *The Commercialization of Genetic Research: Ethical, Legal, and Policy Issues,* eds. Timothy A. Caulfield and Bryn Williams-Jones (New York: Kluwer Academic/Plenum Publishers, 1999), 171–180.

6. Plato, *The Republic* (New York: Barnes & Noble Books, 1999), 151.

7. Ibid., 150.

8. Ibid., 150.

9. Francis Galton, *Hereditary Genius* (Gloucester, MA: Peter Smith, 1972), 41, 45.

10. Francis Galton, "Eugenics: Its Definition, Scope, and Aims," in Galton, *Essays in Eugenics* (London and New York: Garland Publishing Inc., 1985), 35.

11. See Francis Galton, "Hereditary Talent and Character," *Macmillan's Magazine* 12 (1865), 165; Galton, *Hereditary Genius,* 405–415; and Daniel J. Kevles, *In the Name of Eugenics: Genetics and the Uses of Human Heredity* (Cambridge, MA: Harvard University Press, 1995), 4. See Francis Galton, *"Probability, the Foundations of Eugenics," The Herbert Spencer Lecture Delivered on June 5, 1907* (Oxford: Clarendon Press, 1907), 29–30.

12. Karl Pearson, "On the Inheritance of the Mental and Moral Characters in Man, and Its Comparison with the Physical Characters," *Journal of the Royal Anthropological Institute of Great Britain and Ireland* 33 (1903): 207.

13. Theodore Roosevelt, "Address before the National Congress of Mothers," Washington, DC, March 13, 1905, reprinted in *Presidential Addresses and State Papers of Theodore Roosevelt, Part III* (New York: P.F. Collier & Son, 1905), 282–291.

14. Jesse Spaulding Smith, "Marriage, Sterilization and Commitment Laws Aimed at Decreasing Mental Deficiency," *Journal of the American Institute of Criminal Law and Criminology* 5, no. 3 (September 1914): 364–366.

15. Ibid., 367.

16. *Buck v. Bell,* 274 U.S. 200 (1927).

17. For more on this period, see Paul Weindling, "Weimar Eugenics: The Kaiser Wilhelm Institute for Anthropology, Human Heredity and Eugenics in Social Context," *Annals of Science* 42, no. 3 (May 1995): 303–318; and Weindling, *Health, Race and German Politics between National Unification and Nazism, 1870–1945* (New York: Cambridge University Press, 1989).

18. "Eugenical Sterilization in Germany," *Eugenical News* XVIII, no. 5 (September–October 1933): 90.

19. See, for example, C. Thomalla, "The Sterilization Law in Germany," *Scientific American,* September 1934, 126; and Marie E. Kopp, "Legal and Medical Aspects of Eugenic Sterilization in Germany," *American Sociological Review* 1, no. 5 (October 1936): 770.

20. C. G. Campbell, "The German Racial Policy," *Eugenical News* XXI, no. 2 (March–April 1936): 29.

21. Quoted in Benno Muller-Hill, *Murderous Science* (Plainview, NY: Cold Spring Harbor Laboratory Press, 1998), 44.

22. See Robert Proctor, *Racial Hygiene* (Cambridge, MA: Harvard University Press, 1988), 195.

23. See *Skinner v. Oklahoma,* 316 U.S. 535 (1942). Some U.S. states still have laws that allow for involuntary sterilization, even though they are rarely used. See Michael G. Silver, "Eugenics and Compulsory Sterilization Laws: Providing Redress for the Victims

of a Shameful Era in United States History," *George Washington Law Review* 72, no. 4 (April 2004): 862–891.

24. Some early geneticists were harsh critics of the eugenics movement; others were passionate supporters. For a more detailed treatment, see Kevles, *In The Name of Eugenics*, especially 113–128.

25. Hex-A (hexosaminidase A) prevents the abnormal buildup of a fatty substance called GM2 ganglioside. As this substance accumulates, it progressively damages the nervous system and leads inevitably to death. For more on the mechanics of Tay-Sachs transmission, see www.ntsad.org.

26. As with all statistics, exceptions can occur. Theoretically, Joe and Alice could beat the odds, producing, say, eight children without ever conceiving the deadly combination of two recessive genes.

27. See Kevles, *In the Name of Eugenics,* 217.

28. For more on this discovery and its implications, see J. D. Watson and F. H. C. Crick, "Molecular Structure of Nucleic Acids: A Structure for Deoxyribose Nucleic Acid," *Nature* 171 (April 25, 1953): 737–738; and James D. Watson, *The Double Helix: A Personal Account of the Discovery of the Structure of DNA* (New York: Touchstone, 2001).

29. Recounted in Kevles, *In the Name of Eugenics,* 254.

30. Ibid., 257.

31. See Anne Oakley, *The Captured Womb: A History of the Medical Care of Pregnant Women* (Oxford: Basil Blackwell, 1984), 161.

32. See Heidi Evans, "The Debate Over Who Needs a Sonogram," *Wall Street Journal,* June 20, 1995, B1. For a feminist perspective, see Rosalind Pollack Petchesky, "Foetal Images: The Power of Visual Culture in the Politics of Reproduction," in *Reproductive Technologies: Gender, Motherhood and Medicine,* ed. Michelle Stanworth (Cambridge: Polity Press, 1987), 66.

33. Caroline Mansfield et al., "Termination Rates after Prenatal Diagnosis of Down Syndrome, Spina Bifida, Anencephaly, and Turner and Klinefelter Syndromes: A Systematic Literature Review," *Prenatal Diagnosis* 19 (1999): 808–812; and Ralph L. Kramer et al., "Determinants of Parental Decisions After the Prenatal Diagnosis of Down Syndrome," *American Journal of Medical Genetics* 79 (1998): 172–174. For a critical examination of the impact of these technologies, see Rayna Rapp, "Refusing Prenatal Diagnosis: The Meanings of Bioscience in a Multicultural World," *Science, Technology & Human Values* 23, no. 1 (1998): 45–70.

34. Evidence of this practice, along with sex selection methods in Europe and the United States, has attracted intense criticism, particularly from those worried about the long-term implications for gender equality. See, for example, Jodi Danis, "Sexism and the 'Superfluous Female': Arguments for Regulating Pre-Implantation Sex Selection," *Harvard Women's Law Journal* 18 (Spring 1995): 219–264; and Kelly M. Plummer, "Ending Parents' Unlimited Power to Choose," *Saint Louis University Law Journal* 47 (Spring 2003): 517–560.

35. See Heidi Evans, "Womb with a View: Unborn Babies Star in Fetal Film Fests," *Wall Street Journal,* November 30, 1993, A1; and Marc Santora, "Fetal Photos: Keepsake or Health Risk?" *New York Times,* May 17, 2004, B3.

36. Amy Harmon, "Burden of Knowledge: Tracking Prenatal Health," *New York Times,* June 20, 2004, 19.

37. Quoted in ibid., 19.

38. Interview with author, July 2004.

39. See A. H. Handyside et al., "Biopsy of Human Preimplantation Embryos and Sexing by DNA Amplification," *Lancet* (February 18, 1989): 347–349.

40. A. H. Handyside et al., "Pregnancies from Biopsied Human Preimplantation Embryos Sexed by Y-Specific DNA Amplification," *Nature* (April 19, 1990): 768–770.

41. Interview with author, July 2004.

42. A. H. Handyside et al., "Pregnancies from Biopsied Human Preimplantation Embryos Sexed by Y-Specific DNA Amplification." For other early work in this area, see Yury Verlinsky et al., "Analysis of the First Polar Body: Preconception Genetic Diagnosis," *Human Reproduction* 5 (1990): 826–830.

43. Mark Hughes, "Live Talk: A New Way of Making Babies," at www.msnbc.com, June 26, 2003.

44. Lisa Belkin, "The Made-to-Order Savior," *New York Times Sunday Magazine,* July 1, 2001, 39. This section draws heavily on Belkin's excellent account. For complete data on survival rates, see J. E. Wagner, S. M. Davies, and A. D. Auerbach, "Hematopoietic Cell Transplantation in the Treatment of Fanconi Anemia," in *Hematopoietic Cell Transplantation,* eds. E. D. Thomas, K. G. Blume, and S. J. Forman (Malden, MA: Blackwell Science, 1999), 1204–1219.

45. See A. D. Auerbach, "Umbilical Cord Transplants for Genetic Disease: Diagnostic and Ethical Issues in Fetal Studies," *Blood Cells* 20 (1994): 303–309.

46. Kay Lazar, "Shopping for Genes," *Boston Herald,* October 8, 2000, 1.

47. For the team's account of this procedure, see Yury Verlinksy et al., "Preimplantation Diagnosis for Fanconi Anemia Combined with HLA Matching," *Journal of the American Medical Association* 285, no. 24 (June 27, 2001): 3130–3133.

48. Leon R. Kass, *Life, Liberty and the Defense of Dignity: The Challenge of Bioethics* (San Francisco: Encounter Books, 2002), 130–131.

49. See Michael J. Sandel, "The Case Against Perfection," *Atlantic,* April 2004, 52; see also Sandel, "What's Wrong with Enhancement," available at www.bioethics.gov/background.sandelpaper.html; and Sandel, "The Anti-Cloning Conundrum" *New York Times,* May 28, 2002, A19. Other critiques include Nicholas Agar, "Liberal Eugenics," in *Bioethics: An Anthology,* eds. Helga Kuhse and Peter Singer (Oxford: Blackwell Publishers, 1999), 171–181; and Edward O. Wilson, *Consilience: The Unity of Knowledge* (New York: Knopf, 1998), 273–277.

50. Sandel, "The Case Against Perfection," 53.

51. Thomas Barlow, "Body and Mind: I'll Have a Boy—A Clever One," *Financial Times,* September 15, 2001, 2.

52. Wagner himself, however, was very cautious about proceeding too rapidly with the procedure he pioneered. See, for example, the fascinating and balanced review in Susan M. Wolf, Jeffrey P. Kahn, and John E. Wagner, "Using Preimplantation Genetic Diagnosis to Create a Stem Cell Donor: Issues, Guidelines & Limits," *Journal of Law, Medicine & Ethics* 31 (Fall 2003): 327–336.

53. Cited in Roger Dobson, "Five More Designer Babies on Way in UK," *Independent on Sunday*, February 24, 2002, 5.

54. Anver Kuliev and Yury Verlinsky, "Thirteen Years' Experience of Preimplantation Diagnosis: Report of the Fifth International Symposium on Preimplantation Genetics," *Reproductive BioMedicine Online* 8, no. 2 (December 22, 2003): 232.

55. See Gina Kolata, "Fertility Ethics Authority Approves Sex Selection," *New York Times*, September 28, 2001, A16.

56. Reported at www.reproductivegenetics.com. Actual PGD procedures were performed only in the United States and Cyprus.

57. Anthony Browne and Robin McKie, "Designer Babies: We'll Have That One—It's Perfect," *Observer*, October 8, 2000, 20.

58. See "Sex Selection," Postnote Number 198, July 2003 (London: Parliamentary Office of Science and Technology).

59. See Amy Dockser Marcus, "Ensuring Your Baby Will be Healthy," *Wall Street Journal*, July 25, 2002, D1.

60. See Sylvia Pagan Westphal, "The Rush to Pick a Perfect Embryo," *New Scientist*, June 12, 2004, 6.

61. Interview with Dr. Yury Verlinsky, Chicago, August 2004.

62. Quoted in Westphal, "The Rush to Pick a Perfect Embryo," 7.

63. Stéphane Viville and Deborah Pergament, "Results of a Survey of the Legal Status and Attitudes Towards Preimplantation Genetic Diagnosis Conducted in 13 Different Countries," *Prenatal Diagnosis* 18 (1998): 1374–1380.

64. See Catherine Madden, "Women Wait for Perfect Babies," *Sunday Times (Perth)*, June 6, 2004, 18; and Comité Consultatif National d'Ethique pour les Sciences de la Vie et de la Santé, "Reflections on an Extension of Pre-Implantation Genetic Diagnosis," July 4, 2002. Technically, Germany allows intervention only if it is necessary to save the embryo itself.

65. Reported in Rachel Shabi, "Baby Chase," *Guardian*, June 26, 2004, 14. Matters subsequently changed in Italy, where more restrictive legislation was passed in 2004.

66. See Warren Hoge, "Britain: Baby Born to Couple Who Want Stem Cells," *New York Times*, June 20, 2003, A8.

67. Kate O'Hanlon, "Parents Permitted to Screen Embryos to Match Sick Child's Tissue Type," *Independent*, May 20, 2003.

68. Clare Dyer, "All We Wanted Was to Save our Son," *Guardian*, January 14, 2003, 16.

69. Gerard Seenan, " 'Designer Baby' Parents Give Away Male Embryo," *Guardian*, March 5, 2001, 12.

70. Ruth Deech, quoted in Michelle Nichols, "Baby Hope Couple Give Up Fight," *Scotsman*, March 5, 2001, 3.

71. The practice of sex selection is roundly condemned by bioethicists, most practicing fertility specialists, and the public at large. See, for example, E. Scott Sills et al., "Preimplantation Genetic Diagnosis: Considerations for Use in Elective Embryo Sex Selection," *Journal of Assisted Reproduction and Genetics* 16, no. 10 (1999): 509–511; Gina Kolata, "Fertility Society Opposes Choosing Embryos Just for Sex Selection," *New York Times*, February 16, 2002, A16; and David Montgomery, "No Gender Choice in UK,"

Scotsman, October 5, 2000, 2. In the United States, the Ethics Committee of the American Society for Reproductive Medicine initially gave its qualified approval for the use of sex selection in PGD but subsequently revised its opinion. See Ethics Committee of the American Society of Reproductive Medicine, "Sex Selection and Preimplantation Genetic Diagnosis," *Fertility and Sterility* 72, issue 4 (October 1999): 595–598.

72. Robert L. Sinsheimer, "The Prospect of Designed Genetic Change," *Engineering and Science* 32 (April 1969): 8, 13.

73. A similar phenomenon has already occurred as a result of prenatal screening. See Michael Kaback et al., "Tay-Sachs Disease: Carrier Screening, Prenatal Diagnosis, and the Molecular Era," *Journal of the American Medical Association* 270, no. 19 (November 17, 1993): 2307–2315.

74. See Yury Verlinsky et al., "Preimplantation Diagnosis for Early-Onset Alzheimer Disease Caused by V717L Mutation," *Journal of the American Medical Association* 287, no. 8 (February 27, 2002): 1018–1021.

75. See, for example, the discussion with regard to Huntington's disease in Peter R. Braude et al., "Non-Disclosure Preimplantation Genetic Diagnosis for Huntington's Disease: Practical and Ethical Dilemmas," *Obstetrical & Gynecological Survey* 54, no. 7 (July 1999): 432–434; and J. D. Schulman et al., "Preimplantation Genetic Testing for Huntington Disease and Certain Other Dominantly Inherited Disorders," *Clinical Genetics* 49 (1996): 57–58.

76. Celia W. Dugger, "Modern Asia's Anomaly: The Girls Who Don't Get Born," *New York Times,* May 6, 2001, section 4, 4. For a detailed examination of this phenomenon, see Valerie M. Hudson and Andrea M. den Boer, *Bare Branches: Security Implications of Asia's Surplus Male Population* (Cambridge, MA: MIT Press, 2004), especially 171–172; Ansley J. Coale and Judith Banister, "Five Decades of Missing Females in China," *Demography* 31 (1994): 459–479; and Vicki G. Norton, "Unnatural Selection: Nontherapeutic Pre-Implantation Genetic Screening and Proposed Regulation," *UCLA Law Review* 41 (1994): 1600.

77. For an argument along similar lines, see Matt Ridley, "The New Eugenics," *National Review* 52, issue 14 (July 31, 2000): 34–36.

78. Sandel, "The Case Against Perfection," 57.

79. Interview with author, July 2004.

Chapter 5

1. According to a 2002 survey, 10 percent of fertility clinic directors said they were in favor of human reproductive cloning. See Judy E. Stern et al., "Attitudes on Access to Services at Assisted Reproductive Technology Clinics: Comparisons with Clinic Policy," *Fertility & Sterility* 77, no. 3 (March 2002): 537–541.

2. Indeed, the idea of cloning has even earlier precursors in Greek and Roman mythology. The goddess Athena, for example, sprang fully formed from the head of Zeus.

3. For a description of Spemann's work, see Ian Wilmut, Keith Campbell, and Colin Tudge, *The Second Creation: Dolly and the Age of Biological Control* (Cambridge,

MA: Harvard University Press, 2000), 66–73; and Gina Kolata, *Clone: The Road to Dolly and the Path Ahead* (New York: William Morrow and Company, 1998), 57–61. See also Hans Spemann, *Embryonic Development and Induction* (New Haven, CT: Yale University Press, 1938).

4. Reproduced in Kolata, *Clone,* 65.

5. See J. B. S. Haldane, "Biological Possibilities for the Human Species in the Next Ten Thousand Years," reprinted in *Man and His Future,* ed. Gordon Wolstenholme (Boston: Little, Brown and Company, 1963). For additional commentary from this period, see Joshua Lederberg, "Unpredictable Variety Still Rules Human Reproduction," *Washington Post,* September 30, 1967, A16; Leon R. Kass, "Genetic Tampering," *Washington Post,* November 3, 1967, A20; and Paul Ramsey, "Shall We Reproduce?" *Journal of the American Medical Association* (June 12, 1972): 1480–1485.

6. John A. Osmundsen, "Geneticist Asks More Emphasis on Inborn Diversity of Humans," *New York Times,* September 9, 1963, 29; and "The Heretical Professor," *Wall Street Journal,* October 2, 1963, 18.

7. Harris Brotman, "Engineering the Birth of Cattle," *New York Times,* May 15, 1983, 339.

8. See the description in Wilmut et al., *The Second Creation,* 196.

9. See I. Wilmut et al., "Viable Offspring Derived from Fetal and Adult Mammalian Cells," *Nature* 385 (February 27, 1997): 810–813; and K. Campbell et al., "Sheep Cloned by Nuclear Transfer from a Cultured Cell Line," *Nature* 380 (March 7, 1996): 64–66. The breakthroughs that led to Dolly came on the backs of a series of experiments, some of which led to the birth of two other cloned sheep—Megan and Morag—before Dolly. Wilmut and Campbell actually consider their births to be scientifically more important. See Wilmut et al., *The Second Creation,* 183–207.

10. See Wilmut et al., *The Second Creation,* 222.

11. "Remarks by the President at Announcement of Cloning Legislation," June 9, 1997.

12. See Robin Herman, "European Bioethics Panel Denounces Human Cloning," *Washington Post,* June 10, 1997; and Kathy Lewis, "Leaders Wrap up Summit," *Dallas Morning News,* June 23, 1997, 1A.

13. In Leon R. Kass, "The Wisdom of Repugnance," *New Republic,* June 2, 1997, 17–26.

14. Quoted in Kolata, *Clone,* 221.

15. Wilmut et al., *The Second Creation,* 5.

16. See Camillo Fracassini, "Dolly the Sheep's Creator Admits She May Have to Be Put Down," *Scotsman,* January 6, 2002, 1.

17. David Firm and Geoff Dyer, "Disease Leads to Destruction of Dolly the Sheep," *Financial Times,* February 14, 2003, 3; and Charles Arthur, "Early Death of Dolly the Sheep Sparks Warning on Cloning," *Independent,* February 15, 2003, 10.

18. See "Giant Sheep Clones Worry Scientists," *Sunday Times* (London), March 10, 1996, 1; and JoAnn Jacobsen-Wells, "Genetic Mapping Helps Breeders Locate Prime Cattle," *Salt Lake City Tribune,* December 22, 1991, B1.

19. See Stephen Strauss, "Hello Dolly: It's So Scary to See You," *Globe and Mail,* March 1, 1997, A8; and Marj Charlier, "New Breed of Ranchers is Cloning Cows," *Wall Street Journal,* February 22, 1989, Section 2, 5.

20. Gina Kolata, "On Cloning Humans: 'Never' Turns Swiftly into 'Why Not'" *New York Times,* December 2, 1997, A1; and Deborah Kades, "Infigen Introduces Its Golden Calf," *Wisconsin State Journal,* October 6, 2001, F10. The cow was actually sold while still in the womb. She was delivered in September 2001.

21. Trebor Banstetter, "Ranchers Deal with Realities of Cloning," *Fort-Worth Star-Telegram,* January 27, 2002.

22. Denise Gellen, "Biotech Companies Trying to Milk Cloning for Profit," *Los Angeles Times,* December 16, 2001, part 3, 1.

23. Roger Highfield, "World's First Cloned Rabbits," *Vancouver Sun,* March 30, 2002, A8.

24. William Allen, "MU Scientists Alter Pig's Genetic Makeup to Aid in Organ Transplants for People," *St. Louis Post-Dispatch,* January 5, 2002, 15; and Jill Stevenson, "The Six Years Which Transformed Medicine," *Scotsman,* January 5, 2002, 3.

25. The name CC was also short for "copy cat."

26. See the description in Charles Graeber, "How Much Is That Doggy in the Vitro?" *Wired,* March 2000.

27. Gina Kolata, "What Is Warm and Fuzzy Forever? With Cloning, Kitty," *New York Times,* February 15, 2002, A1; and Taeyoung Shin et al., "Cell Biology: A Cat Cloned by Nuclear Transplantation," *Nature.com,* February 14, 2002.

28. Company spokesman Ben Carlson, reported in Joanna Weiss, "Cloned Cat Raises Prospect of Boutique Pet Creation," *Boston Globe,* February 15, 2002, A3.

29. Todd Ackerman, "Pet Owners Think Cloning Is Cat's Meow," *Houston Chronicle,* February 16, 2002, A33.

30. Mary Vallis, "Double Your Cat's Nine Lives for $50,000," *National Post,* May 15, 2004, RB1.

31. Euan Ferguson, "Just What the World Needs—Another Tiddles," *Observer,* February 17, 2002, 28.

32. As mentioned later, small bits of genetic matter remain outside the nucleus, in the cytoplasm of the egg cell. Scientists do not know precisely how this matter interacts with the nucleus.

33. See Jennifer Wolff, "Extreme Baby Making," *SELF,* January 2004, 107–108.

34. Blood tests on two of these children confirmed that they carried mitochondrial DNA from two different maternal sources. See Jason A. Barritt et al., "Mitochondria in Human Offspring Derived from Ooplasmic Transplantation," *Human Reproduction* 16, no. 3 (March 2001): 513–516. See also S. E. Lanzendorf et al., "Pregnancy Following Transfer of Ooplasm from Cryopreserved Thawed Donor Oocytes into Recipient Oocytes," *Fertility & Sterility* 71, no. 3 (March 1999): 575–577.

35. Denise Grady, "Pregnancy Created Using Egg Nucleus of Infertile Woman," *New York Times,* October 14, 2003, A1; and "Not Cloning," *Economist,* October 18, 2003, 79. Initially, there were three fetuses, but selective reduction reduced the number to two.

36. American Society for Reproductive Medicine, "Embryo Splitting for Infertility Treatment," *Fertility & Sterility* 67, issue 5, supplement 1 (May 1997): 4s–5s. For an intriguing discussion of the role cloning could play in fertility treatment, see John A. Robertson, "Liberty, Identity, and Human Cloning," *Texas Law Review* 76 (May 1998): 1371–1456.

37. Conversation with author, September 2004.

38. Conversation with author, July 2004. Seed reports, however, that his greatest demand came from couples suffering from infertility.

39. Wilmut et al., *The Second Creation,* 5.

40. Conversation with author, July 2004.

41. "Profile: Dr. Severino Antinori," BBC News, August 7, 2001. Accessed at http://news.bbc.co.uk/1/hi/sci/tech/1477689.stm.

42. Raja Mishra, "A Try to Clone Human Being Is Set to Start," *Boston Globe,* February 12, 2002, A1.

43. Ibid.

44. Brian Alexander, "(You)²," *Wired,* February 2001.

45. Professor Robert Winston, quoted in Lois Rogers, "Send in the Clones," *Sunday Times* (London), December 29, 2002, 11.

46. For more on the Raëlians, see Margaret Talbot, "A Desire to Duplicate," *New York Times Magazine,* February 4, 2001, 40–45, 67–68.

47. Quoted in ibid., 40.

48. Quoted in Alexander, "(You)²."

49. Arlene Weintraub, "Repairing the Engines of Life," *BusinessWeek,* May 24, 2004, 101; American Diabetes Association, "Economic Costs of Diabetes in the U.S. in 2002," *Diabetes Care* 26, no. 3 (March 2003): 917–932; and www.kingwoodcable.com/martone/parkinson.htm.

50. By way of comparison, worldwide sales for antidepressants like Prozac were nearly $20 billion in 2003; sales for Viagra were around $2 billion.

51. James A. Thomson et al., "Embryonic Stem Cell Lines Derived from Human Blastocysts," *Science* 282, no. 5391 (November 6, 1998): 1145–1147.

52. See Rick Weiss, "Crucial Human Cell Isolated, Multiplied," *Washington Post,* November 6, 1998, A1. One of these teams, based at Johns Hopkins University, actually produced its stem cell lines at the same time as Thomson.

53. For an elaboration of this argument, see Debora L. Spar, "The Business of Stem Cells," *New England Journal of Medicine* 351, no. 3 (July 15, 2004): 211–213.

54. "Remarks by the President at Announcement of Cloning Legislation," The White House, Office of the Press Secretary, June 9, 1997.

55. See Joan Stephenson, "Green Light for Federally Funded Research on Embryonic Stem Cells," *JAMA* 284, no. 14 (October 11, 2000): 1773–1774.

56. See Heidi Forester and Emily Ramsey, "The Law Meets Reproductive Technology: The Prospect of Human Cloning," in *Cloning and the Future of Human Embryo Research,* ed. Paul Lauritzen (New York: Oxford University Press, 2001), 203.

57. Quoted in Rick Weiss and Ceci Connolly, "Experts Urge Ban on Cloned Babies," *Washington Post,* January 19, 2002, A1.

58. See Elias Zerhouni, "Stem Cell Programs," *Science* 300 (May 9, 2003): 911; and Justin Gillis and Rick Weiss, "NIH: Few Stem Cell Colonies Likely Available for Research," *Washington Post,* March 3, 2004, A3.

59. See National Institutes of Health, "Information on Eligibility Criteria for Federal Funding of Research on Embryonic Stem Cells," http://stemcells.nih.gov/research/registry/eligibilityCriteria.asp; and Gillis and Weiss, "Few Stem Cell Colonies Likely Available for Research."

60. See Jonathan Shaw, "Stem-Cell Science," *Harvard Magazine,* July–August 2004, 39. During this time, the Department of Health and Human Services maintained that because stem cells are not capable of sustaining life, they were not subject to a 1996 amendment prohibiting federal funding for embryo research.

61. Quoted in Rick Weiss, "An Uncertain Year for Cloning Laws; Ban on Embryo Research Seen as Unlikely," *Washington Post,* December 26, 2002, A1.

62. See Andrea L. Bonnicksen, "Crafting Cloning Policies," in *Human Cloning: Science, Ethics, and Public Policy,* ed. Barbara MacKinnon (Chicago: University of Illinois Press, 2000), 118–120; and Dan Verango, "States Dive into Stem Cell Debates," *USAToday,* April 21, 2004, D1.

63. Shaw, "Stem-Cell Science," 39.

64. James Q. Wilson, "The Paradox of Cloning," *Weekly Standard,* May 26, 1997, 23.

65. For a discussion of the stem cell "brain drain," see Charles C. Mann, "The First Cloning Superpower," *Wired,* January 2003, 114–123, 142–143; and Peg Brickley, "Scientists Seek Passports to Freer Environments," *The Scientist,* August 20, 2001, 36–39. For a brief description of private sector activity, see President's Council on Bioethics, *Human Cloning and Human Dignity: An Ethical Inquiry* (Washington, DC: The President's Council on Bioethics, 2002); and "The Future of Stem Cells," *Financial Times & Scientific American Special Report,* July 2005, A28–A30.

66. See Rick Weiss, "Free to Be Me: Would-Be Cloners Pushing the Debate," *Washington Post,* May 12, 2001, A1; Steve Mitchell, "Most Americans Favor Therapeutic Cloning," *United Press International,* March 19, 2003; and Lee M. Silver, *Remaking Eden* (New York: Perennial, 2002), 108.

67. Mann, "First Cloning Superpower"; and Carina Dennis, "Stem Cells Rise in the East," *Nature* 419 (September 26, 2002): 334.

68. Andrew Pollack, "Medical and Ethical Issues Cloud Cloning for Therapy," *New York Times,* February 13, 2004, A1.

69. Clive Cookson, "Bright Hopes at Embryonic Stage: Scientists Believe Approval for Human Cloning Research will Make Britain a Leader in Stem Cell Development," *Financial Times,* August 12, 2004, 2; Gareth Cook, "U.S. Stem Cell Research Lagging Without Aid," *Boston Globe,* May 23, 2004, A1.

70. Judy Siegel, "No to Human Cloning, Yes to Stem Cell Research," *Jerusalem Post,* January 1, 2003, 5; and Jane Burgermeister, "Some Success for Czech Biotech," *The Scientist,* July 26, 2004.

71. "Dolly Was a Red Herring," *Economist,* May 3, 2003, 41.

72. See Mann, "The First Cloning Superpower," 114; Chang Ai-Lien, "Local Firm Ties Up with Aussie Centre for Edge in Stem Cell Research," *Straits Times,* July 21, 2004; and "Send in the Clones," 66.

73. For a review of the politics and business of contraception, see Debora L. Spar and Briana Huntsberger, "Midwives, Witches and Quacks: The Business of Birth Control in the Pre-Pill Era," working paper 04-049, Harvard Business School, Boston, 2004; and Andrea Tone, *Devices and Desires* (New York: Hill and Wang, 2001).

74. Charles Krauthammer, "A Secular Argument Against Research Cloning," *The New Republic Online,* April 29, 2002.

75. For example, the Reproductive Cloning Network (www.reproductivecloning .net), the Human Cloning Foundation (www.humancloning.org), and Clone Rights United (www.clonerights.com).

76. See J. Tesarik, "Reproductive Semi-Cloning Respecting Biparental Embryo Origin," *Human Reproduction* 17, no. 8 (August 2002): 1933–1937; and J. Tesarik and C. Mendoza, "Using the Male Gamete for Assisted Reproduction: Past, Present, and Future," *Journal of Andrology* 24, no. 3 (May 1, 2003): 317–328. See also Rick Weiss, "In Laboratory, Ordinary Cells are Turned into Eggs," *Washington Post,* May 2, 2003, A1; William J. Cromie, "Sperm Cells Made in Laboratory Can Fertilize Eggs," *Harvard Gazette,* December 11, 2003.

77. Quoted in Rick Weiss, "Free to Be Me," A1. For a more rigorous examination of this position, see John A. Robertson, "Liberty, Identity and Human Cloning," *Texas Law Review* 76 (May 1998): 1371–1457. Robertson is a leading advocate for defining "procreative liberty" to include reproductive cloning.

Chapter 6

1. From a post at www.frua.org, a chat room for parents interested in adopting from Russia and Ukraine.

2. Quoted on "Internet Adoptions," *CNN: The Point with Greta Van Susteren,* January 22, 2001.

3. For critiques along these lines, see, for example, Jacqueline Bhabha, "Moving Babies: Globalization, Markets, and Transnational Adoption," *Fletcher Forum of World Affairs* 28 (Summer 2004): 181–196; Anne L. Babb, *Ethics in American Adoption* (Westport, CT: Bergin & Garvey, 1999); and Christine Gailey, "Seeking 'Baby Right': Race, Class, and Gender in US International Adoption," in *Yours, Mine, Ours . . . and Theirs: International Adoption,* eds. Anne-Lise Rygvold et al. (Oslo: University of Oslo, 2000).

4. See Drucilla Cornell, *At the Heart of Freedom: Feminism, Sex and Equality* (Princeton, NJ: Princeton University Press, 1998); and Emma Nicholson, "Red Light on Human Traffic," *Guardian Unlimited,* July 1, 2004, available at www.guardian.co.uk/ child/story/0,7369,1250908,00.html. For a critical response, see Carra E. Greenberg and Diane B. Kunz, "Enemies of Intercountry Adoption," mimeo, Center for Adoption Policy, 2005.

5. Adoption data are surprisingly difficult to find, since they are no longer collected in the United States by a single organization. For recent statistics, see National Adoption Information Clearinghouse, "How Many Children Were Adopted in 2000 and 2001?" (Washington, DC: National Adoption Information Clearinghouse, August 2004).

6. Peter Selman, "Trends in Intercountry Adoption 1998–2003: A Review of Recent Statistics for Receiving States," Adoption Working Paper 1, School of Geography, Politics and Sociology, University of Newcastle upon Tyne, work in progress, March 22, 2005.

7. For descriptions of adoption's long history, see E. Wayne Carp, *Family Matters: Secrecy and Disclosure in the History of Adoption* (Cambridge, MA: Harvard University Press, 1998); Leo Albert Huard, "The Law of Adoption: Ancient and Modern," *Vanderbilt Law Review* 9 (1956): 743–763; and Stephen B. Presser, "The Historical Background of the American Law of Adoption," *Journal of Family Law* 11 (1971): 443–516.

8. For more on the apprentice system, see Philippe Ariès, *Centuries of Childhood*, trans. Robert Baldick (London: Pimlico, 1996).

9. Arthur Wallace Calhoun, *A Social History of the American Family from Colonial Times to the Present* (New York: Arno Press, 1973), 306–307, 232.

10. See the description in John Demos, *A Little Commonwealth: Family Life in Plymouth County* (New York: Oxford University Press, 1970), 73–75; see also Margaret Marsh and Wanda Ronner, *The Empty Cradle: Infertility in America from Colonial Times to the Present* (Baltimore: Johns Hopkins University Press, 1996), 17–20.

11. *Vidal v. Commagere,* 13 La. Ann. 516(1858). Cited in Presser, "Historical Background of the American Law of Adoption," 461.

12. See the discussion in Presser, "Historical Background of the American Law of Adoption," 463–464.

13. "An Act to Provide for the Adoption of Children," Acts and Resolves passed by the General Court of Massachusetts, Chapter 324 (1851).

14. Julie Berebitsky, *Like Our Very Own: Adoption and the Changing Culture of Motherhood, 1851–1950* (Lawrence, KS: University Press of Kansas, 2000), 23. For other state laws during this period, see William H. Whitmore, *The Law of Adoption in the United States and Especially Massachusetts* (Albany, NY: Joel Munsell, 1876), 79–83; and Jamil S. Zainaldin, "The Emergence of a Modern American Family Law: Child Custody, Adoption, and the Courts, 1796–1851," *Northwestern University Law Review* 73, no. 6 (1979): 1038–1089.

15. In 1849, for example, Folks reports the following statistics for one New York public almshouse: "514 children were cared for . . . 280 died." See Homer Folks, *The Care of Destitute, Neglected and Delinquent Children* (New York: Macmillan Co., 1902), 21; see also Peter C. English, "Pediatrics and the Unwanted Child in History: Foundling Homes, Disease and the Origins of Foster Care in New York City, 1860–1920," *Pediatrics* 73 (1984): 699–711.

16. For more on the movement to reform orphanages and the care of abandoned children, see David M. Rothman, *The Discovery of the Asylum: Social Order and Disorder in the New Republic* (Boston: Little, Brown, 1971), especially 206–236; and William I. Trattner, *From Poor Law to Welfare State: A History of Social Welfare in America*, 5th ed. (New York: Free Press, 1994), 112–127.

17. For example, in the first forty-five years of operation, the Boston Female Asylum, an orphanage in Boston, placed only 4.9 percent of its charges for adoption. See Susan Lynne Porter, "The Benevolent Asylum—Image and Reality: The Care and Training of Female Orphans in Boston, 1800–1840" (PhD diss., Boston University, 1984). See also E. Wayne Carp, "Orphanages vs. Adoption: The Triumph of Biological Kinship, 1800–1933," in *With Us Always: A History of Private Charity and Public Welfare,* eds. Donald T. Chritchlow and Charles H. Parker (New York: Rowman & Littlefield Publishers, Inc., 1998), 123–144; and Peter Romanofsky, "The Early History of Adoption Practices, 1870–1930" (PhD diss., University of Missouri at Columbia, 1969). Some charitable institutions did rely on adoption, but they were few in number and generally under attack. See Marsh and Ronner, *The Empty Cradle,* 106–107.

18. From Charles Loring Brace, *The Dangerous Classes of New York,* quoted in Miriam Z. Langsam, *Children West: A History of the Placing-Out System of the New York Children's Aid Society, 1853–1890* (Madison: State Historical Society of Wisconsin, 1964), v.

19. The bulk of the orphan trains ran from 1854 to 1904, although a handful traveled as late as 1929. See Burton Z. Sokoloff, "Antecedents of American Adoption," *Adoption* 3, no. 1 (Spring 1993): 20.

20. For more on Brace and the orphan trains, see also Marilyn Irvin Holt, *The Orphan Trains: Placing Out in America* (Lincoln: University of Nebraska Press, 1992); Langsam, *Children West;* and Henry Thurston, *The Dependent Child: A Story of Changing Aims and Methods in the Care of Dependent Children* (New York: Columbia University Press, 1930).

21. Sokoloff, "Antecedents of American Adoption," 20.

22. Brace himself argued that "very many" of his charges were adopted. Yet the historical record strongly suggests otherwise. See Joan Heifetz Hollinger, "Introduction to Adoption Law and Practice," in *Adoption Law and Practice,* ed. Hollinger (New York: Matthew Bender & Co., Inc., 1991), 1–32. For Brace's account, see Charles L. Brace, "The 'Placing Out' Plan for Homeless and Vagrant Children," *Proceedings of the Conference of Charities and Correction* (Albany, NY: Joel Munsell, 1876), 140.

23. See the discussion in Carp, *Family Matters,* 10–11; Bruce Bellingham, "Institution and Family: An Alternative View of Nineteenth-Century Child Saving," *Social Problems* 33 (December 1986): S33–S57; and Langsam, *Children West,* 45–67.

24. For a description of this proliferation, see Folks, *The Care of Destitute, Neglected, and Delinquent Children,* 64–71, 179–197; LeRoy Ashby, *Saving the Waifs: Reformers and Dependent Children, 1890–1917* (Philadelphia: Temple University Press, 1984); and Holt, *The Orphan Trains,* 106–117.

25. See, for example, Katherine P. Hewins and L. Josephine Webster, "The Work of Child-Placing Agencies," Children's Bureau publication 171 (Washington, DC: Government Printing Office, 1927); W. H. Slingerland, *Child-Placing in Families: A Manual for Students and Social Workers* (New York: Russell Sage Foundation, 1919); and Romanofsky, "The Early History of Adoption Practices," 66–104. For a description of the growing role of sentiment in child placement and the eventual embrace of foster care,

see Viviana Zelizer, *Pricing the Priceless Child: The Changing Social Value of Children* (Princeton, NJ: Princeton University Press, 1985), 177–184; and Susan Tiffin, *In Whose Best Interest? Child Welfare Reform in the Progressive Era* (Westport, CT: Greenwood Press, 1982), 61–109.

26. See Berebitsky, *Like Our Very Own,* 130; and Romanofsky, "The Early History of Adoption Practices," 117–123.

27. See the description in Carp, "Orphanages vs. Adoption," 134.

28. From *Delineator,* May 1908, 808, quoted in Berebitsky, *Like Our Very Own,* 62.

29. Ada Elliot Sheffield, quoted in Carp, *Family Matters,* 18.

30. Robert Grant, "Domestic Relations and the Child," *Scribner's Magazine* 65, May 1919, 527; cited in Zelizer, *Pricing the Priceless Child,* 190.

31. For a description of this shift, see Elizabeth S. Cole and Kathryn S. Donley, "History, Values, and Placement Policy Issues in Adoption," in *The Psychology of Adoption,* eds. David M. Brodzinsky and Marshall D. Schecter (New York: Oxford University Press, 1990), 276–278; and E. Wayne Carp, ed., *Adoption in America: Historical Perspectives* (Ann Arbor: University of Michigan Press, 2002), 199.

32. A similar process occurred in Great Britain, where adoption was legalized in 1926. See Margaret Kornitzer, *Child Adoption in the Modern World* (New York: Philosophical Library, 1952), xi–xiii.

33. See Tiffin, *In Whose Best Interest?* 207–208.

34. Barbara Melosh, *Strangers and Kin: The American Way of Adoption* (Cambridge, MA: Harvard University Press, 2002), 26.

35. For more on the more general embrace of professional social work during this period, see Tiffin, *In Whose Best Interest?* 253–280.

36. During most of this period, professional social workers were adamant about not separating infants from their mothers for at least several months. See E. Wayne Carp, "Professional Social Workers, Adoption, and the Problem of Illegitimacy, 1915–1945," *Journal of Policy History* 6, no. 3 (1994): 161–184. For an alternative view, see Regina Kunzel, "The Professionalization of Benevolence: Evangelicals and Social Workers in the Florence Crittenton Homes, 1915 to 1945," *Journal of Social History* 22 (1988): 21–43.

37. See Melosh, *Strangers and Kin,* 36–38; and Zelizer, *Pricing the Priceless Child,* 169–207.

38. Zelizer, *Pricing the Priceless Child,* 199. For a related picture but lower estimated prices, see Frederick G. Brownell, "Why You Can't Adopt a Baby," *Reader's Digest,* September 1948, 55–59.

39. See *Hearings Before the Subcommittee to Investigate Juvenile Delinquency of the Committee on the Judiciary,* United States Senate, 84th Congress, 1st session, July 15 and 16, 1955 (hereafter cited as Kefauver Commission), 50–71.

40. Kefauver Commission, 10, 110; and "Adoption Tale Told by Unwed Mother," *New York Times,* July 17, 1955, 32.

41. Vera Connolly, "Bargain-Counter Babies," *Pictorial Review* 38 (March 1937), quoted in Zelizer, *Pricing the Priceless Child,* 192–193.

42. Cited in Carp, *Family Matters,* 26. For similar estimates in the late 1940s and early 1950s, see Huard, "The Law of Adoption," 761; and Richard Perlman and Jack Wiener, "Adoption of Children, 1953: A Statistical Analysis," *Iowa Law Review* 40 (1955): 339–340.

43. "Regarding Adoptions," Children's Welfare League of America, Special Bulletin (March 1937), 8, cited in Carp, *Family Matters,* 31.

44. See, for example, "Moppets on the Market: The Problem of Unregulated Adoption," *59 Yale Law Review* (1950), 715–736. Although not written by a social worker, this article lays out the standard argument that many social workers and licensed agencies put forth.

45. Much of this shift was driven by postwar embarrassment over Nazi atrocities committed under the banner of eugenics. See the discussion in chapter 4.

46. They also began charging for their services. See Zelizer, *Pricing the Priceless Child,* 201–207.

47. Clark Vincent, "Illegitimacy in the Next Decade: Trends and Implications," *Child Welfare* 43 (December 1964): 515.

48. In the days before infant formula, removing a baby from her mother also often meant condemning the child to death.

49. See, for example, Alice Lake, "Babies for the Brave," *Saturday Evening Post,* July 31, 1954, 26–27, 65; and Michael Schapiro, *A Study of Adoption Practice: Adoption of Children with Special Needs* (New York: Child Welfare League of America, 1957).

50. Because out-of-wedlock births have historically been higher among African Americans, and because African American couples have tended to be less interested than whites in adoption, adoption agencies in the United States typically have had trouble finding a sufficient number of black families to adopt all the available black children.

51. Carp, *Family Matters,* 28.

52. For more on changing views toward childlessness during this period, see Elaine Tyler May, *Barren in the Promised Land: Childless Americans and the Pursuit of Happiness* (Cambridge, MA: Harvard University Press, 1997), 127–179.

53. See Arthur D. Sorosky, Annette Baran, and Reuben Pannor, *The Adoption Triangle: The Effects of the Sealed Record on Adoptees, Birth Parents and Adoptive Parents* (Garden City, NY: Anchor Books, 1979), 35.

54. See Kefauver Commission; and Linda Tollett Austin, *Babies for Sale: The Tennessee Children's Home Adoption Scandal* (Westport, CT: Praeger, 1993), 109–127.

55. Lincoln Caplan, *An Open Adoption* (New York: Farrar, Straus & Giroux, 1990), 87; and Austin, *Babies for Sale,* 152–153.

56. By 1976, only four states—Connecticut, Delaware, Massachusetts, and Minnesota—explicitly prohibited private placement. See Margaret V. Turano, "Black-Market Adoptions," *Catholic Lawyer* 22 (Winter 1976): 54.

57. Generally, statutes against baby-selling are expressed as prohibitions against receiving compensation for relinquishing maternal legal rights. For an overview of the relevant statutes, see Avi Katz, "Surrogate Motherhood and the Baby-Selling Laws," *Columbia Journal of Law and Social Problems* 20, no. 1 (1986): 1–53; Turano, "Black-Market Adoptions"; and Daniel G. Grove, "Independent Adoption: The Case for the Gray Market," *Villanova Law Review* 13 (Fall 1967): 116–136.

58. These are very rough estimates based on voluntary disclosure. No data exists for 1945–1950, 1952–1954, or 1956. See Penelope L. Manza, "Adoption Trends: 1944–1975," *Child Welfare Research Notes* #9 (U.S. Children's Bureau, August 1984), 1–4.

59. Berebitsky, *Like Our Very Own,* 173. Kathy S. Stolley, "Statistics on Adoption in the United States," *Future of Children* 3 (Spring 1993): 30–33.

60. Between 1973 and 1983, the number of abortions performed on teenaged girls rose from 244,000 to 412,000. See Alfred Kadushin and Judith A. Martin, *Child Welfare Services* (New York: Macmillan Publishing Co., 1988), 471.

61. Kadushin and Martin, *Child Welfare Services,* 495.

62. Christine Bachrach, "Adoption Plans, Adopted Children and Adoptive Mothers," *Journal of Marriage and the Family* 48 (May 1986): 243–253.

63. Kadushin and Martin, *Child Welfare Services,* 539.

64. This debate became one of the most contested issues in the history of U.S. adoption. For a discussion, see Andrew Billingsly and Jeanne M. Giovannoni, *Children of the Storm: Black Children and American Child Welfare* (New York: Harcourt Brace Jovanovich, 1972); Elizabeth Bartholet, *Nobody's Children: Abuse and Neglect, Foster Drift, and the Adoption Alternative* (Boston: Beacon, 1999); Randall Kennedy, "Orphans of Separatism: The Painful Politics of Transracial Adoption," *American Prospect* 17 (Spring 1994): 38–45; and Lucille J. Grow and Deborah Shapiro, *Black Children—White Parents: A Study of Transracial Adoption* (New York: Child Welfare League of America, 1974).

65. Carp, *Family Matters,* 34; Howard Altstein and Rita J. Simon, *Intercountry Adoption: A Multinational Perspective* (New York: Praeger, 1990), 3.

66. The process was not necessarily simple, because adoptive parents had to document, first, that they satisfied federal criteria for parental fitness; second, that they had fulfilled all requirements of their child's home country; and third, that their child fit a narrow definition of "orphan." For a review and critique of these requirements, see Elizabeth Bartholet, "International Adoption: Current Status and Future Prospects," *The Future of Children: Adoption* 3, no. 1 (Spring 1993): 89–103.

67. INS data, as reported in Adam Pertman, *Adoption Nation: How the Adoption Revolution is Transforming America* (New York: Basic Books, 2000), 23.

68. In 1979, China instituted a draconian "one child" policy that prohibited couples from bearing more than a single child. Although there were some exceptions, couples were generally required to receive birth permits prior to attempting to conceive, and women either had to be sterilized or use an IUD after the birth of their child. For a discussion of how this policy has affected both adoption and China's own demographics, see Valerie M. Hudson and Andrea M. den Boer, *Bare Branches: Security Implications of Asia's Surplus Male Population* (Cambridge, MA: MIT Press, 2004); and Karin Evans, *The Lost Daughters of China: Abandoned Girls, Their Journey to America and the Search for a Missing Past* (New York: J.P. Tarcher/Putnam, 2000).

69. See Carol Sisco, "Strict Romanian Birth Rules Bred Orphanages, Says Expert," *Salt Lake City Tribune,* November 14, 1991, B1; and Bill Snead, "The Abandoned Children of Romania's Orphanages," *Washington Post,* September 17, 1991, 6.

70. Pertman, *Adoption Nation,* 73; and John Taylor, "Romania's Lost Children . . . Omahans Challenge System, Bring Home Maria," *Omaha World-Herald,* July 2, 1991, 29.

71. *Immigrant Visas Issued to Orphans Coming to the U.S.*, available at http://travel.state.gov/family/adoption/stat/stats_451.html.

72. W. Tyree, "The Business of International Adoption," *Japan Times,* June 9, 1999, 1–2; and Madelyn Freundlich, *The Market Forces in Adoption* (New York: Child Welfare League of America, 2000), 43.

73. Statistics on intercountry adoption are notoriously difficult to find. No international institution collects them, and researchers have thus been forced to cobble together estimates from sending and receiving countries, many of which also have no central collection mechanism. For a discussion of this problem, see R. H. Weil, "International Adoptions: The Quiet Migration," *International Migration Review* 18, no. 2 (1984): 276–293; and S. Kane, "The Movement of Children for International Adoption: An Epidemiological Perspective," *Social Science Journal* 30, no. 4 (1993): 323–339. For the best recent estimates, see Peter Selman, "The Movement of Children for Intercountry Adoption: A Demographic Perspective," Poster Presentation P275, at XXIVth IUSSP General Population Conference, Salvador, Bahia, Brazil, August 18–24, 2001. Figures for 2003 come directly from Selman, personal conversation with author, February 9, 2005. See also Selman, "Trends in Intercountry Adoption 1998–2003."

74. Precise data are unavailable, because no U.S. agency collects adoption statistics regularly. See *How Many Children Were Adopted in 2000 and 2001?* (Washington, DC: National Adoption Information Clearinghouse, 2004).

75. A fourth category—adoption by a relative or stepparent—is not considered here.

76. Susan Freivalds, "What's New in Adoption?" in "2005 Adoption Guide," special issue, *Adoptive Families* (2005): 11.

77. Complaints about the U.S. foster care system are voluminous. See, for example, Carole A. McKelvey and JoEllen Stevens, *Adoption Crisis: The Truth behind Adoption and Foster Care* (Golden, CO: Fulcrum Publishing, 1994); and "Health Care of Young Children in Foster Care," *Pediatrics* 109, no. 3 (March 2002): 536–541.

78. The Adoption and Foster Care Analysis and Reporting System (AFCARS), estimated as of August 2004, available at http://www.acf.hhs.gov/programs/cb/publications/afcars/report9.htm.

79. For more on parental preferences, see Mark E. Courtney, "The Politics and Realities of Transracial Adoption," *Child Welfare* 76, no. 6 (1997): 749–780.

80. Freundlich, *Market Forces in Adoption,* 68–73.

81. Adoption and Safe Families Act (ASFA) of 1997, P.L. 105-89, November 19, 1997.

82. See Hollinger, "Introduction to Adoption Law and Practice," 1–56; and *How Many Children Were Adopted in 2000 and 2001?* (Washington, DC: National Adoption Information Clearinghouse, 2004).

83. Hollinger, "Introduction to Adoption Law and Practice," 1–68.

84. These costs vary widely. For estimates, see http://costs.adoption.com.

85. For the growth of independent adoption and an argument for its merits, see Mark T. McDermott, "Agency Versus Independent Adoption: The Case for Independent Adoption," *Adoption* 3, no. 1 (Spring 1993): 146–151.

86. See the description in Caplan, *An Open Adoption,* 14–15; and Laura Mansnerus, "Market Puts Price Tags on the Priceless," *New York Times,* October 26, 1998, A1.

87. Interview with Mark T. McDermott, Washington, DC, January 7, 2005. The rate of $350 is at the very high end of the market.

88. See Annette Baran and Reuben Pannor, "Open Adoption," in *The Psychology of Adoption,* eds. Brodzinsky and Schecter, 316–331; and Annette Baran, Reuben Pannor, and Arthur D. Sorosky, "Open Adoption," *Social Work* 21 (1976): 97–105.

89. *2005 Adoption Guide,* 40; *Costs of Adopting: A Factsheet for Families* (Washington, DC: National Adoption Information Clearinghouse, June 2004).

90. Mansnerus, "Market Puts Price Tags on the Priceless," A1.

91. See William L. Pierce, "Accreditation of Those Who Arrange Adoptions Under the Hague Convention on Intercountry Adoption as a Means of Protecting, Through Private International Law, the Rights of Children," *Journal of Contemporary Health Law and Policy* 12 (1996): 535–559.

92. Formally, the Hague Convention on the Protection of Children and Cooperation in Respect of Intercountry Adoption. See Ethan B. Kapstein, "The Baby Trade," *Foreign Affairs,* November 1, 2003, 115–125; and Peter Selman, "Intercountry Adoption in Europe after the Hague Convention," in *Developments in European Social Policy: Convergence and Diversity,* eds. Rob Sykes and Pete Alcock (Bristol: The Policy Press, 1998), 147–169.

93. The United States has approved the treaty but has yet to formally ratify it.

94. These particular fees are from Wide Horizons for Children, available at www.whfc.org. Other agencies' fees vary but follow a similar pattern.

95. Conversation with author, April 2005.

96. In economic terms, they reduce the information asymmetries that would otherwise exist. For a critical examination of this process, see Lisa Cartwright, "Photographs of 'Waiting Children': The Transnational Adoption Market," *Social Text* 74, vol. 21, no. 1 (Spring 2003): 83–109.

97. Twila L. Perry, "Transracial and International Adoption: Mothers, Hierarchy, Race and Feminist Legal Theory," *Yale Journal of Law and Feminism* 10 (1998): 105.

98. Janice G. Raymond, "The International Traffic in Women: Women Used in Systems of Surrogacy and Reproduction," in *Reconstructing Babylon: Essays on Women and Technology,* ed. H. Patricia Hynes (Bloomington, IN: Indiana University Press, 1991), 97. Italics in original. For similar arguments, see Raymond, *Women as Wombs* (North Melbourne, Australia: Spinifex Press, 1995), 144–154; and Kenneth J. Herrmann Jr. and Barbara Kasper, "International Adoption: The Exploitation of Women and Children," *Affilia* 7, no. 1 (Spring 1992): 45–58.

99. For a balanced argument along these lines, see Madelyn Freundlich, "Families without Borders—I," *UN Chronicle* no. 2 (1999): 88.

100. See, for example, Bartholet, "International Adoption."

101. For Tann, see Zelizer, *Pricing the Priceless Child,* 199; and Austin, *Babies for Sale.* For Silverton and similar cases, see Lynne McTaggart, *The Baby Brokers: The Marketing of White Babies in America* (New York: The Dial Press, 1980); and Nancy C. Baker, *Babyselling: The Scandal of Black Market Adoption* (New York: Vanguard Press, 1978).

102. See, for example, Holly C. Kennard, "Curtailing the Sale and Trafficking of Children: A Discussion of the Hague Conference Convention in Respect of Intercoun-

try Adoptions," *University of Pennsylvania Journal of International Business Law* 14, no. 4 (1994): 623–649.

103. Hearings before the Subcommittee on Children and Youth of the Committee on Labor and Public Welfare, 94th Congress, 1st session (1975), 141–145.

104. Author interviews with Mark T. McDermott, past president of American Academy of Adoption Attorneys; and Thomas C. Atwood, president and CEO, National Council for Adoption, Washington, DC, January 7, 2005.

105. For Cambodia, see Sara Corbett, "Where Do Babies Come From?" *New York Times Sunday Magazine,* June 16, 2002, 42; for India, see Raymond Bonner, "For Poor Families, Selling Baby Girls was Economic Boon," *New York Times,* June 23, 2003, A3; and Gregory Katz, "The £18 Babies," *FT Magazine,* June 19, 2004, 20–23.

106. Even groups critical of international adoption tend to agree that cases of outright kidnapping are extremely rare. See, for example, Marie-Françoise Lucker-Bubel, "Inter-Country Adoption and Trafficking in Children: An Initial Assessment of the Adequacy of the International Protection of Children and Their Rights" (Geneva: Defense for Children International, 1990), 2. For a discussion of how trafficking allegations skew the debate over international adoption, see Elizabeth Bartholet, *Family Bonds: Adoption and the Politics of Parenting* (Boston: Houghton Mifflin Company, 1993), 150–160.

107. See Corbett, "Where Do Babies Come From?" and Thomas Fields-Meyer et al., "Whose Kids Are They?" *People,* January 19, 2004, 74–78. For earlier allegations, see Marlise Simons, "Abductions in Salvador Fill a Demand: Adoption," *New York Times,* December 17, 1985; and *International Children's Rights Monitor* 5, no. 4 (1988).

108. McTaggart, *The Baby Brokers,* 1. See also the discussion in Daniel G. Grove, "Independent Adoption: The Case for the Gray Market," *Villanova Law Review* 13 (Fall 1967): 116–136.

109. For individual cases, see McTaggart, *The Baby Brokers*; and Robert D. McFadden, "Adoption Lawyer Throws a Party," *New York Times,* March 3, 1979, 26.

110. For a legal discussion of these ambiguities, see James B. Boskey and Joan Heifetz Hollinger, "Placing Children for Adoption," in *Adoption Law and Practice,* ed. Hollinger, 3–26, 3–39.

111. For a classic argument along these lines, see Margaret Jane Radin, "Market Inalienability," *Harvard Law Review* 100 (June 1987): 1849–1937. For a rare and extremely controversial argument in favor of the marketplace, see Elisabeth M. Landes and Richard A. Posner, "The Economics of the Baby Shortage," *Journal of Legal Studies* 7, no. 2 (June 1978): 323–348.

112. For arguments that baby markets are inherently bad, see J. Robert S. Prichard, "A Market for Babies?" *University of Toronto Law Journal* 34 (1984): 341–357; Robin West, "Submission, Choice and Ethics: A Rejoinder to Judge Posner," *Harvard Law Review* 99 (1986): 1449–1456; and Tamar Frankel and Francis H. Miller, "The Inapplicability of Market Theory to Adoptions," *Boston University Law Review* 67 (1987): 99–103.

113. See, for example, Perry, "Transracial and International Adoption," 147.

114. Of course, theoretically it is possible that funds and efforts could be devoted to helping the child's relatives or neighbors care for him. This is the option offered by many

critics of international adoption. Under current circumstances, however, it seems highly improbable that sufficient monies will flow in this direction.

115. For a discussion, see E. Wayne Carp, "Two Cheers for Orphanages," *Reviews in American History* 24, no. 2 (1996); and Deborah A. Frank et al., "Infants and Young Children in Orphanages: One View from Pediatrics and Child Psychiatry," *Pediatrics* 97 (April 1996): 569–578.

116. As Posner asks rhetorically, "Are the infertile to be blamed for a glut of unwanted children?" See Richard A. Posner, "The Ethics and Economics of Enforcing Contracts of Surrogate Motherhood," *Journal of Contemporary Health Law and Policy* 21 (April 1989): 21–31.

117. For a compelling argument along these lines, see Bartholet, *Family Bonds.*

118. There is a voluminous literature evaluating the success of adoptive placements. See, for example, Rita J. Simon and Howard Altstein, *Transracial Adoptees and Their Families: A Study of Identity and Commitment* (New York: Praeger, 1987); Barbara Tizard, "Intercountry Adoption: A Review of the Evidence," *Journal of Child Psychology and Psychiatry* 32, no. 5 (1991): 743–756; William Feigelman and Arnold R. Silverman, *Chosen Children* (Westport, CT: Praeger Publishers, 1983); Janet L. Hoopes, "Adoption and Identity Formation," in *The Psychology of Adoption,* eds. Brodzinsky and Schecter, 144–166; and James A. Rosenthal, "Outcomes of Adoption of Children with Special Needs," *The Future of Children: Adoption* 3, no. 1 (Spring 1993): 77–88.

119. For one argument along these lines, see Hearings before the Subcommittee on Children and Youth (1975), 579–581.

120. See Betty Jean Lifton, *Lost and Found: The Adoption Experience* (New York: Dial Press, 1979); and Arthur D. Sorosky, Annette Baran, and Reuben Pannor, "Identity Conflicts in Adoptees," *American Journal of Orthopsychiatry* 45, no. 1 (1975): 18–27.

121. For the classic argument in favor of open adoption, see Annette Baran and Reuben Pannor, "Open Adoption," in *The Psychology of Adoption,* eds. Brodzinsky and Schecter, 316–331; and Annette Baran, Reuben Pannor, and Arthur D. Sorosky, "Open Adoption," *Social Work* 21 (1976): 97–105. For a discussion of the politics behind the open adoption movement, see E. Wayne Carp, *Adoption Politics: Bastard Nation and Ballot Initiative 58* (Lawrence, KS: University Press of Kansas, 2004).

122. See Anne B. Brodzinsky, "Surrendering an Infant for Adoption: The Birthmother Experience," in *The Psychology of Adoption,* eds. Brodzinsky and Schecter, 295–315.

123. See, for example, the arguments made in Bhabha, "Moving Babies"; and Perry, "Transracial and International Adoption," 101–164.

Chapter 7

1. For an intriguing discussion of how opposition to the use of market language may drive opposition to the market itself, see Ronald A. Cass, "Adoption and Market Theory: Coping with Life, Law, and Markets," *Boston University Law Review* 67 (January 1987): 73–96.

2. Leon Kass, *Toward a More Natural Science: Biology and Human Affairs* (New York: Free Press, 1985), 31.

3. Classic arguments along these lines include Douglass C. North, "Institutions," *Journal of Economic Perspectives* 5, no. 1 (Winter 1991): 97–112; North and Robert Thomas, *The Rise of the Western World: A New Economic History* (Cambridge: Cambridge University Press, 1973); John A. James and Mark Thomas, eds., *Capitalism in Context* (Chicago: University of Chicago Press, 1994); John L. Campbell and Leon N. Lindberg, "Property Rights and the Organization of Economic Activity by the State," *American Sociological Review* 55, no 5 (1990): 634–647; and Harry N. Schreiber, "Regulation, Property Rights, and the Definition of 'The Market': Law and the American Economy," *Journal of Economic History* XLI, no. 1 (March 1981): 103–109.

4. In some societies, scholars like North have argued, family ties or barter can take the place of a more formal system of property rights. But once society becomes sophisticated enough to support impersonal exchange, property rights become necessary. See Douglass C. North, "Institutions, Transaction Costs and Economic Growth," *Economic Inquiry* XXV (July 1987): 419–428.

5. See Warren Hoge, "British Judge Sends Infants Adopted on the Web Back to St. Louis," *New York Times,* April 10, 2001, A3; and Chris Gray, "Internet Twins Taken into US Foster Care," *Independent,* April 20, 2001, 11.

6. Steve Patterson and Abdon M. Pallasch, "Embryo Mistakenly Destroyed by Lab Was a Human, Judge Rules," *Chicago Sun-Times,* February 6, 2005, 9.

7. The father eventually received compensation of $108,000: $98,000 for the cost of raising the child, and $10,000 for emotional distress. See John Ellement and Thanassis Cambanis, "Ex-Husband Sues Clinic over Birth of Daughter," *Boston Globe,* January 15, 2004, B1; and Thanassis Cambanis, "Father Wins Case Against Fertility Clinic," *Boston Globe,* January 31, 2004, A1.

8. As the case developed, serious questions emerged about the suitability of both sets of parents. Eventually, the American couple withdrew their claim after allegations surfaced that the father had molested two young babysitters.

9. Kari L. Karsjens, "Boutique Egg Donation: A New Form of Racism and Patriarchy," *DePaul Journal of Health Care Law* 5 (Summer 2002): 73.

10. See Michael Sandel, "The Baby Bazaar," *New Republic,* October 20, 1997, 25; and Margaret Jane Radin, *Contested Commodities: The Trouble with Trade in Sex, Children, Body Parts and Other Things* (Cambridge, MA: Harvard University Press, 1996), 139. For similar arguments, see Tamar Frankel and Francis H. Miller, "The Inapplicability of Market Theory to Adoptions," *Boston University Law Review* 67 (1987): 99–103; Jane Maslow Cohen, "Adoption and Market Theory: Posnerism, Pluralism, Pessimism," *Boston University Law Review* 67 (1987): 105–175; and J. Robert S. Prichard, "A Market for Babies?" *University of Toronto Law Review* 34 (1984): 341–357. Interestingly, Professor Cohen, author of one of these antimarket arguments, is the same woman profiled earlier, who conceived twins by using eggs from two unrelated donors.

11. See Marilyn Gardner, "Sperm Donors No Longer Bank on Anonymity," *Christian Science Monitor,* March 30, 2005, 11.

12. For surrogates, see Helena Ragoné, *Surrogate Motherhood: Conception in the Heart* (Boulder, CO: Westview Press, 1994); and Lori Andrews, "Beyond Doctrinal Boundaries: A Legal Framework for Surrogate Motherhood," *Virginia Law Review* 81 (1995): 2343–2375. For sperm donors, see David Plotz, "No Nobels, One 'Failure,' a Few Regrets," *Slate,* March 30, 2001, at http://slate.msn.com/is/103402/; Plotz, *The Genius Factory: The Curious History of the Nobel Prize Sperm Bank* (New York: Random House, 2005); and K. Daniels et al., "Previous Semen Donors and their Views Regarding the Sharing of Information with Their Offspring," *Human Reproduction* 20, no. 6 (March 10, 2005): 1670–1675.

13. Ertman adds a related point: that the market for assisted reproduction allows gay and single people to become parents as well. See Martha M. Ertman, "What's Wrong with a Parenthood Market? A New and Improved Theory of Commodification," *North Carolina Law Review* 82 (December 2003): 1–59.

14. See Sheridan McCoid, "Donation: The Medical Facts," *Observer,* July 6, 2003, 4; Cherry Norton, "Top Specialist Wants Sperm and Egg Donors Paid," *Independent,* March 24, 2000, 7; "Hopeful Parents go to U.S. as Sperm Payments Dry Up," *Ottawa Citizen,* August 6, 2004, A2; and Charlie Fidelman, "Law Bans the Baby Business," *The Gazette* (Montreal), June 28, 2004, A8.

15. For a similar and intriguing argument in the realm of human tissue, see Julia D. Mahoney, "The Market for Human Tissue," *Virginia Law Review* 86, no. 2 (March 2000): 163–223.

16. See Constance Holden, "Two Fertilized Eggs Stir Global Furor," *Science* 225, no. 4657 (July 1984): 35; and Peter Coster, "State of the Orphans," *Sunday Tasmanian,* April 28, 1996. For a broader discussion of how ART affects inheritance, see Sharona Hoffman, "Birth After Death: Perpetuities and the New Reproductive Technologies," *Georgia Law Review* 38 (Winter 2004): 575–631; and Margaret Ward Scott, "A Look at the Rights and Entitlements of Posthumously Conceived Children," *Emory Law Journal* 52 (Spring 2003): 963–996.

17. The literature here, in both the law and ethics, is voluminous. For a review and discussion of the various approaches, see John A. Robertson, "In the Beginning: The Legal Status of Early Embryos," *Virginia Law Review* 76 (April 1990): 437–517; Jill R. Gorny, "The Fate of Surplus Cryopreserved Embryos: What Is the Superior Alternative for their Disposition?" *Suffolk University Law Review* 37 (2004): 459–477; President's Council on Bioethics, "Human Cloning: Policy Considerations," Staff Working Paper, January 2002, Appendix A; and Jens David Ohlin, "Is the Concept of the Person Necessary for Human Rights?" *Columbia Law Review* 105 (January 2005): 209–249.

18. For a broader discussion of the role of property rights in all body parts, see Michelle Bourianoff Bray, "Personalizing Personalty: Toward a Property Right in Human Bodies," *Texas Law Review* 69 (1990): 209–244; Thomas H. Murray, "On the Human Body as Property: The Meaning of Embodiment, Markets, and the Meaning of Strangers," *Journal of Law Reform* 20, no. 4 (Summer 1987): 1055–1088; and Julia D. Mahoney, "The Market for Human Tissue," *Virginia Law Review* 86, no. 2 (March 2000): 163–223.

19. This, indeed, is the criticism raised against several high-profile surrogacy cases, in which the financial situation of the contracting couple has arguably been used to determine the child's best interest.

20. Emerging case law in the United States suggests that individuals have some basic property rights in their sperm or eggs and that they are not prohibited from selling this property. See Karsjens, "Boutique Egg Donation," 57–89; and Amy S. Pignatella Cain, "Property Rights in Human Biological Materials: Studies in Species Reproduction and Biomedical Technology," *Arizona Journal of International and Comparative Law* 17 (Spring 2000): 449–481.

21. For more on the role that rules play in society, see Frederick Schauer, *Playing by the Rules* (Oxford: Clarendon Press, 1991); H. L. A. Hart, "Definition and Theory in Jurisprudence," in *Essays in Jurisprudence and Philosophy* (Oxford: Clarendon Press, 1983); and Debora Spar, "Note on Rules," Case 799-013 (Boston: Harvard Business School, 1999).

22. See, for example, Gena Corea, *The Mother Machine* (London: The Women's Press, Ltd., 1977); Janice G. Raymond, *Women as Wombs* (San Francisco: Harper San Francisco, 1993); and S. Roach Anleu, "Surrogacy: For Love but Not for Money?" *Gender & Society* 6 (1992): 30–48.

23. The classic treatments of this division are Charles Lindblom, *Politics and Markets: The World's Political-Economic Systems* (New York: Basic Books, 1977); and Oliver E. Williamson, *Markets and Hierarchies* (New York: Free Press, 1975).

24. See R. H. Coase, "The Lighthouse in Economics," *Journal of Law and Economics* 17, no. 2 (October 1974): 357–376.

25. See, for example, the discussion in Willis Emmons, *The Evolving Bargain: Strategic Implications of Deregulation and Privatization* (Boston: Harvard Business School Press, 2000).

26. Recently, economists have proposed innovative markets that would allow for the noncommercial exchange of kidneys. See Alvin E. Roth, Tayfun Sönmez, and M. Utku Ünver, "Kidney Exchange," *Quarterly Journal of Economics* 119, issue 2 (May 1, 2004): 457–488; and Alvin E. Roth, Tayfun Sönmez, and M. Utku Ünver, "Pairwise Kidney Exchange," working paper 10698, National Bureau of Economic Research, Cambridge, MA, August 2004. For arguments in favor of a commercial market in kidneys and other vital organs, see Lloyd R. Cohen, "Increasing the Supply of Transplant Organs: The Virtues of a Futures Market," *George Washington Law Review* 58, no. 1 (November 1989): 1–51.

27. One is a legitimate market in the provision of children to parent; the others are trade in things that we, as a society, can clearly choose to ban.

28. Interview with author, November 2003.

29. If the surrogate is both gestational and traditional, then she is more closely akin to the birth mother in a traditional adoption. Yet even here there are differences, because traditional birth mothers do not plan beforehand to become pregnant.

30. See, for example, the discussions at http://infertility.adoption.com and www.siblingsadoption.com.

31. See Genetics & Public Policy Center, "The Regulatory Environment for Assisted Reproductive Technology," April 2003. Available at www.dnapolicy.org/policy/art.jhtml.html.

32. Chicago-Kent College of Law, "The Laws of Reproductive Technology," Institute for Science, Law and Technology. Available at www.kentlaw.edu/islt/TABLEII.htm.

33. For an overview of state-by-state differences, see Gail Dutton, *A Matter of Trust: The Guide to Gestational Surrogacy* (Irvine, CA: Clouds Publishing, 1997).

34. Technically, pregnancy is treated as a disability, and exclusion of pregnant women from employee health benefits is deemed, under the Pregnancy Discrimination Act of 1978, an act of sex discrimination. See Brietta R. Clark, "Erickson v. Bartell Drug Co.: A Roadmap for Gender Equity in Reproductive Health Care or an Empty Promise?" *Law and Inequality* 23 (Summer 2005): 304–311.

35. In the United States, Medicaid covers services related to pregnancy and delivery for women whose family income falls below 133 percent of the federal poverty line. For those whose incomes are greater than the Medicaid eligibility but who still cannot afford private insurance, there is CHIP (State Children's Health Insurance Program), a federal program administered on a state level.

36. Most people have two functioning kidneys but need only one to survive.

37. For a description of NOTA and its implications, see Gregory S. Crespi, "Overcoming the Legal Obstacles to the Creation of a Futures Market in Bodily Organs," *Ohio State Law Journal* 55 (Winter 1994): 1–77.

38. For data on transplants, see http://www.optn.org/latestData/rptData.asp.

39. See Michael Finkel, "Complications," *New York Times,* May 27, 2001, 26; and Larry Rohter, "Tracking the Sale of a Kidney on a Path of Poverty and Hope," *New York Times,* May 23, 2004, 1.

40. Legislation has been introduced at the federal level that would mandate insurance coverage for the treatment of infertility. No federal bill, however, has yet been passed. See The Family Building Act of 2003 (HR 3014) and The Family Building Act of 2005 (HR 735). For a description of state-level coverage, see Lucie Schmidt, "Effects of Infertility Insurance Mandates on Fertility," mimeo, Williams College, February 2005.

41. According to one 1995 analysis, the estimated cost of including IVF coverage in standard insurance coverage was $3.14 per family per year. See J. A. Collins et al., "An Estimate of the Cost of In Vitro Fertilization Services in the United States in 1995," *Fertility & Sterility* 64 (1995): 538–545. Also Tarun Jain et al., "Insurance Coverage and Outcomes of in Vitro Fertilization," *New England Journal of Medicine* 347, no. 9 (29 August 2002): 661–666.

42. Comment to author, November 2003.

43. Interview with author, February 2004.

44. Fukuyama is actually borrowing the terms from, and critiquing the views of, Lee Silver. See Francis Fukuyama, *Our Posthuman Future: Consequences of the Biotechnology Revolution* (New York: Farrar, Straus and Giroux, 2002), especially 153–154; and Lee Silver, *Remaking Eden: How Genetic Engineering and Cloning will Transform the American Family* (New York: Perennial, 2002).

45. The memorable phrase "the pulling and hauling that is politics" comes from Graham Allison, *Essence of Decision: Explaining the Cuban Missile Crisis* (Boston: Little, Brown, 1971), 144.

46. For an argument along similar lines, see Lars Noah, "Assisted Reproductive Technologies and the Pitfalls of Unregulated Biomedical Innovation," *Florida Law Review* 55 (April 2003): 603–665; and "Executive Summary of the Task Force on Life and the Law," New York State Task Force on Life and the Law, October 2001, available at http://www.health.state.ny.us/nysdoh/taskfce/execsum.htm.

47. The President's Council on Bioethics, *Reproduction and Responsibility: The Regulation of New Biotechnologies* (Washington, DC: 2004), 205–224.

48. In this context, "equity" refers to the principle that allocates kidneys by waiting time and medical condition rather than by a patient's social standing or ability to pay.

49. She also declined, in the end, to receive payment, citing the extraordinary expenses that she knew the couple would face. See Michelle Roberts, "Quintuplets are Born to Surrogate Mother," *Boston Globe,* April 27, 2005, A3.

50. This is an estimate based on aggregate studies. In this particular case, total costs may well have been much higher. See James M. Goldfarb et al., "Cost Effectiveness of In-Vitro Fertilization," *Obstetrics & Gynecology* 87 (January 1996): 18–21.

51. The range in this study is determined by how many cycles of IVF the woman undergoes, as well as the timing of these cycles. See Ben W. J. Mol et al., "Cost-effectiveness of In Vitro Fertilization and Embryo Transfer," *Fertility & Sterility* 73, no. 4 (April 2000): 748–754.

52. Centers for Disease Control and Prevention, *2002 Assisted Reproductive Technology Success Rates: National Summary and Fertility Clinic Reports,* December 2004.

53. See Laura Schieve et al., "Live-Birth Rates and Multiple-Birth Rates Using In Vitro Fertilization," *Journal of the American Medical Association* 282, no. 19 (November 17, 1999): 1832–1838; Nanette Elster, "Less is More: The Risks of Multiple Births," *Fertility & Sterility* 74 (2000): 617–618; and Ezekiel Emanuel, "Eight is Too Many," *New Republic,* January 25, 1999, 11.

54. For a discussion of how to evaluate these costs, see Peter J. Neumann et al., "The Cost of a Successful Delivery with in Vitro Fertilization," *New England Journal of Medicine* 331, no. 4 (July 28, 1994): 239–243.

55. *Griswold v. Connecticut,* 381 U.S. 479 (1965). The glaring exception, of course, is abortion, where the federal government imposes limits on both time and, to some extent, method: under the Partial-Birth Abortion Ban Act of 2003, any doctor who delivers a living fetus in order to perform an abortion faces a fine and up to two years in prison. See Alissa Schecter, "Choosing Balance: Congressional Powers and the Partial-Birth Abortion Ban Act of 2003," *Fordham Law Review* 73 (March 2005): 1991–1993.

56. Currently, there is no way to identify the genetic component of intelligence, because it derives from a complex interplay of characteristics. In time, however, such markers could become more distinguishable.

Acknowledgments

IN 2001, I published a book called *Ruling the Waves*. It was a book about the politics of high technology, and in particular about the political evolution of the Internet and e-commerce. I argued that the Internet, like the telegraph and radio before it, was destined to undergo certain predictable cycles, moving from an initial period of market anarchy to an eventual demand for rules. After the book's release, I spent many months describing its arguments to various groups and audiences. And inevitably, the same question emerged: what did I think was the next technology that would follow a similar route? What was the next technological wave that would create new markets and unleash political demands?

It took me a while to arrive at an answer. But eventually I became convinced that this next technological wave would come from biology, and especially from ongoing breakthroughs in genetics and reproductive medicine. Like the Internet technologies that preceded them, these technologies had the potential to generate vast commercial opportunity, to sell products and services that simply were not available before. At the same time, though, these technologies were certain to attract an equally vast political reaction, a reaction that, in this case, might well be devoted to shutting down the market.

So I began to explore the world of reproductive medicine, a world I knew little about. I became fascinated by the developments under way and convinced that the science of baby-making was already generating a market for baby production. Meanwhile, ironically, my husband and I were also contemplating the prospect of adoption. We had had two boys the old-fashioned way, and, as they approached adolescence, we became intrigued with the thought of adding another child—an older child, a girl—to our family. As we ventured along what I had presumed would be a very personal journey, I discovered that the world of adoption over-lapped considerably with the world of reproductive science; that adoption had created a market for babies and children, and that this market even competed to some extent with the higher-tech forms of family building.

For the next three years, I continued to wander through these worlds. I marveled at the science that was emerging from some of the world's most sophisticated laboratories, and at the researchers who were probing into the very origins of life. I met the people who are trying to write the rules of this new field, and those who are trying, with equal perseverance, to break them. And I was drawn time after time into the tragedies that mark the baby trade: the heart-breaking tales of people who desperately want a child to love, and of children who have never known a home. *The Baby Business* is my sixth book. It's the only one that's ever made me cry.

Because the research for this book was new to me, moreover, I de-pended more than usual on the kindness and expertise of others. Be-cause I promised anonymity to most of my sources, I will not mention them by name here. But I am exceedingly grateful to the doctors and re-searchers who spoke with me; to the fertility clinics, sperm banks, and egg brokers who graciously opened their doors; and to the adoption agencies and attorneys who generously described their work. I am also grateful to the individuals—also left anonymous here—who shared with me their very personal stories.

Outside the baby trade, this book also benefited from the wisdom of those who read and critiqued it. I am grateful for the advice of Rawi Ab-delal, Constance Bagley, Vicki Baldwin, Traci Battle, Jacqueline Bhabha, Diane Clapp, Susan Crockin, Adam Day, Laurie Gould, Charles Jennings, Ronald Mann, Al Roth, David Shaywitz, Rise Shepsle, Richard Tedlow, Leslie Williams, and Allegra Young. Peter Selman of the University of Newcastle generously shared his data on international adoption statistics; Anjani Chandra of the National Institutes of Health did likewise with her research on the incidence and treatment of infertility in the United States.

Several wonderful research assistants also played a vital role in bringing the book into being. Briana Huntsberger worked with me in the earliest years to tease out the commercial history of contraception. Although this research is not explicitly included in the book, it was critical in introducing me to the politics and business of reproduction. Adam ("AJ") Plotkin doggedly tracked the surrogacy market and explored its economic drivers; Cate Reavis provided key background research for the cloning and adoption chapters. Anna Harrington, meanwhile, was indispensable throughout. She combed through medical and legal materials with equal aplomb and brought her considerable energies to all the book's research and analysis. David Han provided legal insights during the final stages of research, Chris Bebenek helped ready the book for publication, and Chris Grosse ably kept watch over a myriad of details and processes. I am grateful for the assistance of all these people, as well as for the support and professionalism of Jacque Murphy and her colleagues at Harvard Business School Press. I am also grateful to Kim Clark and the Division of Research and Faculty Development at Harvard Business School, which generously provided financial support for the project.

As usual, my greatest debts remain at home. For my sons, this was a tough book. Because not only was Mom traveling and writing and worrying as she always does; this time, she was writing on a topic that was way too embarrassing to contemplate, much less mention to their friends. The only redeeming factor for them was their development of a strange new family pastime: betting how long, at any given dinner party, it would take before their mother started talking about sperm banks or egg sales. I thank them for their patience and their fortitude, and for bringing such joy to my life. I am likewise grateful to my parents, Judy and Marty Spar, who encouraged this endeavor as they have all others, and to my husband, Miltos, whose love and support feel never-ending.

It seems appropriate to end with my daughter, who arrived from Russia halfway through the production of this book. Her grace and enthusiasm remind me daily of the potential for families to grow beyond the bounds of conventional biology. Her journey shows how remarkable the baby business can be—and how important it is to make it work.

Index

Note: page numbers followed by *t* indicate tables; page numbers followed by *n* indicate footnotes.

About the Author

DEBORA SPAR is the Spangler Family Professor and Senior Associate Dean, Director of Research, at Harvard Business School. She teaches courses on the politics of international business and is Chair of Making Markets Work, an executive education program devoted to public and private sector leaders in Africa.

Dr. Spar's previous books include *Ruling the Waves: Cycles of Discovery, Chaos, and Wealth from the Compass to the Internet* and *The Cooperative Edge: The Internal Politics of International Cartels*. She is also coauthor, with Raymond Vernon, of *Beyond Globalism: Remaking American Foreign Economic Policy*. She lives outside Boston with her husband and three children.